Drugs and Politics

Drugs and Politics

Edited by Paul E. Rock

Transaction Books
New Brunswick, New Jersey

Library of Congress Catalog Number: 76-1766.
ISBN: 0-87855-076-3 (cloth); 0-87855-572-2 (paper).
Printed in the United States of America.

Library of Congress Cataloging in Publication Data

Main entry under title:

Drugs and politics.

    Includes bibliographical references and index.
    1.   Drug abuse–United States–Addresses, essays,
lectures. 2.   Drug abuse–Social aspects–United
States–Addresses, essays, lectures. 3.   Narcotics,
Control of–United States–Addresses, essays, lec-
tures. I.   Rock. Paul Elliott.
HV5825.D789   362.2'9'0973   76-1766
ISBN 0-87855-076-3
ISBN 0-87855-572-2 pbk.

Contents

Introduction*

Paul E. Rock

Reconstructing and reporting the history of a social problem is always a difficult and speculative enterprise. Substantial areas of the problem may never have been recorded because they were covert or concealed. Those unknown areas form an uncertain context for interpreting the residue that was intentionally or unwittingly left for others to examine. The residue itself is composed of contributions made by people who were often engaged in masking or transforming the possible significance of what they were doing. The worlds of legislators, control agents, and deviants tend to be complex, ambiguous, and marked by internal contradiction. They revolve around practices that are variously discredited or discreditable; designed for very diverse audiences; expressly public or intensely private; and shaped by conflicting, perhaps irreconcilable, imperatives and principles. Each practice assumes a different meaning when it is individually evaluated. Only a few facets of such worlds will ever become visible, they

*I am indebted to Robert Scott and Irving Louis Horowitz for comments on earlier drafts of this introduction.

7

are politically laden, and those facets that can be inspected must be treated circumspectly.

The perspectives offered on one major American problem, the consumption and regulation of illegal drugs, have been particularly confusing. Although the history of the problem remains largely opaque, few forms of deviancy have ever been made to seem so totally or lavishly revealed. The perspectives flowed from almost all the groups whose lives have been touched by drugs: sociologists, psychiatrists, lawyers, legislators, police officials, drugtakers, and others have attempted to impose a definitive form on the social problem. The perspectives are numerous, contrasting, and couched in such discrepant vocabularies that they defy all neat synthesis or summary. Their discord emphasizes the political and contentious nature of drugtaking. The criminal law has rarely been so exposed to dissent.

Although laws manifestly do change, they typically do so because they fall into disuse or are made to undergo an orderly, restrained process of modification or repeal. The buttresses of law are massively powerful: they are built around force, the mobilization of much symbolism and ritual, and the capacity of law to become a reified moral entity. Very few people are able to provide effective resistance: even if they break the law with impunity, they cannot destroy its legitimacy or moral authority. Thus, in the main, the latent ambiguities of lawbreaking are controlled and suppressed. When laws are first drafted and debated, certain conceptions of social order are systematically denied credibility and relevance. A legal system can retain coherence only at the cost of a restricted vision of social life. When breaches of laws are judged, there may be institutional provision for dispute about the circumstances surrounding the possible transgression, but there cannot be a detailed scrutiny of the political and ethical propriety of the rules themselves. Most instances of crime and deviancy are thus enveloped by a canopy of formal definitions and understandings that receive no overt or effective challenge. Isolated attempts to negotiate the significance of law are continually being made, yet they lack much impact. When a Genet, de Sade, or Cleaver issues some alternative construction of the meanings of sexual deviancy, his interpretation is generally held to be peripheral, perverse, and insubstantial. When limited collective action is initiated by a Gay Liberation Front or the Black Panthers, it is most usually without any immediate consequence. Over time, such challenges may lead to a revision, but their effects can rarely be minutely traced or ascertained.Even when the opposition flows from some segment of the state itself, it tends to be rapidly discredited. Canadian, British, and American commissions produced reports on drugs that were dismissed as contaminated, foolish, and unworkable. Moreover, concerted and sustained opposition to a set of criminal laws is uncommon because those people who might offer it are normally constrained to be secretive, ill-organized, and committed to a show of compliance. A readiness to champion the stigmatized can itself confer stigma and rob the advocate of his authority and plausibility. Publicly, at least, the criminal law reflects and supports a monolithic consensus.

In part, the extraordinary variety and subversiveness of the ideas that were raised about drugs may be attributed to the peculiar qualities of those people who were led to experience legal control. Most of the drugtaking population was politically mute, as all deviant populations are. Many may even have acquiesced in the formal interpretations of their activity. Edwin Schur's work in Britain certainly suggests that this has been so. But the dramatization and negotiation of the public significance of a phenomenon have never depended on the intervention of the mass of people who are affected by it. The work of undermining the official definitions of drug use was taken up by a relatively small number who were somewhat socially distant from the common user. Indeed, controversy became salient only when drugtaking was embraced by this rather distinct group. The contribution that was made by the articulate lent a special gloss to the meanings of drugs. Other versions that might have complemented or competed with such accounts can only be derived indirectly from the ethnographic work that was undertaken among the relatively mute users. The early article by Finestone, "Cats, Kicks, and Color," and the ones by Sutter and Feldman that are reprinted in this book, provide some understanding of alternative organizations of the drug experience.

A consequential denial of the authority and plausibility of the law on drugs had to stem from groups that were themselves unusually plausible and authoritative. The critics had to have a firm anchorage in the public moral order. That order is constructed and maintained by an array of governmental and extragovernmental interpreters of style, morals, and politics. The interpreters give form to otherwise formless and strange phenomena. They have acquired institutional, professional, or artistic mandates to fashion understanding and taste. It is a sign of their mandate that their pronouncements are publicly disseminated and discussed. Indeed, their doings constitute a substantial proportion of "news." There is no necessary harmony between their schemes of interpretation. Some, especially those who have no formal connection with the state or civil administration, tend to a greater flexibility, inconsistency, and innovativeness. In a sense, they are less encumbered by organizational rationality, by the practical consequences of their actions, or by the demands of controlling and controlled publics. They are comparatively free to assume a playfulness that encourages experimentation and the comparatively rapid adoption and shedding of styles. As dissectors and manipulators of the forms of social life, they have also achieved a distance from the commonplace world that leads to a companion moral alienation. Their production of ideas is correspondingly marked by a fluidity and a volatility that can generate tension between the interpretative forms of the administrative community and members of the unestablished community. Such strains can bring about accompanying ideological and political schism. In America, at least, the public moral order is not settled but changeable and emergent. It is the subject of disputation. For a while, those disputes centered on drugs and the protagonists were members of the rival interpreting communities.

Division does not characterize relations between the administrators and the unestablished alone. Neither community is entirely cohesive nor sealed. The two may merge into one another or fragment into smaller competing factions. It is a distinguishing feature of the unestablished world that it is

chiefly composed of small circles or solitary individuals who
have only the most tenuous links with one another. At a critical
phase in the evolution of the drug problem, the groups
clustered around legislation and social control also fractured.

During the 1960s, an elective affinity emerged between
the world of drugtaking and the world of the relatively
unburdened interpreters. The widely communicated alternatives to the conventional meanings of use were constructed,
in great measure, by people who studied and taught in
universities; painted; played and composed music; wrote
essays, commentaries, and poetry; or were involved in
organized political action. Such a group could not be effort-
lessly translated into a malleable and deferential subject of
police and judicial control. The attempt to subjugate it was
construed as a matter for contest rather than simple submis-
sion. Contest took the guise of an active questioning of the
illegality and impropriety of drugtaking. Thus any reading of
the development of drugs as a political problem must place
some emphasis on its importance for the relations between
competing moral authorities. That development represents, in
part, a dispute about the right to legislate experience and
interpret the social world. As Horowitz remarks in his article
in this book, "stylistic considerations [had] become politically
substantial." Two major units of the reality-building machinery of American society confronted one another; the established being challenged by the unestablished.

The dispute flowered during a period of much wider
public contention about the proper ordering of American
society. The collective representations of the late 1940s and
1950s, once apparently taken for granted, were treated by
many as arbitrary and oppressive. For at least a decade, there
has been an unprecedented exploration of the contents and
forms of the major classifying principles in American social
life. The public organization of the beliefs upon which
American society had appeared to rest were surveyed in ways
that suggested a substantial upheaval. The meanings of
poverty, sex, work, equality, power, and race became
politically unstable. Not only was there an attack upon
previously sure symbolic universes, but doubts were also
raised about the very authority on which those universes

rested. How much all this confrontation upset the fabric of everyday American life is uncertain. It is not clear whether the disputes were phrased in terms that mirrored apprehensions experienced in that life. But it is evident that truths that had hitherto been silently presupposed could no longer have seemed so firm.

Drugtaking infused particular sectors and layers of that larger controversy. Possibilities could be discovered in the drugtaking experience that were entirely congruent with the attack on established classification. It has been claimed that such experience can destroy existing structures of intellectual organization, revealing them as absurd or irrelevant. The cosmology of some drugtakers revolves around an understanding of nature and society as relatively undifferentiated and whole, not as a series of discontinuous and bounded parts. The apprehension of the arbitrary and inauthentic nature of classification, its sheer conventionality, encouraged the elective affinity among the drugtaking experience, explorations conducted by the public mediators of style, and the political movements of the late 1950s and 1960s. Indeed, Horowitz styles the whole an "experiential revolution."

That affinity was further stimulated by the regions of thought upon which drugs were held to work. As an unstable and probably ineffable experience, drug-use works on consciousness in ways that can never be definitely described. John Auld argues that the routine practices of use were to eventually render that experience banal. Yet in the earlier stages of the history of the phenomenon, drug-induced meanings were thought to be symbolically fertile, evocative, and shifting. They varied from group to group and from setting to setting. As a medium of changed consciousness, they operated expressly within the spheres of reality-building. Thus conceived, they were taken by some to represent a vital machinery for the production of ideas and ideology. At a time when much attention was addressed to the reconstruction of consciousness, and the liberation of man from an alienated world, drugs became one of the central agents in an idealist politics. Much of the political activity in America was framed around idealist concerns, and drugs took on potency within that context. They were construed as the augurs and vehicles of liberation, regeneration, spiritual renaissance, revolution, repression, or moral decay. A politics that pitched conscious-ness against consciousness found in drugs both a symbol and a producer of symbols.

Affinity was increased, too, by the growing experience of police and penal regulations. Encounters with these bans and the risk of prosecution, the threat to jobs and moral standing, lent drugs an urgency and centrality in many users' lives. In time, what might have been a flirtation with the taboo became an organizing preoccupation. Thus Jock Young illustrates how the amplification of drug-focused deviance in Britain led to an orderly rearrangement of users' existences and schemes of thought. The peripheral became pivotal, repression became a major theme, and drugtakers came to see themselves as embattled. Their routine experiences became tied to issues of power, freedom, oppression, and libertarianism. Similarities could be found among the situations of the blacks, homosex-uals, women, and poor, and the circumstances of the user. The whole could be made intelligible by an analysis that stressed alienation, the exercise of force by ruling minorities, and the rigid censorship of experience. For a while, the Head Liberation Front was consort to the black movements, and welfare-rights organizations, and the Gay Activists Alliance. The politically marginal and the deviant coalesced and exchanged vocabularies of motive. Deviant phenomena could achieve an importance within a range of political visions. Szasz and Dumont, for instance, demonstrate the possibilities that drugs offered for a reading of political process in America. The chief source of opposition to such a political interpretation came from radicals who emphasized material-ism rather than idealism. The Maoists, conventional commun-ists, and Trotskyites had no commerce with libertarianism, anarchism, or people who viewed consciousness as a histori-cal force.

Drugs could not only bear personally on users who discussed them during this period, but drugs were also taken to have widely ramifying connotations that swamped over into conflicts about the legitimacy of law, the permissible boundaries of individual freedom, and the very nature of rationality. As Horowitz observes, the politics of drugs subordinated reason to experience. Statements about drugs could not be enclosed. They became statements about moral, existential, and political realms. In turn, analyses of drugs were construed as having political implications that were more generous than those flowing from the treatment of most other forms of deviancy.

The multiplicity of perspectives on drugs may also be traced to the manner in which the settings and significance of the problem evolved over the last two decades. Far from being fixed, the meanings of use have undergone a continuous series of transformations that furnished ever more abundant commentary. As drug-centered symbolism changed, as the availability and range of drugs increased, as the scale and patterns of use grew, so new formalized interpretations of drugs were offered. Becker has chronicled the marked growth in the collective knowledge and competence of users. There have also been some changes in the composition of the using population itself. Over time, and among sections of the using community, there has been an evolving set of structurally available vantage points from which the issue may be viewed. Drugs cannot signify the same things when they are taken by jazz musicians, or by black youth, or by university students, or by the middle aged and conventional. Perspectives feed on other perspectives, producing an increasingly complicated spectrum of existential and intellectual possibilities.

The heterogeneity of meanings has been further reinforced by the manner in which they may become tethered to specific times and places. Forceful and immediate, permeated by their contexts, and permitting only inadequate articulation, drug experiences are generally focused and local. Yet, because they are forceful and immediate, they engender particularly intense responses that color the political and ideological statements made about them. The analysis of drugs has been occasionally distinguished by an involvement and seriousness that are not awarded to writings on juvenile delinquency, theft, prostitution, or automobile offenses.

Staggered over the history of the problem, therefore, are

a number of commentaries that are deeply embedded in the situations that gave rise to them. Like writings on the black riots of the 1960s, or on student protest, observations on drugs often attached a central and set importance to what now appears to have been a shifting, and relatively ephemeral, phenomenon. Changes in expressive fashion are probably more frequent and abrupt than those writers who describe them realize. Too much permanence and significance may have been bestowed on events that were evanescent and ultimately peripheral in their participants' lives. Indeed, part of the fascination of some of the articles in this book derives from the recapturing of a sense of urgency that has now largely vanished.

So multifaceted a phenomenon as drugs lends itself to virtually endless cabalistic interpretation. People scrutinized it for what it documented about the present and portended for the future. Drugs laid the basis for a renewed examination of the American zeitgeist. The age was variously construed as one of absurdity, spirituality, psychic liberation, or symbolic collapse. In retrospect, many of those readings appear too simplistic and confident in their reduction of an ambiguous and situated phenomenon to one master trait. They also appear to generate irony because they displayed a piety that was unbecoming the group that proffered them. Hofstadter has alleged that American intellectuals tend to be playful rather than pious. The seemingly enduring quality of their commitment to drugs proved short-lived. As John Auld and Howard Becker suggest, the stabilization and diffusion of drug experiences transformed the novel and the open into predictable and repetitious routines.

Of course, it is the case that much writing, and academic writing in particular, took its themes and styles from sources other than those provided directly by the world of drugs. Much was not charged by this special meeting of worlds, nor was it wholly immersed in one standpoint. Indeed, intellectual traditions had been laid down by such sociologists as Lindesmith long before drugs were more widely adopted as an interpretative vehicle. Yet the very nature of drugtaking phenomenon was constituted by this distinctive congregation of meanings, and that nature had to be accommodated in analysis. Simultaneously, the models and strategies that were being applied by the major branch of sociology that approached deviance, symbolic interactionism, also shared some common conceptions with the new critiques. The interactionists were occupied with the business of demystification; with the exploration of meaning; with the abandonment of coherent and systematic descriptions of social life; and with the jettisoning of the rationality of the natural sciences and mechanistic metaphor. They, too, leaned toward a mild anarchism and a rewriting of the social contract. Thus, Becker and Horowitz's extolling of culture and civility in San Francisco may be read as a mapping out of a world in which a social compact embraces the deviant as an insider.

Many interactionists were personally involved in the drug-using world. Even if some were not, their students were bound up in it. Use, and the problems that attended it, formed a very real presence in their lives. The efflorescence of the "Labeling School" of sociology was not an incongruous intellectual event in the 1960s. Its stress on the ontological tyranny of administratively imposed classifications, its attempt to replace "hard determinism" by a more existentially authentic "soft determinism," and its focus on the grounded experience displayed a considerable affinity with the other currents of thought. Indeed, the work of the school paid much attention to drugs. Drugs were to become the exemplary or archetypal case for the explanation of deviance. They were to serve as a model for the routine analysis of all rule-breaking. The school's approach took a deal of its form from a few essays that had dwelt on facets of the problem. Howard Becker's "Becoming a Marihuana User" and "Marihuana Use and Social Control" led to a reanimation of the idea of dialectical process in criminology. David Matza's Becoming Deviant, a general thesis founded on "Becoming a Marihuana User," was to galvanize thinking about the nature of causality and the appropriateness of conventional analogical reasoning. Edwin Schur's Narcotic Addiction in Britain and America underscored ideas about secondary deviation and the self-fulfilling prophecies of social control. Altogether, they conferred authority on speculation about the entire span of deviant affairs.

One other important network was to work on the evolution of the drug problem. Around the boundaries of the formal social control apparatus there are a number of special groups that mediate the effects of law. These groups are partially autonomous of legislation and control agencies. The medical, psychiatric, and legal professions are awarded substantial command over large areas of social problems. It is a mark of their particular competence that they are expected to know more about those problems than the inhabitants of the areas themselves. It is their procedures and vocabularies that lend organization to the development of deviancy. Their members are imputational experts who shape individual and collective understandings about the nature of such matters as drug-taking. They can translate legislative intent and they can bestow legitimacy on law. Their work was no simple mirroring of legislative conceptions of the problem. It was structured by the unique concerns and practices of the professions; by the fashion in which the drug issue was to intersect with those concerns and transform them; and by the peculiar contradictions and dilemmas that were encountered in the effort to control drugs. Drugs did not maintain a stable place in that context. They were continually reviewed as attempts were made to manage them. As John Clausen shows, from an early stage in the recent history of drugs significant sections of the professions were to publicly represent them as unmanageable. Marihuana, at least, was ultimately dismissed as an unworthy and impractical subject for professional attention.

Most of these major mediating bodies became implicated in the emerging character of the drug phenomenon. It was their actions and interpretations that shaped the conventional handling of the user. Who and what a drugtaker was depended heavily on models provided by doctors and lawyers. In the larger negotiation of the significance of use, too, representatives of those professions organized perspectives, wrote manuals and textbooks, engaged in political debate, and provided the substance of press reports.

Although there was never an unbroken consensus, it is

possible to discern some systematic shifts in the public ideas offered by the American Medical Association, the National Academy of Sciences, the American Bar Association, and the American Public Health Association. Those bodies never lent a completely unequivocal support to the official stance that cast the drugtaker as a pathological and dangerous outsider. Yet, over time, even that meager support was progressively withdrawn, leaving the stance stripped of much of its coherence and authority.

There are no closed frontiers around the worlds of the official and unofficial interpreters of morality. Internally, those worlds are fluid and incompletely integrated. Their separate segments display a limited independence and different capacities for change. Connections are made and unmade between the two worlds. Groups such as the medical and legal professions occupy a sometimes marginal position, being specially exposed to knowledge that is conveyed by universities, research institutes, and academic journals. They sponsor their own intellectual work, adopting academic research styles. Their openness led them to become caught up in the main movements of ideas about drugs. Engaged in the larger debate and confronting their own problems in control work, they detached themselves from the official portrayal of the user as a demonic figure. Indeed, David Downes's warning about the manufacture of drugtaking folk devils was addressed precisely to the British equivalent of the American Medical Association.

Increasingly, in the 1960s, administrative institutions such as the federal Bureau of Narcotics appeared remote and isolated from the perspectives that were forming around the problem. In time, parts of the professions contributing to the business of social control were themselves to locate the prime cause of the problem in legislative and enforcement policies. This defection was not uniform, but it led to an important fusion between the different sources of subversion. Thus, the American Bar Association supported work such as William Eldridge's *Narcotics and the Law*, which was most critical of established ideas and procedures. Similarly, the Ford Foundation sponsored research by lawyers that was to result in the

Drug Abuse Survey Project's *Dealing with Drug Abuse*. John
Kaplan's *Marihuana—the New Prohibition* constituted another major attack on an erstwhile dominant construction of
the proper control of drugs. Such fractures within the legal
world were of massive importance. They led, for instance, to
the scrutiny and questioning of search procedures, the use of
urine tests, entrapment tactics, the employment of informants,
and the like. Most particularly, they contributed to the
credibility of the contention that the coercive quality of
enforcement exacerbated and perpetuated pathologies that
had once been attributed to defects in the user alone. They
may well have led to the Department of Justice announcement
that the crime of possessing small amounts of marihuana
would no longer be prosecuted.[1]

The medical profession, too, began to distinguish between
types and consequences of drugs. Once discussed by many as
an undifferentiated group of harmful substances, drugs
became the subject of even finer discrimination. Erich Goode
remarks:

> It is fair to say that prior to the late 1960s, nearly all
> medical writings on marihuana, apart from a small and out-
> standing number of exceptions, adopted a pathology model
> to explain the causes and consequences of the drug's use.
> Marihuana use was a phenomenon typically thought to be
> very much like a disease . . . . Today, this tradition is dying
> . . . . Physicians, and especially the profession's younger
> half, have largely abandoned the view that, in the typical
> case, the "social" marihuana user will experience psychia-
> tric or medical pathologies. Dominant medical opinion today
> holds that marihuana is used recreationally, episodically,
> noncompulsively, socially, hedonistically, and frivolously.[2]

In effect, there would seem to have been a considerable
interpenetration of ideas that has affected all but the most
isolated members of legislatures and enforcement agencies.
There has been appreciable desertion from the camp of hard-
line proscribers to that of the advocates of a liberal or
libertarian policy. Doctors are in some measure attempting to
regain their control over the administration of drugs. Becker,

Clausen, and Dickson describe how that original control was eroded by interpretations put upon court decisions sought by the federal Bureau of Narcotics. There now appears to be a resurgence of effort to define addiction as a medical state and the user as one who might either be managed as a medical problem or simply shepherded away from the effects of social control altogether. Even medical advisers within the White House have advocated a relaxation of the laws on marihuana. Dr. Jerome Jaffe, at one time the director of the White House Office for Drug Abuse Prevention, was reported to have urged President Nixon to remove the sanction of imprisonment from offenses connected with the consumption of marihuana. He stated:

> In my opinion, it serves largely to clutter the courts, divert the police from more important responsibilities, and enrich the legal profession . . . . Those arguments were not sufficiently persuasive, and the decision to hold the line on criminal penalties came from the Oval Office.[3]

Although drugs remain under the aegis of an ostensibly static set of official definitions, there has been an apparent dilution of social control effort. The use of marihuana is not quite as zealously patrolled or punished as it once was, and restraints on it are about to be significantly removed. Prohibition has effectively ceased in some geographical and social areas. As Becker and Horowitz show, much enforcement in San Francisco is confined to a ritual beating of the bounds of deviancy, a discreet use of drugs having become practically tolerated. In John Auld's argument, too, there may be seen support for the assertion that drugs are no longer dramatic, contentious, or politically pregnant. Having become neutered and accommodated, they are being partially superseded by experiences that are as yet existentially ill organized. Most important, many forms of drugtaking may prove to be the symbolic artifacts of particular generations. Those who are most flirtatious with expressive styles seem to be dismissing drugs as anachronistic. Confronting new anxieties about life-chances, students at least appear to treat much drug use as an eccentricity of a historically dead leisure class. The organized memory of the young is short.

At one level, then, the evolution of the drugs problem has all the appearance of two analytically distinct movements. It is possible to trace out the history of ideas about drugs and the social history of drugtaking itself. Because the history of ideas must be treated both as a resource and as a problem, its connections with the history of use are most difficult to unravel. No clear conceptions of the latter process can be gained without resorting to the former, but there is only an uncertain correspondence between them. In one sense, any distinction between the two processes can never be less than highly contrived because they form a whole that cannot be properly wrenched apart. Yet such a separation serves some purposes well, and it may dispel a little of the confusion that surrounds the accumulated writings on drugs.

All history shapes and is shaped by publicly available reflection, but the scientific and political commentary on drugs has been most intimately fused with the manner in which their control and use has developed. At critical stages in that development, the history of ideas and the social history have been substantially one. Thus the writings of Timothy Leary and Harry Anslinger gave structure to both processes. Indeed, as I have argued, drugs have been interpreted by some as chiefly important on the plane of ideas and ideology. At other stages, the two histories may usefully be conceived as undergoing parallel courses that reflect but do not appreciably affect one another. The work of Lindesmith, Becker, or Sutter may not have made any pronounced impact on the routine experience of users and regulators. How great the degree of interpenetration might be is beyond appraisal. Drugs and ideas about drugs have often been courted by the same groups. University students have explored both, for example. Occasionally, too, there has been an apparent abyss between the evolving commentary and the evolving phenomenon. While any perspective cannot ultimately be divorced from what it surveys, it is as if some of the thinking about drugs has become part of an autonomous universe of beliefs that has acquired its own schemes of relevance, styles of interpretation, and patterns of change.

All writings on drugs may then achieve importance in different ways. They may be read as sources of instruction, as part of the problem itself, as perspectives on the history of ideas about the problem, or as some variable combination of the three. The chapters that make up this *Transaction* collection do not therefore make a simple contribution to the understanding of American and other drugtaking. Each has its own bearing on the two histories of the problem, each is more or less temporally restricted in scope, and each lends a· different sense to the others. Collectively, they represent a range of examples of the rhetorics and political vocabularies that have been utilized in the examination of drugs. So vast and discordant are the treatments of the problem that no one book could ever pretend to be comprehensive. In the main, *Drugs and Politics* should be taken as a sample of the manner in which one loosely coherent set of models was applied during the evolution of recent events. As a whole, the book may serve as documentation of central features of the problem.

NOTES

1. *New York Times*, 21 November 1974.

2. E. Goode, review of *Marihuana and Social Evolution* by J. Hochman, *Contemporary Sociology* 3, no. 5 (September 1974): 457.

3. Quoted in *New York Times*, 20 November 1974.

Drugs and Politics

1

Early History of Narcotics Use and Narcotics Legislation in the United States *

John A. Clausen

The opium poppy has been the source of sleep-inducing drugs and soothing beverages since antiquity.[1] Eventually it was learned that the ingredients responsible for the soporific properties were contained in the juice that exudes from the ripe poppy head when it is lanced. This juice, collected and dried, is opium. The opium itself contains two major components (alkaloids) that are distinct though related in drug action: morphine and codeine. They were first identified early in the nineteenth century.

Opium and its derivatives were inexpensive drugs and were used for a wide variety of human ills with almost no limitation until the early twentieth century. Indeed, the bold

*From "Drug Addiction" by John A. Clausen, in *Contemporary Social Problems,* edited by Robert K. Merton and Robert A. Nisbet, ©1961 by Harcourt Brace Jovanovich, Inc., and reprinted with their permission.

use of opium appears to have been the basis for the reputations of a number of famous physicians of earlier times. Not confined to use by physicians, however, opium and its derivatives were included in almost every patent medicine for the relief of painful conditions, in "soothing syrups" for babies, and in a variety of confections. Not all users received a sufficiently large or regular dosage to become addicted to these drugs, but many did. As one writer has commented:

> Addicted persons have enjoyed the appellation "dope fiend" for only some forty years, while the pusher of pre-World War I society was usually the local pharmacist, grocer, confectioner, or general store keeper. In fact, until the turn of the twentieth century, the use of opium and its derivatives was generally less offensive to Anglo-American public morals than the smoking of cigarettes. [2]

Some physicians had begun to warn against the dangers of the opiates as early as the 1830s, but by and large during the nineteenth century the problem of dependency was simply dealt with by continued consumption of the drug. The discomforts of abstinence were then just another set of aches and pains that could be alleviated by this panacea for all ills.

As an increasing number of physicians became aware of the dangers of habitual use of opium and its derivatives, there was a search for ways of using the drugs so as to avoid an "opium appetite." The introduction of the hypodermic needle was thought to afford such a means. It was only after the habitual hypodermic use of morphine to relieve pain by Civil War veterans that the dangers of addiction through this channel were recognized. So widespread was morphine use among ex-soldiers that it was known for a time as "army disease."

No sooner had awareness of this danger been achieved than a new one appeared. A new opiate, heroin, was produced in Germany in 1898. It was widely heralded as being free from addiction-producing properties, possessing all of the virtues but none of the dangers of morphine. It took several years' use of heroin to disprove these erroneous beliefs. Terry and Pellens observe that the widespread use of heroin as a substitute for morphine and as a more stimulating narcotic took place "first in the underworld, . . . long before the average physician had become aware of the dangers of the drug."[3] Heroin was especially convenient for underworld use, in that it was both highly potent and easy to adulterate with sugar and milk (lactose). While these characteristics were useful even before heroin could no longer be purchased freely, they became especially important after federal control of narcotics had been established.

Use of opium primarily for the sake of psychological effects achieved a vogue in some circles as a consequence of De Quincey's famous *Confessions of an English Opium-Eater*, which had appeared in 1821. Later in the century, the Chinese pattern of opium smoking was introduced to "sporting circles" in San Francisco. It spread especially among gamblers, prostitutes, and other frequenters of the demimonde. Although local ordinances were passed forbidding the practice, imports of smoking opium increased sharply and exceeded 100,000 pounds per year for every year from 1890 to 1909, when legal importation was terminated. Interestingly enough, prior to the passage of federal legislation in 1909, the only measure employed for the control of this importation of opium for nonmedicinal use was the imposition of import duties. When these became heavy, legal importation diminished and smuggling increased.

The Harrison Act

The first significant federal legislation to deal with the problems posed by narcotics addiction was an outgrowth of concern about opium smoking in Far Eastern territories. Theodore Roosevelt established a commission that met in Shanghai in 1908 to discuss the abuse of drugs and recommend possible solutions. This in turn led to the first international drug conference. The Hague Opium Convention of 1912 constituted an agreement among nations to control the traffic of opium and other addicting drugs. As an expression of our adherence to that convention, Congress in 1914 passed the Harrison Act to control the domestic sale, use, and transfer of opium and coca products. The act provided at the same time for an excise tax and for registration of, and maintenance of exact records by, persons handling drugs; and prohibited possession of the drugs, except for "legitimate medical purposes," on the part of persons not registered under the provisions of the act.

The primary purpose of the act, then, appeared to be to bring the drug traffic into observable and controllable channels. The lack of adequate control and the earlier indiscriminate use of opiates by physicians had resulted in a large number of addicted persons. Estimates vary, but almost certainly there were more than 100,000 addicts in the United States in 1914, many of whom were highly respected members of society. Prior to passage of the Harrison Act, these persons could apply to any member of the medical profession for treatment, including gradual drug withdrawal, or they could purchase drugs at moderate prices direct from any supplier. At a stroke, the Harrison Act cut off the latter source of supply and left the question of medical dosage for addicts to legal interpretation. That is, the direct dispensing of drugs by a physician was permitted only "for legitimate medical purposes" but it was not clear whether a physician could provide drugs to prevent the abstinence syndrome in persons previously addicted. World War I intervened before this issue was resolved. It would appear that many addicts did receive drugs through physicians, but that the short supply of opiates during the war led to some diminution of the number of addicted persons.

Since the Harrison Act was a revenue act, enforcement of its provisions was vested in a special police unit, the Narcotics Division of the Treasury Department. In 1919, after Treasury Department officials had charged that the drug menace had greatly increased, the government brought action against a number of physicians who had prescribed opiates for addicted persons. Several of these physicians had written prescriptions for addicts on a wholesale scale, without regard for medical responsibility. They were convicted; and, on appeal, the convictions were sustained by the Supreme Court. Unfortunately, these convictions were interpreted as denying to physicians the right to prescribe narcotics to relieve

suffering due to addiction. Justices Holmes, Brandeis, and
McReynolds vigorously dissented from this interpretation.
Overnight, the government's action, put into effect by the
Treasury Department, created a new dimension of the problem
of drug addiction. The former chairman of the Committee on
Narcotics and Alcohol of the American Bar Association
presents one view of the consequences:

> Armed with what came to be known as the Behrman
> indictment, the Narcotics Divison launched a reign of terror.
> Doctors were bullied and threatened, and those who were
> adamant went to prison. Any prescribing for an addict,
> unless he had some other ailment that called for narcotiza-
> tion, was likely to mean trouble with the Treasury agents.
> The addict-patient vanished; the addict-criminal emerged in
> his place. Instead of policing a small domain of petty stamp-
> tax chiselers, the Narcotics Division expanded its activities
> until it was swelling our prison population with thousands of
> felony convictions each year. Many of those who were
> caught had been respected members of their communities
> until the T-men packed them off.

> Simultaneously with its campaign to cut the addict off
> from the recourse to medical help, the Narcotics Division
> launched an attack on him along another line as well. He
> was portrayed as a moral degenerate, a criminal type, and
> the public was told that he could only be dealt with by being
> isolated from all normal contacts with society; if left at
> large, one of his main preoccupations was allegedly contriv-
> ing ways to induce others to share his misery by becoming
> addicted themselves. In short, he should be caught and
> locked up.[4]

The consequences of the interpretation and implementation of the Harrison Act was, then, to discourage the medical
professional from dealing with a legitimate medical problem,
to define the addict as a criminal rather than as an afflicted
person, and, by branding them "dope fiends," degenerates,
enemies of society, greatly to increase the difficulty of rehabilitating addicts and assimilating them into normal society. In
1925 the Supreme Court unequivocally rejected the interpreta-

tion that physicians were prohibited by the Harrison Act from treating addicts by prescribing drugs. In a unanimous decision, the Court disclaimed that the previous rulings could be:

> accepted as authority for holding that a physician who acts bona fide and according to fair medical standards, may never give an addict moderate amounts of drugs for self-administration in order to relieve conditions incident to addiction. Enforcement of the tax demands no such drastic rule, and if the act had such scope it would certainly encounter grave Constitutional difficulties.[5]

Unfortunately, by the time this ruling was handed down, the medical profession had withdrawn from attempting to treat addicts; the field was left to the illicit drug peddler.

There were occasional waves of public concern about drug addiction between the early 1920s and World War II, even though the available evidence suggests that there was a gradual decrease in the number of addicts during this period. World War II brought about a further decline, as the channels of illegal drug distribution were disrupted by the war. It is not clear whether any substantial number of addicts were thereby freed from the drug habit or whether they became merely quiescent for a time. It does appear, however, that relatively fewer new addicts were being created during the decade before World War II and during the war itself. Within five years of the end of World War II, however, there was unmistakable evidence of a substantial increase in narcotics use. Increasing proportions of young delinquents and criminals either had on their persons the characteristic bent spoon and hypodermic needle that are the addict's standard equipment for preparing and injecting heroin, or manifested the abstinence syndrome when jailed. Increasing numbers of parents appealed to police, to hospitals, and to social agencies for help in dealing with older adolescents and young adults who had become addicted to heroin. There were reports that heroin was being peddled to high school and even junior high school students and that addiction was rife in many parts of major cities. These reports were grossly exaggerated. There can be no question, however, that within relatively limited areas a major epidemic of drug use was in process. By 1960 the rate of new cases of addiction seems to have diminished, but the population of relatively young, recent addicts remains a threat to new outbreaks.

NOTES

1. Based largely on Charles E. Terry and Mildred Pellens, *The Opium Problem* (New York: The Committee on Drug Addiction, 1928), ch. 2.

2. Rufus King, "Narcotic Drug Laws and Enforcement Policies," *Law and Contemporary Problems* 22 (Winter 1957): 113.

3. Terry and Pellens, p. 84.

4. King, pp. 122-23.

5. Ibid., p. 123, quoted from the Supreme Court ruling in *Linder vs United States*, 268 U.S. 5 (1925).

2

Bureaucracy and Morality: An Organizational Perspective on a Moral Crusade*

Donald T. Dickson

The occurrence of a moral commitment within a bureaucratic setting is not an uncommon phenomenon, especially in our federal bureaucratic system. Examples abound, including the Federal Bureau of Investigation, the Bureau of Narcotics, the Selective Service System, the Central Intelligence Agency, the Internal Revenue Service, and—on a different scale—the Departments of State and Justice. In fact, one could argue that some sort of moral commitment is necessary for the effective functioning of any bureaucratic body. Usually this moral

*This work first appeared in *Social Problems* 16, no. 2 (Fall 1968): 143-56; it is reprinted with the permission of the author and The Society for the Study of Social Problems. The author gratefully acknowledges the assistance of Professors John Lofland and Leon Mayhew for both their encouragement and their critical comments on previous drafts, and of Professor Albert J. Reiss, Jr., whose several suggestions strengthened the focus of the paper.

commitment is termed an *ideology* and is translated into goals for the bureaucracy. Anthony Downs suggests four uses for an ideology: 1) to influence outsiders to support the bureau or at least not attack it; 2) to develop a goal consensus among the bureau members; 3) to facilitate a selective recruitment of staff, that is, to attract those who will support and further the goals of the bureau and repel those who would detract from those goals; and 4) to provide an alternative in decision making where other choice criteria are impractical or ambiguous.[1]

While most if not all bureaucracies attempt to maintain this moral commitment or ideology for the above mentioned reasons, some go further and initiate moral crusades, whereby they attempt to instill this commitment into groups and individuals outside their bureaus. The Narcotics Bureau in its efforts to mold public and congressional opinion against drug use is one bureaucratic example, the F.B.I. in its antisubversive and anticommunist crusades another.[2] The question then becomes, under what conditions does this transference of ideology from the bureaucracy to its environment or specific groups within its environment take place? Howard S. Becker supplies one answer to this, suggesting that this is the work of a "moral entrepreneur," either in the role of a crusading reformer or a rule enforcer.[3] In either role, the moral entrepreneur as an individual takes the initiative and generates a "moral enterprise."

This explanation has appeal. It is reminiscent of Weber's charismatic leader, and can be used to account for the genesis of most moral crusades and entire social movements. Further, it is very difficult to refute. A complete refutation would not only have to indicate an alternative, but also demonstrate that the bureaucratic leader is not a "moral entrepreneur"—is not a major factor in this transference of ideology. The purpose of this chapter is to accomplish the former only—to provide an equally if not more persuasive alternative based upon organizational research and theory. The difficulty in separating the two approaches is similar to the historian's dilemma of whether the historical incident makes the man great or the great man makes the historical incident. Here the question becomes: does the moral crusader create the morally committed bureaucracy or is he a product of that bureaucracy?

The difference between the moral entrepreneur situation and a situation wherein the moral crusade results primarily from a bureaucratic response to environmental factors, is that in the latter instance moral considerations are secondary to bureaucratic survival and growth, while in the former instance moral considerations are primary. Further, the end results of either of these crusades may vary considerably since each is in response to different stimuli. Other conditions being equal, the bureaucratic crusade will continue only as long as bureaucratic considerations dictate, while the moral crusade will continue as long as the individual moral crusader's zealotry requires.

In this chapter, the work of the Bureau of Narcotics and its former commissioner, Harry J. Anslinger, are examined in light of Becker's conclusion that Anslinger was a moral entrepreneur who led his Bureau on a moral crusade against the use of marihuana, culminating in an Anslinger-instigated publicity campaign that persuaded first the general public and then Congress that marihuana use was a vicious habit that should be outlawed and severely penalized.[4] Given the short time span Becker chose and his individualized focus, this seems to be a logical explanation of the Bureau's efforts. Given a broader organizational perspective, however, the passage of the Marihuana Tax Act and the Bureau's part in that passage appear to be only one phase of a larger organizational process, that of environmental change. Using this focus it is necessary first to examine briefly the relationships between organizations and their environments with special emphasis on adaptation and to discuss a special case of these organizations, the public bureaucracy. The results of this analysis are then applied to the Narcotics Bureau and narcotics legislation in conjunction with an examination of Becker's findings. Finally, the implications of this analysis are examined.

Organizations and Environments

One ongoing problem an organization must cope with is its relationship with its environment.[5] For the incipient organization this means an initial decision as to the type of relationship it desires to establish with its environment, an assessment of the type of relationship it is able to establish, and the working out of some acceptable compromise between the two. For the established organization, this means maintaining this relationship either through normal boundary defenses or through other means, or establishing a more favorable one. The consequences of these—decision, assessment, and compromise—for the organization are far reaching; for if the organization wishes to grow and expand or even continue to exist, it must come to terms with its environment, and where necessary insure acceptance by it. No doubt a few organizations with substantial resources may exist for some time in a hostile environment, but the more normal case seems to be that an organization must at least establish an environmentally neutral relationship if not an environmentally supportive one.

Of course when the organization is in its incipient stages, the problems are magnified. Environmental support is more necessary, environmental hostility more of a threat to survival. Usually the organization will adapt to the demands of the environment, but occasionally Starbuck's observation, "Adaptation is an obvious precondition of survival,"[6] is ignored and the organization either chooses to attempt to alter these demands, or chooses to ignore them. Not uncommonly such a decision results in drastic consequences for the organization. The Women's Christian Temperance Union failed in its efforts to gain wide acceptance for its programs and has only been able to continue with its operations severely curtailed. The counseling organization at Western Electric that grew out of the Hawthorne Studies felt it could not function properly if it adapted to the requirements of the larger organization and was eventually discontinued, though adaptation was part of a more complex problem.[7]

An organization may attempt to alter the demands of its environment when such an attempt would not draw too heavily upon the organization's resources, or when the alternative, adaptation to the environment, would mean a substantial loss to the organization or perhaps dissolution. Selznick's study of the T.V.A. and Clark's study of adult education in California are examples of organizations that chose to try to alter their environments rather than adapt to them. [8] In Selznick's case, the organization itself was altered through these efforts. Clark argues that a number of organizations undergoing a similar value transformation may alter the values of the society in which they exist. He focuses on what he calls "precarious values" and discusses under what conditions these may be changed.

It is clear then that some attempts to alter the environment succeed and others fail. Why is this so? An organization's environment may be very simple or highly complex, but in general every environment when viewed as a system will contain the following elements: 1) pragmatic day-to-day decisions categorized as policies or practices; 2) long-range goals; 3) a clearly defined normative system; and 4) a generalized value system. [9]

If placed in a hierarchy in this order, each succeeding category would influence its predecessors. That is, values in the environment are in part the basis of the other three, norms influence both goals and policies and practices, and so forth. Further, any member of any category may be strongly or weakly held. Some of the reasons for weakness are outlined by Clark—that is, not legitimated, undefined, or not widely accepted. [10]

Any organization that chooses to alter its environment will have to make a decision as to where along the hierarchy to focus its efforts. Attempts to alter some policy of an environmental element may be more successful and less costly than attempts to alter some value of an environment, but the latter might result in a long-term change while the former might be the more unstable—since the goals, norms, and values underlying it were not changed. A change in the value system, where possible, would eventually result in changes throughout the system.

Organizational attempts at environmental change will depend upon a number of factors:

(a) The necessity for change—is environmental change a prerequisite for organizational survival, or is it not necessary but merely desirable?

(b) The amount of resources available—can the organization afford to attempt the change effort?

(c) The size and complexity of the environment—would change be necessary in only a small element in the environment, or would a whole complex of elements need to be altered?

(d) The extent to which change must take place—is it necessary to change only some environmental policy or practice, or is it necessary to totally revamp the environmental structure from values on down?

(e) Is the policy, goal, norm, or value to be changed, strongly or weakly held—is it firmly entrenched and legitimated, or is it "precarious?"

It is clear, then, that when one is talking about organizations changing their environment, one should make explicit what elements in the environment are being focused upon, how extensively they are being changed, and how strongly held they were to begin with. Clark's adult education study was concerned with weakly held values. The W.C.T.U. as discussed by Gusfield was concerned with strongly held values and this may in some degree account for its failure.[11] In his discussion of the Marihuana Tax Act as a "moral enterprise," Becker was concerned with a weakly held value, as will be shown, though he did not discuss it in these terms.

A Case Study: The U.S. Bureau of Narcotics

The Bureau as a Public Bureaucracy

This case study will be limited to an analysis of the policies of the Narcotics Bureau and the effects of these policies on salient elements of its environment. This approach is preferable to a more general organizational analysis of the Bureau—examining its structure, recruitment, boundary defenses, and myriad environmental transactions—because in these respects the Bureau is not unlike most other governmental bureaucracies. Further, in its efforts to mold public opinion in support of its policies, it is not unlike many organizations, especially those with a moral commitment. The

W.C.T.U. carried on the same sort of campaign—including propaganda, attacks on its critics, and legislative lobbying. What makes the Bureau unique from many other organizations that have tried to influence their environments is that the campaign was and is carried out by a governmental organ.

Several ramifications of this difference are immediately apparent. There is the element of legitimation. The public is far more likely to accept the pronouncements of a federal department than a voluntary private organization. There is the element of propaganda development. Due to its public nature, a federal department is more skilled in dealing with the public and in preparing propaganda for public consumption. There is the element of communication. A federal organization has far more means available for the dissemination of the information than a private one—by press releases, publications, or lectures and speeches—and it is likely to have representatives based in major population centers to disseminate the information. There is the element of coercion. A federal department can bring a wide range of pressures to bear on its critics.

Finally, at a different level, a federal bureau differs in the area of survival. Private organizations have considerable control over their future. They may decide to expand, continue as before, disband, merge, alter their aims, or reduce their activities. The attitude of their environments will have great bearing on this decision, to be sure, but the final decision rests with the organization. A federal department may go through any of the above stages, but frequently the final decision does not rest within the department but with the congressional, executive, or judicial body that created it. A bureau created by congressional enactment will continue to be unaltered except by internal decision only as long as Congress can be convinced that there is no need to alter it. Although there may be some question of degree, there is no question that public opinion will be a major factor in the congressional decision.

Therefore the federal department must convince the public and Congress: 1) that it serves a useful, or if possible, a necessary function; and 2) that it is uniquely qualified to do so. The less the department is sure of its future status, the more it will try to convince Congress and the public of these.

Background in Environment Change: The Emergence and Development of the Bureau

In the late nineteenth and early twentieth centuries, narcotics were widely available: through doctors who indiscriminately prescribed morphine and later heroin as pain killers, through druggists who sold them openly, or through a wide variety of patent medicines.

The public. . .[in the early twentieth century] had an altogether different conception of drug addiction from that which prevails today. The habit was not approved, but neither was it regarded as criminal or monstrous. It was usually looked upon as a vice or personal misfortune, or much as alcoholism is viewed today. Narcotics users were pitied rather than loathed as criminals or degenerates....[12]

In 1914 Congress through the passage of the Harrison Act attempted to exert some control over the narcotics traffic. This act remains today the cornerstone of narcotics legislation. Rather than eliminate the use of narcotic drugs, the act was passed in order to honor a previous international obligation stemming from the Hague Convention of 1912, and to control the criminal encroachments into the drug trade. Nowhere in the act is there direct reference to addicts or addiction.

Its ostensible purpose appeared to be simply to make the entire process of drug distribution within the country a matter of record. The nominal excise tax (one cent per ounce), the requirement that persons and firms handling drugs register and pay fees, all seemed designed to accomplish this purpose. There is no indication of a legislative intention to deny addicts access to legal drugs or to interfere in any way with medical practices in this area.[13]

Medical practices were specifically exempted:

Nothing contained in this section. . .shall. . .apply. . .
[t]o the dispensing or distribution of any drugs mentioned...
to a patient by a physician, dentist, or veterinary surgeon
registered under section 4722 in the course of his professional practice only.[14]

Thus, the act did not make addiction illegal. All it required
was that addicts should obtain drugs from registered physicians who made a record of the transaction.

A narcotics division was created in the Internal Revenue
Bureau of the Treasury Department to collect revenue and
enforce the Harrison Act. In 1920 it merged into the Prohibition
Unit of that department and upon its creation in 1927 into the
Prohibition Bureau. In 1930 the Bureau of Narcotics was
formed as a separate bureau in the Treasury Department.

Legitimation: The Process of Changing an Environment

After 1914 the powers of the Narcotics Division were clear
and limited: to enforce registration and recordkeeping, violation of which could result in imprisonment for up to ten years,
and to supervise revenue collection. The large number of
addicts who secured their drugs from physicians were
excluded from the Division's jurisdiction. The public's attitude
toward drug use had not changed much with the passage of the
Act—there was some opposition to drug use, some support of
it, and a great many who did not care one way or the other. In
fact, the Harrison Act was passed with very little publicity or
news coverage.[15]

Thus at this time the Narcotics Division was faced with a
severely restricted scope of operations. Acceptance of the
legislation as envisioned by Congress would mean that the
Division would at best continue as a marginal operation with
limited enforcement duties. Given the normal, well-docu-
mented bureaucratic tendency toward growth and expansion,
and given the fact that the Division was a public bureaucracy
and needed to justify its operations and usefulness before
Congress, it would seem that increased power and jurisdiction

in the area of drug control would be a desirable and, in fact, necessary goal. Adaptation to the Harrison Act limitations would preclude attainment of this goal. Operating under a legislative mandate, the logical alternative to adaptation would be to persuade the Congress and public that expansion was necessary and to extend the provisions of the Harrison Act.

Also at this point, the public's attitude toward narcotics use could be characterized as only slightly opposed. Faced with a situation where adaptation to the existing legislation was bureaucratically unfeasible, where expansion was desirable, and where environmental support—from both Congress and the public—was necessary for continued existence, the Division launched a two-pronged campaign: 1) a barrage of reports and newspaper articles that generated a substantial public outcry against narcotics use; and 2) a series of Division-sponsored test cases in the courts, which resulted in a reinterpretation of the Harrison Act and substantially broadened powers for the Narcotics Division.[16] Thus the Division attained its goals by altering a weakly held public value regarding narcotics use from neutrality or slight opposition to strong opposition, and by persuading the courts that it should have increased powers.[17]

Though the resources of the Division were limited, it was able to accomplish its goals because it was a public bureaucracy and as such had the aforementioned advantages that arise from that status. Since the ability to develop propaganda and the means to communicate it were inherent in this status, as was the propensity by the public to accept this propaganda, environmental support could be generated with less resource expenditure. Further, the Division as a public bureaucracy would be assumed to have a familiarity with governmental processes not only in its own executive branch, but also in the congressional and judicial branches as well. This built-in expertise necessary for the Division's expansion might be quite costly in time and resources for the private bureaucracy, but again was inherent in the Division's status.

One typical example of the public campaign was a report cited and relied upon by the Narcotics Division for some years.

It is an interesting combination of truth, speculation, and fiction, a mix that the Division and the Bureau that succeeded it found to be an effective public persuader for many years. In a report dated June 1919, a committee appointed by the Treasury Department to study narcotics reported inter alia that there were 237,665 addicts in the United States treated by physicians (based upon a 30 percent response by physicians queried), that there were over one million addicts in the country in 1919 (a figure based upon a compromise between projections based on the percentage of addicts in Jacksonville, Florida in 1913 and New York City in 1918) that there was extensive addiction among children, that narcotics were harmful to health and morals, and that they were directly connected with crime and abject poverty. Among the physical effects noted were insanity; diseased lungs, hearts, and kidneys; rotting of the skin; and sterility.[18]

This "scholarly report" is an interesting example of the propaganda effort, for it appears to the casual reader to be credible (especially given its source), and contains charges that seem to be designed to generate widespread public disgust toward narcotics users and support for the Division and its efforts. Many of the same charges were applied to marihuana when the Bureau campaigned against its use.

While the Division was carrying out its public campaign, it was also busy in the courts. Between 1918 and 1921 the Narcotics Division won three important cases in the Supreme Court and persuaded the Court, essentially, to delete the medical exception from the Harrison Act thereby broadening its position as an enforcement agency. In the first case, *Webb vs United States*,[19] the court held that a physician could not supply narcotics to an addict unless he was attempting to cure him and in so doing made illegal the work of a large number of physicians who were supplying addicts with drugs under the registration procedures of the Harrison Act. This decision was supported in the two following cases: *Jin Fuey Moy vs United States*[20] and *United States vs Behrman*.[21] In *Behrman*, it was held that physicians could not even supply drugs to addicts in an attempt to cure them. The medical exception was nullified. The cases were skillfully chosen and presented to the court.

Each was a flagrant abuse of the statute—in *Webb* the physician's professional practice seemed to be limited to supplying narcotics to whoever wanted them. In the other two cases, the physicians supplied huge amounts of drugs over short periods of time to a small number of patients—patently for resale at a later time. Yet the Division did not argue for and the court did not rule on the cases as violations of the statute as it was intended, but instead regarded all of these as normal professional practices by physicians and held that, as such, they were illegal.

Three years after *Behrman*, the court somewhat reversed itself in *Linder vs United States*.[22] Here the doctor supplied a small dosage to a patient who was a government informer. The court rejected the government's case in a unanimous opinion, holding:

> The enactment under consideration. . .says nothing of "addicts" and does not undertake to prescribe methods for their medical treatment, and we cannot possibly conclude that a physician acted improperly or unwisely or for other than medical purposes solely because he has dispensed to one of them, in the ordinary course and in good faith, four small tablets of morphine or cocaine for relief of condition incident to addiction.[23]

The court went on to warn the Division:

> Federal power is delegated, and its prescribed limits must not be transcended even though the ends seem desirable. The unfortunate condition of the recipient certainly created no reasonable probability that she would sell or otherwise dispose of the few tablets entrusted to her and we cannot say that by so dispensing them the doctor necessarily transcended the limits of that professional conduct with which Congress never intended to interfere.[24]

Though *Linder* might have reintroduced doctors into the area, the Narcotics Division successfully prevented this by refusing to recognize *Linder* in its regulations, thus creating a situation where few would accept the risks involved in testing the doctrine, and by launching an all-out campaign against doctors—closing the remaining narcotics clinics, imprisoning rebellious doctors, and publicizing records and convictions of physician addicts.[25]

Rufus King comments on this period of growth:

> In sum, the Narcotics Division succeeded in creating a very large criminal class for itself to police. . .instead of the very small one Congress has intended.[26]

The success of this campaign was reflected not only in the increased number of potential criminals, but in financial growth as well. Between 1918 and 1925, the Bureau's budgetary appropriations increased from $325,000 to $1,329,440, a rise of over 400 percent.[27] (See Table 1.)

The Marihuana Tax Act of 1937: A Bureaucratic Response

There are many other examples of efforts by the Bureau to create and maintain a friendly and supportive environment—through other publicity campaigns, through lobbying in Cong. ess, and through continued and diligent attacks upon and harassments of its critics—which have been amply chronicled by others, although not as part of an organizational process.[28] The Bureau's efforts to induce passage of the Marihuana Tax Act deserve special mention, however, in light of Becker's finding that the legislation was the result of what he terms a "moral enterprise." [29] Becker concludes that Narcotics Commissioner Anslinger and his Bureau were the motive forces behind the original 1937 legislation and the increasingly severe penalties that have since been imposed. This is readily conceded.[30] But he argues that the motivation behind this desire for the marihuana legislation was a moral one. He presents a picture of a society totally indifferent to the use of marihuana until Anslinger, in the role of a moral entrepreneur, "blows the whistle" on marihuana smoking. Again, it is conceded that Commissioner Anslinger throughout his long career with the Narcotics Bureau has opposed drug and narcotics use on moral grounds. This theme runs consistently through his writings.[31] What Becker ignores is that Anslinger was also a bureaucrat and thus responsive to bureaucratic

DRUGS AND POLITICS
TABLE 1

Budgetary Appropriations for
the U.S. Narcotics Bureau
(1915-44)*

Year**	Total Appropriation
1915	$ 292,000
1916	300,000
1917	325,000
1918	750,000
1919	750,000
1920	750,000
1921	750,000
1922	750,000
1923	750,000
1924	1,250,000
1925	1,329,440
1926	1,329,440
1927	1,329,440
1928	1,329,440
1929	1,350,440
1930	1,411,260
1931	1,611,260
1932	1,708,528
1933	1,525,000
1934	1,400,000
1935	1,244,899
1936	1,249,470
1937	1,275,000
1938	1,267,000
1939	1,267,600
1940	1,306,700
1941	1,303,280
1942	1,283,975
1943	1,289,060
1944	1,150,000

*Source: Appropriations Committee, U.S. Senate, *Appropriations, New Offices, etc., Statements Showing Appropriations Made, New Offices Created, etc., 1915-1923*; U.S. Bureau of the Budget, *The Budget of the United States Government*, Washington, D.C.: Government Printing Office, 1923-45.

**Fiscal year the appropriation was made. Each sum was appropriated for the following fiscal year.

pressures and demands as well. The distinction between these roles is difficult to make but it is fundamental in analyzing the legislation.

To understand whether the marihuana legislation was to a large degree the result of bureaucratic processes similar to the Bureau's expansion after the Harrison Act or whether it was instead the result of an individual's moral crusade, it is necessary to focus not only on the individual, as Becker has done, but upon the Bureau and its environment during this period as well. Through this method, certain parallels with the post-Harrison Act period become evident.

The Marihuana Tax Act that imposed a prohibitively costly tax on the sale of marihuana was passed by both houses of Congress with practically no debate [32] and signed into law on 2 August 1937. While Becker seems to argue that the Bureau generated a great public outcry against marihuana use prior to the passage of the Tax Act, his data supporting this argument are misleading if not erroneously interpreted. [33] While marihuana use seems to have increased since the early 1930s, there appears to have been little public concern expressed in the news media, even in 1937. Few magazine articles were written about the subject, and if the *New York Times* is any indication, newspaper coverage was also slight. [34] The final presidential signing of the act received minimal coverage from the *New York Times*. [35] In short, rather than the Bureau-generated public turmoil the Becker indicates, it seems that public awareness of the problem, as well as public opposition to it, was slight.

While it cannot be shown conclusively that the Marihuana Tax Act was the result of a bureaucratic response to environmental conditions, similarities between this period and the post-Harrison Act period are evident. Marihuana opposition, like narcotics opposition before, appears to have resulted from a weakly held value. In both situations, publicity campaigns were launched. In both cases, one through the courts and one through Congress, efforts were exerted to expand the power of the Bureau. In both cases, there were substantial numbers of potential criminals who could be incorporated into the Bureau's jurisdiction.

Perhaps more convincing than similarities are the budgetary appropriations for the Bureau from 1915 to 1944 presented
in Table 1. In 1932, when the Bureau's appropriations were
approaching an all-time high, the Bureau stated:

> The present Constitutional limitations would seem to
> require control measures directed against the intrastate
> traffic of Indian hemp (marihuana) to be adopted by the
> several State governments rather than by the Federal
> Government, and the policy has been to urge the State
> authorities generally to provide the necessary legislation,
> with supporting enforcement activity, to prohibit the traffic
> except for bona fide medical purposes. The proposed
> uniform State narcotic law. . .with operational text apply-
> ing to restriction of traffic in Indian hemp, has been
> recommended as an adequate law to accomplish the desired
> purpose. [36]

At this time, according to the Bureau, sixteen states had
enacted legislation in which "the sale or possession (of
marihuana) is prohibited except for medical purposes."[37] One
year later, 18 more states had enacted the desired legislation,
and by 1936, it appears that the Bureau's policy had
succeeded completely, for all 48 states had enacted legislation
that governed the sale or possession of marihuana.[38]

Despite this apparent success and despite former questions concerning the Constitutionality of the measure, the
Bureau in 1937 pressed for the enactment of the federal
marihuana act. For Anslinger, the moral entrepreneur, 1936
should have been a year of victory. In every state the
marihuana menace was subjected to statutory control.[39] But
for Anslinger, the bureaucrat, 1936 seems to have been
another year of defeat. His budgetary appropriation remained
near a low point that had not been seen in over a decade,
which to some extent reflected the general economic conditions of the time. His request for fiscal 1933 had been cut
$100,000 below the general Treasury Department reduction
for all bureaus.[40] In succeeding years, reductions in actual
operating expenses were greater than those reflected in Table
1, for varying sums were deducted from the appropriations
and held in a general trust fund as part of the government's

anti-Depression program. The Bureau's actual operating funds remained at about one million dollars from fiscal 1934 to fiscal 1936.[41] In his appearances before the House Subcommittee of the Committee on Appropriations that considered the Treasury Department budget, Anslinger repeatedly warned that the limited budget was curtailing his enforcement activities.[42] By 1936, his budget had decreased over $450,000 from its high four years before, a fall of almost 26 percent.

Again in 1937 Anslinger, the moralist, would be expected first to convince the general public that marihuana use was evil and immoral, while Anslinger, the bureaucrat, would be more concerned with attaining passage of legislation that would increase the Bureau's powers and then proceed to generate environmental support for these powers. In fact, the latter occurred. The great bulk of Bureau-inspired publicity came after the passage of the act, not before.[43]

Faced with a steadily decreasing budget, the Bureau responded as any organization so threatened might react: it tried to appear more necessary, and it tried to increase its scope of operations. As a result of this response, the Marihuana Tax Act of 1937 was passed.[44] Whether the Bureau's efforts were entirely successful is questionable. One beneficial result for the Bureau was that violations and seizures under the Marihuana Tax Act contributed substantially to the Bureau's totals, which had been declining for some time. (When arrests, convictions, and seizures were on the increase, these were faithfully reported to the House Subcommittee as evidence of the Bureau's effective use of funds.) In 1938, the first full year under the Marihuana Tax Act, one out of every four federal drug and narcotic convictions was for a marihuana violation.[45]

Financially, the enterprise was less successful. Though the budgetary decline was halted, expected increases for enforcing the new legislation did not immediately materialize. Anslinger pointed out this problem in a 1937 subcommittee hearing in connection with the fiscal 1939 appropriation:

Comm. Anslinger: We took on the administration of the marihuana law and did not get any increase for that purpose. The way we are running we may have to request a deficiency of $100,000 at the end of the year; but I sincerely hope you will not see me here for a deficit. Beginning the first of the year, Mr. Chairman, I shall control all travel out of Washington. That is a hard job. I have to do that to make up some of this money. We went ahead at high speed and broke up ten big distributing rings, and now we find ourselves in the hole financially.

Mr. Ludlow: You have to find some way to recoup?

Comm. Anslinger: Yes; and keep the enforcement of the Marihuana Act going. Not a dollar has been appropriated in connection with the enforcement of the marihuana law. We have taken on the work in connection with the Marihuana Act in addition to our other duties.[46]

While the Bureau's budgetary appropriations since that time have in general increased, the period of the late 1930s and early 1940s, where increases might be expected to be the largest, was a period of small advances and then a gradual decline. Of course the major factor in that period was the massive redirection of funds from nonmilitary areas, and thus these figures do not accurately reflect the Bureau's enterprise.

In conclusion, it should be reiterated that this chapter does not presume to refute the moral entrepreneur approach —for in many instances it is a valid and useful means of analysis—but rather it attempts to demonstrate an alternative explanation that may frequently be appropriate. It would be either naive or presumptuous to deny that some combination of both moral and bureaucratic factors exist in any given crusade. The problem for analysis is to determine the relative importance of each, and the consequences stemming from a particular combination. The utility of the organizational approach lies in that it can be extended to other similar moral crusades or to entire social movements, where the emphasis so far has been on the work of individual crusaders rather than on the organizations and their environments. Further, to the extent these movements follow the general societal pattern and become increasingly complex, organized, and bureaucratic, the organizational approach will become even more important in analysis and prediction.

NOTES

1. Anthony Downs, *Inside Bureaucracy* (Boston: Little, Brown, 1967).

2. Fred J. Cook, *The FBI Nobody Knows* (New York: Macmillan, 1964).

3. Howard S. Becker, *The Outsiders: Studies in the Sociology of Deviance* (New York: Free Press, 1963), pp. 147-63.

4. Becker, pp. 135-46.

5. See especially Peter M. Blau and W. Richard Scott, *Formal Organizations: A Comparative Approach* (San Francisco: Chandler, 1962), pp. 222-54; William H. Starbuck, "Organizational Growth and Development," in *Handbook of Organizations,* edited by James G. March (Chicago: Rand McNally, 1965), pp. 450-533; Philip Selznick, *T.V.A. and the Grassroots: A Case Study in the Sociology of Formal Organizations* (Berkeley, California: University of California Press, 1949).

6. W. Starbuck, p. 468.

7. William J. Dickson and F. J. Roethlisberger, *Counseling in an Organization: A Sequel to the Hawthorne Researches* (Boston: Harvard Business School, 1966), ch. 14, 16.

8. Selznick; Burton Clark, "Organizational Adaptation and Precarious Values," *American Sociological Review* 21 (1956): 327-36.

9. Adapted from Talcott Parsons, "An Outline of the Social System," in *Theories of Society: Foundations of Modern Sociological Theory,* volume 1, edited by Talcott Parsons, Edward Shils, Kasper D. Nagele, and Jesse N. Pitts (New York: Free Press, 1961), pp. 30-79.

10. Clark, pp. 328-29.

11. Joseph R. Gusfield, *Symbolic Crusade: Status Politics and the American Temperance Movement* (Urbana, Illinois: University of Illinois Press, 1963).

12. Alfred R. Lindesmith, *Opiate Addiction* (Bloomington, Indiana: Principia, 1947), p. 183.

13. Lindesmith, p. 4. See also Rufus King, "The Narcotics Bureau and the Harrison Act: Jailing the Healers and the Sick," *Yale Law Journal* 62 (1953): 736; William B. Eldridge, *Narcotics and the Law* (New York: American Bar Foundation, 1961). The Harrison Act is placed in a statutory perspective in "Note: Narcotics Regulations," *Yale Law Journal* 62 (1953):751-87.

14. 26 U.S.C. 4705(c) (1954 Code).

15. The *New York Times Index* for 1914 lists only two brief articles on the federal legislation, one in June and one in August when the Senate adopted the Harrison Act. It should be noted that there was

also discussion of a broadened New York State narcotics act and articles publicizing the arrest of violators of an earlier New York statute at that time.

16. King, pp. 737-48; Lindesmith, pp. 5-11.

17. In focusing on judicial expansion of existing legislation rather than on further congressional action, the Division was able to avoid the lobbies of doctors and pharmacists who strongly opposed the Harrison Act in the first place and who successfully lobbied for the medical exception. See the New York Times, 28 June 1914, sec. 2, p. 5.

18. U.S. Treasury Department, Report of Special Committee to Investigate the Traffic in Narcotic Drugs (15 April 1919).

19. 249 U.S. 96 (1918).

20. 254 U.S. 189 (1920).

21. 258 U.S. 280 (1921).

22. 268 U.S. 5 (1924).

23. 268 U.S. 5 at 15 (1924).

24. 268 U.S. 5 at 20 (1924).

25. King, pp. 744-45; "Note: Narcotics Regulation," pp. 784-87. The Bureau's yearly report, Traffic in Opium and Other Dangerous Drugs, carries numerous reports of addiction among physicians during this period. See also Lindesmith, pp. 135-61.

26. King, p. 738.

27. See Table 1. During this period, two pieces of legislation were enacted that affected the Bureau's scope of operation: The Revenue Act of 1918, and the Narcotic Drug Import and Export Act of 1922.

28. Along with the works of Lindesmith and King above, see the Bureau's publication, Comments on Narcotic Drugs (undated), the Bureau's reply to the A.B.A.—A.M.A. committee interim report "Narcotic Drugs." This publication was described by DeMott as "perhaps the crudest publication yet produced by a government agency . . ." and was later taken out of print. Benjamin DeMott, "The Great Narcotics Muddle," Harper's Magazine, March 1962, p. 53. For a vivid account of the Bureau's methods with its critics, see Lindesmith, pp. 242-68.

29. Becker, p. 135.

30. It seems clear from examining periodicals, newspapers, and the Congressional Record that the Bureau was primarily responsible for the passage of the act, though Becker's almost exclusive reliance on the claims of the Bureau in its official publication, Traffic in Opium and Other Dangerous Drugs, does not seem warranted given the previously discussed tendency of a public bureaucracy to emphasize its necessity and successful functioning.

31. See especially Harry Anslinger and Will Osborne, *The Murderers: The Story of the Narcotic Gang* (New York: Farrar, Straus, 1961), ch. 1; and also the other writings of the Commissioner, among them: Harry Anslinger and William F. Tompkins, *The Traffic in Narcotics* (New York: Funk and Wagnalls, 1953); Harry Anslinger and J. Gregory, *The Protectors: The Heroic Story of the Narcotic Agents, Citizens, and Officials in Their Unending, Unsung Battle Against Organized Crime in America* (New York: Farrar, Straus, 1964).

32. This is not unusual in the area of moral legislation, as Becker points out. Furthermore, unlike noncriminal legislation where the losing party still has a variety of remedies available to challenge the law, few remedies are available to those who are legislated against in criminal areas. Legitimate lobbies cannot be formed and test cases are dangerous.

However, Becker gives the impression that the only opposition to the marihuana legislation came from hemp growers, and that no one argued for the marihuana users (pp. 144-45). This is erroneous. The legislative counsel for the A.M.A., Dr. William C. Woodward, challenged the Bureau's conclusions that marihuana use was harmful to health and widespread among children, and demanded evidence to support these assertions. While he was not representing the marihuana users, he was certainly arguing their case and questioning the need for legislation. See *Taxation of Marihuana*, Hearings Before the Committee on Ways and Means of the House of Representatives, 75th Congress, 1st Session, on H.R. 6385, April 27-30 and May 4, 1937, esp. p. 92. It should be noted that this opposition was ignored by the committee members.

33. Becker's data consist of a survey of the *Readers Guide to Periodical Literature*, in which he found that no magazine articles appeared before July 1935; four appeared between July 1935 and June 1937; and 17 between July 1937 and June 1939 (p. 141). While this is correct, it is misleading due to the time intervals used. The four articles in the second period all appeared before 1937, no articles appeared in the five months preceding the House committee hearings on the act in late April and early May, one appeared in July 1937, and the rest appeared after the bill was signed into law on 2 August 1937. In short, of the articles that Becker asserts provided the impetus to congressional action, only one appeared in the seven months of 1937 before the marihuana bill was signed into law.

34. A survey of the *New York Times Index* shows: one article discussed marihuana in 1936 and eight discussed the subject between January and August 1937. There were no articles about or coverage of any of the congressional hearings. Contrary to Becker's assertion,

perhaps the most significant thing about this period was the lack of publicity involved.

35. The total coverage by the *New York Times* consisted of a four-line A.P. dispatch near the bottom of page four, titled "Signs Bill to Curb Marihuana," and reading in its entirety: "President Roosevelt signed today a bill to curb traffic in the narcotic, marihuana, through heavy taxes on transactions" (3 August 1937).

36. U.S. Bureau of Narcotics, *Traffic in Opium and Other Dangerous Drugs For the Year Ending December 31, 1932* (Washington, D.C.: Government Printing Office), p. 43.

37. Ibid., p. 43.

38. U.S. Bureau of Narcotics, *Traffic,* 1932-36.

39. It can be argued that a federal measure was still necessary because: 1) state legislation was poorly drawn, or 2) state enforcement was inadequate. The former is doubtful since by 1937, thirty-nine states (as compared to four in 1933) had enacted the Uniform Narcotic Drug Act, the very legislation the Bureau felt would best control marihuana use. The latter situation, even if true, could have been rectified by means other than federal legislation.

40. *Hearings Before the Subcommittee of the House Committee on Appropriations,* 72nd Congress, 1st Session, in charge of the Treasury Department Appropriations Bill for 1933, January 14, 1932, pp. 375-93.

41. *Hearings Before the Subcommittee of the House Committee on Apropriations,* for fiscal 1934: 72nd Congress, 2nd Session, November 23, 1932, pp. 171-80; for fiscal 1935: 73rd Congress, 2nd Session, December 18, 1933, pp. 178-98; for fiscal 1936: 74th Congress, 1st Session, December 17, 1934, pp. 201-225.

42. Thus in the hearing for the 1935 appropriation:

Mr. Arnold: How are you getting by with that $1,000,000 after those deductions?
Comm Anslinger: I am getting by, but I have had to cut back enforcement activities so sharply that it has reached a point where I think it has been harmful .... (1935 *Hearings,* p. 189)

In his opening statement at the hearing for the 1936 appropriation, Anslinger stated: "Mr. Chairman, and distinguished members of the committee, during the past fiscal year we have been operating under a very restricted appropriation. Our enforcement did not fall off too much although it did suffer somewhat" (1936 *Hearings,* p. 201). A decrease in seizures and fines levied was attributed to the limited budget (ibid., pp. 213-14).

43. See note 32.

44. While Commissioner Anslinger as leader of this bureaucratic response might be characterized as a "bureaucratic entrepreneur," such characterization would be misleading, for similar to Becker's characterization it still simplifies the problem by emphasizing the individual's importance rather than that of the Bureau and its environment.

45. U.S. Bureau of Narcotics, *Traffic in Opium and Other Dangerous Drugs For the Year Ending December 31, 1938* (Washington, D.C.: Government Printing Office), pp. 77-79.

46. *Hearings Before the Subcommittee of the House Committee on Appropriations*, 75th Congress, 3rd Session, in charge of the Treasury Department Appropriations Bill for 1939, December 14, 1937, p. 380.

3

The Marihuana Tax Act *

Howard S. Becker

The Marihuana Tax Act

It is generally assumed that the practice of smoking marihuana was imported into the United States from Mexico, by way of the Southwestern states of Arizona, New Mexico, and Texas, all of which had sizable Spanish-speaking populations. People first began to notice marihuana use in the nineteen-twenties but, since it was a new phenomenon and one apparently confined to Mexican immigrants, did not express much concern about it. (The medical compound prepared from the marihuana plant had been known for some time, but was

*This work originally appeared in *The Outsiders* by Howard S. Becker, pp. 135-46. Reprinted with permission of Macmillan Publishing Co., Inc., ©1963 by The Free Press of Glencoe, a division of the Macmillan Company.

not often prescribed by U.S. physicians.) As late as 1930, only sixteen states had passed laws prohibiting the use of marihuana.

In 1937, however, the United States Congress passed the Marihuana Tax Act, designed to stamp out use of the drug. According to the theory outlined above, we should find in the history of this Act the story of an entrepreneur whose initiative and enterprise overcame public apathy and indifference and culminated in the passage of federal legislation. Before turning to the history of the Act itself, we should perhaps look at the way similar substances had been treated in American law, in order to understand the context in which the attempt to suppress marihuana use proceeded.

The use of alcohol and opium in the United States had a long history, punctuated by attempts at suppression.[1] Three values provided legitimacy for attempts to prevent the use of intoxicants and narcotics. One legitimizing value, a component of what has been called the *Protestant ethic*, holds that the individual should exercise complete responsibility for what he does and what happens to him; he should never do anything that might cause loss of self-control. Alcohol and the opiate drugs, in varying degrees and ways, cause people to lose control of themselves; their use, therefore, is evil. A person intoxicated with alcohol often loses control over his physical activity; the centers of judgment in the brain are also affected. Users of opiates are more likely to be anesthetized and thus less likely to commit rash acts. But they become dependent on the drug to prevent withdrawal symptoms and in this sense have lost control of their actions; insofar as it is difficult to obtain the drug, they must subordinate other interests to its pursuit.

Another American value legitimized attempts to suppress the use of alcohol and opiates: disapproval of action taken solely to achieve states of ecstasy. Perhaps because of our strong cultural emphases on pragmatism and utilitarianism, Americans usually feel uneasy and ambivalent about ecstatic experiences of any kind. But we do not condemn ecstatic experience when it is the by-product or reward of actions we consider proper in their own right, such as hard work or religious fervor. It is only when people pursue ecstasy for its own sake that we condemn their action as a search for "illicit pleasure," an expression that has real meaning to us.

The third value that provided a basis for attempts at suppression was humanitarianism. Reformers believed that people enslaved by the use of alcohol and opium would benefit from laws making it impossible for them to give in to their weaknesses. The families of drunkards and drug addicts would likewise benefit.

These values provided the basis for specific rules. The Eighteenth Amendment and the Volstead Act forbade the importation of alcoholic beverages into the United States and their manufacture within the country. The Harrison Act in effect prohibited the use of opiate drugs for all but medical purposes.

In formulating these laws, care was taken not to interfere with what were regarded as the legitimate interests of other groups in the society. The Harrison Act, for instance, was so drawn as to allow medical personnel to continue using morphine and other opium derivatives for the relief of pain and such other medical purposes as seemed to them appropriate. Furthermore, the law was carefully drawn in order to avoid running afoul of the Constitutional provision reserving police powers to the several states. In line with this restriction, the Act was presented as a revenue measure, taxing unlicensed purveyors of opiate drugs at an exorbitant rate while permitting licensed purveyors (primarily physicians, dentists, veterinarians, and pharmacists) to pay a nominal tax. Though it was justified Constitutionally as a revenue measure, the Harrison Act was in fact a police measure and was so interpreted by those to whom its enforcement was entrusted. One consequence of the passage of the Act was the establishment, in the Treasury Department of the federal Bureau of Narcotics in 1930.

The same values that led to the banning of the use of alcohol and opiates could, of course, be applied to the case of marihuana and it seems logical that this should have been done. Yet what little I have been told, by people familiar with the period, about the use of marihuana in the late twenties and early thirties leads me to believe that there was relatively lax enforcement of the existing local laws. This, after all, was the era of Prohibition and the police had more pressing matters to attend to. Neither the public nor law-enforcement officers, apparently, considered the use of marihuana a serious problem. When they noticed it at all, they probably dismissed it as not warranting major attempts at enforcement. One index of how feebly the laws were enforced is that the price of marihuana is said to have been very much lower prior to the passage of federal legislation. This indicates that there was little danger in selling it and that enforcement was not seriously undertaken.

Even the Treasury Department, in its report on the year 1931, minimized the importance of the problem:

A great deal of public interest has been aroused by newspaper articles appearing from time to time on the evils of the abuse of marihuana, or Indian hemp, and more attention has been focused on specific cases reported of the abuse of the drug than would otherwise have been the case. This publicity tends to magnify the extent of the evil and lends color to an inference that there is an alarming spread of the improper use of the drug, whereas the actual increase in such use may not have been inordinately large.[2]

The Treasury Department's Bureau of Narcotics furnished most of the enterprise that produced the Marihuana Tax Act. While it is, of course, difficult to know what the motives of Bureau officials were, we need assume no more than that they perceived an area of wrongdoing that properly belonged in their jurisdiction and moved to put it there. The personal interest they satisfied in pressing for marihuana legislation was one common to many officials: the interest in successfully accomplishing the task one has been assigned and in acquiring the best tools with which to accomplish it. The Bureau's efforts took two forms: cooperating in the development of state legislation affecting the use of marihuana, and providing facts and figures for journalistic accounts of the problem. These are two important modes of action available to all entrepreneurs seeking the adoption of rules: they can enlist the support of other interested organizations and develop, through the use of the press and other communications media, a favorable public attitude toward the proposed rule. If the efforts are successful, the public becomes aware of a definite problem and the appropriate organizations act in concert to produce the desired rule.

The federal Bureau of Narcotics cooperated actively with the National Conference of Commissioners on Uniform State Laws in developing uniform laws on narcotics, stressing among other matters the need to control marihuana use.[3] In 1932, the Conference approved a draft law. The Bureau commented:

> The present Constitutional limitations would seem to require control measures directed against the intrastate traffic in Indian hemp to be adopted by the several State governments rather than by the Federal Government, and the policy has been to urge the State authorities generally to provide the necessary legislation, with supporting enforcement activity, to prohibit the traffic except for bona fide medical purposes. The proposed uniform State narcotic law. . .with optional text applying to the restriction of traffic in Indian hemp, has been recommended as an adequate law to accomplish the desired purposes. [4]

In its report for the year 1936, the Bureau urged its partners in this cooperative effort to exert themselves more strongly and hinted that federal intervention might perhaps be necessary:

> In the absence of additional Federal legislation the Bureau of Narcotics can therefore carry on no war of its own against this traffic. . .the drug has come into wide and increasing abuse in many states, and the Bureau of Narcotics has therefore been endeavoring to impress upon the various States the urgent need for vigorous enforcement of local cannabis [marihuana] laws.[5]

The second prong of the Bureau's attack on the marihuana problem consisted of an effort to arouse the public to the danger confronting it by means of "an educational campaign describing the drug, its identification, and evil effects."[6] Apparently hoping that public interest might spur the states and cities to greater efforts, the Bureau said:

In the absence of Federal legislation on the subject, the States and cities should rightfully assume the responsibility of providing vigorous measures for the extinction of this lethal weed, and it is therefore hoped that all public-spirited citizens will earnestly enlist in the movement urged by the Treasury Department to adjure intensified enforcement of marihuana laws.[7]

The Bureau did not confine itself to exhortation in departmental reports. Its methods in pursuing desired legislation are described in a passage dealing with the campaign for a uniform state narcotic law:

Articles were prepared in the Federal Bureau of Narcotics, at the request of a number of organizations dealing with this general subject [uniform state laws] for publication by such organizations in magazines and newspapers. An intelligent and sympathetic public interest, helpful to the administration of the narcotic laws, has been aroused and maintained.[8]

As the campaign for federal legislation against marihuana drew to a successful close, the Bureau's efforts to communicate its sense of the urgency of the problem to the public bore plentiful fruit. The number of articles about marihuana that appeared in popular magazines indicated by the number indexed in the *Reader's Guide* reached a record high. Seventeen articles appeared in a two-year period, many more than in any similar period before or after.

Of the seventeen, ten either explicitly acknowledged the help of the Bureau in furnishing facts and figures or gave implicit evidence of having received help by using facts and figures that had appeared earlier, either in Bureau publications or in testimony before the Congress on the Marihuana Tax Act. (We shall consider the congressional hearings on the bill in a moment.)

Articles on Marihuana Indexed in
The Reader's Guide to Periodical Literature

Time Period	Number of Articles
January 1925-December 1928	0
January 1929-June 1932	0
July 1932-June 1935	0
July 1935-June 1937	4
July 1937-June 1939	17
July 1939-June 1941	4
July 1941-June 1943	1
July 1943-April 1945	4
May 1945-April 1947	6
May 1947-April 1949	0
May 1949-March 1951	1

One clear indication of Bureau influence in the preparation of journalistic articles can be found in the recurrence of certain atrocity stories first reported by the Bureau. For instance, in an article published in the *American Magazine*, Anslinger, the Commissioner of Narcotics, related the following incident:

An entire family was murdered by a youthful [marihuana] addict in Florida. When officers arrived at the home they found the youth staggering about in a human slaughterhouse. With an ax he had killed his father, mother, two brothers, and a sister. He seemed to be in a daze. . . .He had no recollection of having committed the multiple crime. The officers knew him ordinarily as a sane, rather quiet young man; now he was pitifully crazed. They sought the reason. The boy said he had been in the habit of smoking something which youthful friends called "muggles," a childish name for marihuana. [9]

Five of the seventeen articles printed during the period repeated this story, and thus showed the influence of the Bureau.

The articles designed to arouse the public to the dangers of marihuana identified use of the drug as a violation of the value of self-control and the prohibition on search for "illicit pleasure," thus legitimizing the drive against marihuana in the eyes of the public. These, of course, were the same values that had been appealed to in the course of the quest for legislation prohibiting use of alcohol and opiates for illicit purposes.

The federal Bureau of Narcotics, then, provided most of the enterprise that produced public awareness of the problem and coordinated action by other enforcement organizations. Armed with the results of their enterprise, representatives of the Treasury Department went to Congress with a draft of the Marihuana Tax Act and requested its passage. The hearings of the House Committee on Ways and Means, which considered the bill for five days during April and May of 1937, furnish a clear case of the operation of enterprise and of the way it must accommodate other interests.

The Assistant General Counsel of the Treasury Department introduced the bill to the Congressmen with these words: "The leading newspapers of the United States have recognized the seriousness of this problem and many of them have advocated Federal legislation to control the traffic in marihuana." [10] After explaining the Constitutional basis of the bill—like the Harrison Act, it was framed as a revenue measure—he reassured them about its possible effects on legitimate businesses:

The form of the bill is such, however, as not to interfere materially with any industrial, medical, or scientific uses which the plant may have. Since hemp fiber and articles manufactured therefrom [twine and light cordage] are obtained from the harmless mature stalk of the plant, all such products have been completely eliminated from the purview of the bill by defining the term marihuana in the bill so as to exclude from its provisions the mature stalk and its compounds or manufacturers. There are also some dealings in marihuana seeds for planting purposes and for use in the manufacture of oil, which is ultimately employed by the paint and varnish industry. As the seeds, unlike the mature stalk, contain the drug, the same complete exemption could not be applied in this instance. [11]

He further assured them that the medical profession rarely used the drug, so that its prohibition would work no hardship on them or on the pharmaceutical industry.

The committee members were ready to do what was necessary and, in fact, queried the Commissioner of Narcotics as to why this legislation had been proposed only now. He explained:

> Ten years ago we only heard about it throughout the Southwest. It is only in the last few years that it has become a national menace. . . .We have been urging uniform State legislation on the several States, and it was only last month that the last State legislature adopted such legislation.[12]

The commissioner reported that many crimes were committed under the influence of marihuana, and gave examples, including the story of the Florida mass murderer. He pointed out that the present low prices of the drug made it doubly dangerous, because it was available to anyone who had a dime to spare.

Manufacturers of hempseed oil voiced certain objections to the language of the bill, which was quickly changed to meet their specifications. But a more serious objection came from the birdseed industry, which at that time used some four million pounds of hempseed a year. Its representative apologized to the Congressmen for appearing at the last minute, stating that he and his colleagues had not realized until just then that the marihuana plant referred to in the bill was the same plant from which they got an important ingredient of their product. Government witnesses had insisted that the seeds of the plant required prohibition, as well as the flowering tops smokers usually used, because they contained a small amount of the active principle of the drug and might possibly be used for smoking. The birdseed manufacturers contended that inclusion of seed under the provisions of the bill would damage their business.

To justify his request for exemption, the manufacturers' representative pointed to the beneficial effect of hempseed on pigeons:

[It] is a necessary ingredient in pigeon feed because it contains an oil substance that is a valuable ingredient of pigeon feed, and we have not been able to find any seed that will take its place. If you substitute anything for the hemp, it has a tendency to change the character of the squabs produced. [13]

Congressman Robert L. Doughton of North Carolina inquired: "Does that seed have the same effect on pigeons as the drug has on human beings?" The manufacturers' representative said: "I have never noticed it. It has a tendency to bring back the feathers and improve the birds." [14]

Faced with serious opposition, the Government modified its stern insistence on the seed provision, noting that sterilization of the seeds might render them harmless: "It seems to us that the burden of proof is on the Government there, when we might injure a legitimate industry." [15]

Once these difficulties had been ironed out, the bill had easy sailing. Marihuana smokers, powerless, unorganized, and lacking publicly legitimate grounds for attack, sent no representatives to the hearings and their point of view found no place in the record. Unopposed, the bill passed both the House and Senate the following July. The enterprise of the Bureau had produced a new rule, whose subsequent enforcement would help create a new class of outsiders—marihuana users.

I have given an extended illustration from the field of federal legislation. But the basic parameters of this case should be equally applicable not only to legislation in general, but to the development of rules of a more informal kind. Wherever rules are created and applied, we should be alive to the possible presence of an enterprising individual or group. Their activities can properly be called *moral enterprise*, for what they are enterprising about is the creation of a new fragment of the moral constitution of society, its code of right and wrong.

Wherever rules are created and applied we should expect to find people attempting to enlist the support of coordinate groups and using the available media of communication to develop a favorable climate of opinion. Where they do not develop such support, we may expect to find their enterprise unsuccessful.[16]

And, wherever rules are created and applied, we expect that the processes of enforcement will be shaped by the complexity of the organization, resting on a basis of shared understandings in simpler groups and resulting from political maneuvering and bargaining in complex structures.

NOTES

1. See John Krout, *The Origins of Prohibition* (New York: Columbia University Press, 1928); Charles Terry and Mildred Pellens, *The Opium Problem* (New York: The Committee on Drug Addiction with the Bureau of Social Hygiene, Inc., 1928); and *Drug Addiction: Crime or Disease?*, Interim and Final Reports of the Joint Committee of the American Bar Associaton and the American Medical Association on Narcotic Drugs (Bloomington, Indiana: Indiana University Press, 1961).

2. U.S. Treasury Department, *Traffic in Opium and Other Dangerous Drugs for the Year ended December 31, 1931* (Washington, D.C.: Government Printing Office, 1932), p. 51.

3. Ibid., pp. 16-17.

4. Bureau of Narcotics, U.S. Treasury Department, *Traffic in Opium and Other Dangerous Drugs for the Year ended December 31, 1932* (Washington, D.C.: Government Printing Office, 1933), p. 13.

5. Bureau of Narcotics, U.S. Treasury Department, *Traffic in Opium and Other Dangerous Drugs for the Year ended December 31, 1936* (Washington, D.C.: Government Printing Office, 1937), p. 59.

6. Ibid.

7. Bureau of Narcotics, U.S. Treasury Department, *Traffic in Opium and Other Dangerous Drugs for the Year ended December 31, 1935* (Washington, D.C.: Government Printing Office, 1936), p. 30.

8. Bureau of Narcotics, U.S. Treasury Department, *Traffic in Opium and Other Dangerous Drugs for the Year ended December 31, 1933* (Washington, D.C.: Government Printing Office, 1934), p. 61.

9. H. J. Anslinger, with Courtney Ryley Cooper, "Marihuana: Assassin of Youth," *American Magazine* 124 (July 1937): 19, 150.

10. *Taxation of Marihuana,* Hearings before the Committee on Ways and Means of the House of Representatives, 75th Congress, 1st Session, on H.R. 6385, April 27-30 and May 4, 1937, p. 7.

11. Ibid., p. 8.

12. Ibid., p. 20.

13. Ibid., pp. 73-74.

14. Ibid.

15. Ibid., p. 85.

16. Gouldner has described a relevant case in industry, where a new manager's attempt to enforce rules that had not been enforced for a long time (and thus, in effect, create new rules) had as its immediate consequence a disruptive wildcat strike; he had not built support through the manipulation of other groups in the factory and the development of a favorable climate of opinion. See Alvin W. Gouldner, *Wildcat Strike* (Yellow Springs, Ohio: Antioch Press, 1954).

4

On Capturing an Opium King: The Politics of Law Sik Han's Arrest*

William P. Delaney

In July 1973, Thai Border Patrol Police announced the arrest of one of the biggest opium-heroin tycoons in Southeast Asia's Golden Triangle: Law Sik Han of Kokang State, Burma. Law's empire alone was purported to account for one-third of the world's illicit drugs. Although probably an exaggerated estimate, the effect of his arrest nevertheless sent drug prices soaring in the world market and severely disrupted Asian smuggling networks.

Newspapers and magazines naturally portrayed the event as an unexpected victory over drug-trafficking involving, in the words of *Time*, a "rare display of cooperation" among Burmese, Thai, and American authorities. However, true to the nature of Southeast Asian politics, a much deeper story lay behind Law's arrest involving the confusing political condi-

*This work originally appeared in *Transaction/Society* 11, no. 6 (September -October 1974): 62-71.

tions within the Shan states of Burma that make grand-scale opium smuggling possible. The political negotiations Law was conducting shortly before his arrest represent a modus operandi among entrepreneurial armies in this area who continue to sell their anticommunist military services in exchange for covert rights to opium smuggling. This negotiating process has been repeated many times in the past and probably will continue. Despite the press reports, the political conditions that create the need for these buy-and-sell armies have not changed, and any one of many rebel leaders remains available to replace Law Sik Han as the Golden Triangle's opium king.

The Shan States of Burma: Chaos and Intrigue

Lying on a rugged hilly plateau in eastern central Burma, the Shan states contain an amazing number of tribal and linguistic groups. The largest group are the Shans themselves, a Tai-speaking people that has traditionally governed the low-lying valleys through a system of hereditary princes who accepted tribute from the tribes settled in the surrounding hills. The latter include the Lahu, Lisu, Palaung, and Wa, among others, and the Kokang Chinese from whom Law Sik Han traces his ancestry.

The Shans have historically been a problem to the Burmese government for several reasons. Linguistically and culturally, the Shans share more similarities with their neighbors across the border in Thailand than they do with the Burmese. In addition, the rugged terrain and remoteness of the Shan states traditionally made the area impossible for the Burmese to control and therefore fostered the development of independent political and cultural institutions among the proud Shans. The British recognized this fact during the colonial years (1886-1948) by adminstering the Shan states independently from Burma proper and granting the Shan princes considerable control over their own affairs.

At the time of Burma's independence in 1948, therefore, the Shans, along with many other minority groups, had traditional misgivings about joining the proposed "Union of Burma," a loose federation that seemed completely dominated by Burmese military and political leaders and slow to recognize the rights of other indigenous ethnic groups. However, through the clever diplomacy of Aung San, the Burmese hero who led the independence movement, the Shans cautiously agreed to join the Union in return for statehood status and the granting of a number of national ministry posts to Shans.

Later, after Aung San's assassination, U Nu gained power and continued this diplomacy by presenting the Shans with a ten-year trial program (1947-57), which gave the Shans the right to secede from the Union at the end of this period.

Shan nationalist revolutionaries now view this ten-year period from 1947 to 1957 as the political and economic rape of the Shan states by the Burmese government and the disruption of all levels of traditional Shan social and cultural life. Because of the Burmese government's crudely implemented programs, their increasing reliance on military and police power, and their stubborn disregard for the political and cultural rights of the minorities, the background for civil war was established in the Shan states as well as throughout Burma.

Moreover, out of this period there emerged in the Shan states a hodgepodge of political factions: unorganized Shan nationalist guerrillas, communist fighters, marauding bandits and warlords, government spies, religious messianic cults, and the ubiquitous opium smuggler and his counterpart, the corrupt police and military official. Along with this political chaos the economy of the Shan states also suffered gross imbalances caused by the Burmese government's tax programs and fixed prices for the area's rich supply of teak, gold, silver, precious gems, mining ores, rice, and cattle. One result of these ruinous government policies was to push the hillfarmer to turn more and more to the production of opium for a market, which remained predominantly outside of government control. Finally, many Shans blamed their hereditary princes for buckling under to the government's demands; thus, the traditional system of authority began to erode and with it the morale of the peasantry.

One foreign group that abetted the disintegration of the

Shan states and figured monumentally, then as now, in the opium-smuggling business was the Chinese Nationalist troops (Kuomingtang or K.M.T.), which fled southward into the Shan states after Chiang Kai-shek's regime collapsed in Yunnan in late 1949. Taking advantage of the debilitated conditions of the Shan states, these troops eventually dominated opium smuggling there, impressing young Shans and other ethnics into their ranks, and frequently bilking the peasants by introducing counterfeit money into the already overly strained financial dealings of the petty traders and producers.

In 1961 the Chinese Nationalist KMT fled from a Burmese Army offensive and settled in Thailand where they sold their counterinsurgency services to the joint Thai Army-C.I.A. establishment and thereby gained some legitimacy by fighting communists while still covertly holding a tight rein on their smuggling operations in the Shan states.

Eventually, the continued presence of the Chinese KMT opium operations in the Shan states helped convince the unorganized and bickering Shan nationalists by the late 1960s that a more definite form of unity and organization must be created if they ever hoped to regain political and cultural autonomy for the Shan people. In the eyes of the Shan revolutionaries this meant throwing the Burmese government and communists out of their land and preventing the Chinese KMT from running smuggling operations into the Shan states from Thailand. The organization created to do this was the Shan State Army (S.S.A.) and its political arm, the Shan State Progress party. However, besides the number of enemies the Shans must fight and their lack of funds and fledgling military organization, they also suffer seriously from the fact that even among their own ethnic Shan revolutionaries and rebels there exist widely contrasting levels of political consciousness. Although the SSA spends a great deal of time trying to politically educate Shan peasants and the many independent Shan rebel groups, many of the latter still choose the path of petty warlordism rather than join a truly unified Shan revolutionary movement. Thus beset by myriad problems the SSA's operations are marked by desperation and frustration.

The story of Law Sik Han's rise and fall is less interesting as the saga of an opium king than as a study of the political confusion and armed conflict in the area that allow Law Sik Han and others like him to build opium-heroin empires and to rule them at the national government's pleasure.

Hopefully, the details and background of Law's arrest, especially the politics and intrigue they reveal, will illustrate how the anarchic conditions in the Shan states have spawned a system in which drugs and politics are so deeply enmeshed.

Law's Capture

The details surrounding Law's arrest in 1973 were so simple that it became difficult for local observers not to speculate about a possible double cross. The *Bangkok Post* claimed that a small group of Thai Border Police inadvertently stumbled on Law in the woods of Thailand's Maehongson province. *Time* magazine reported Burmese troops forced him across the border into the hands of the Thai Special Narcotics Organization. On the other hand, members of the revolutionary Shan State Army who had been negotiating with Law before his arrest gave the following description of events:

Law freely entered Thailand from the Burmese border town of Mong Mah accompanied by seventy of his men armed with automatic weapons. He left billeted on the Burmese side of the border a combined force of Wa, Shan, and Kokangese rebels numbering 1,500 strong. Although Law's troops had just had a serious skirmish with the Burmese army at Mong Mah, they had regrouped and remained camped on the Burmese side of the border.

Prior to his departure Law had received a long radio cable from Jao Nhu, head of the revolutionary Shan State Army, explaining that special arrangements had been made with the Thai authorities and Law had been granted permission to enter Thailand. After crossing into Thailand, Law and his men went to a small Thai Border Police post in Maehongson province. There they were met by twenty Thai Border Police who nervously began to negotiate with Law. At this point, a critical link that ultimately led to Law's arrest emerged in the person of Sai Krue, an interpreter whom the Shan State Army had assigned to Law to help him translate from Chinese to Shan and Thai.

Following Sai Krue's advice but against the misgivings of his own men, Law agreed to leave his men and accompany the Thai police to the main road at the town of Ban Mae Suya. After further conversations, Law went with the police to Mae Rim town in order to clear up what appeared to be a minor technicality. Upon his arrival, Law was officially arrested and charged with illegal entry; however, he managed to smuggle out two letters to his troops telling them to remain calm and that he was still convinced everything would be all right. Shortly after this, Law was suddenly whisked off to the Thai Border Police camp, Dara Rasmee, and the Thais broke the story to the press.

To understand Sai Krue's important role in Law's arrest and why Law, the notorious opium king, did not feel it a major risk to deal with the Thai authorities, requires a closer look at Law—however, not so much as an opium king but as the political symbol he had become to the many rebel groups in the Shan states who still grope in desperation for a figure powerful enough to unite them against their common enemies: the Burmese government, the Chinese KMTs, and the communists.

Law's Rise to Power

Kokang State, located in the northeast corner of the Shan states, represents a small pocket of ethnic Chinese who claim to have been relocated into their mountainous homeland by the last Ming emperor in 1642. In accordance with the Peking Convention of 1897, China agreed to cede Kokang to the British. However, previous to and throughout the British administration of the Shan states, Kokang remained under the suzerainty of the strong Shan princes of Northern Hsenwii. This is an important factor for understanding why the Kokang Chinese habitually refer to themselves as "Shans" and have historically formed alliances with ethnic Shan groups of the neighboring states. It was not until the time of Burma's independence that the Kokang Chinese along with the larger Shan groups pressured for and achieved statehood within the newly formed Union of Burma.

Tucked between the border of China and Burma's Salween River, the thrifty Kokang settlers prospered by relying on two primary exports—tea and opium—which were hauled out on mules forming ribbons of trade into China and Burma proper. By World War II, a powerful opium syndicate had emerged under the careful control of a leading Kokang family, the Yangs. Utilizing the vast opium production of the fierce Wa tribesmen both in Burma and southern China, the Yang syndicate garnered an unprecedented amount of wealth. However, because it has not been granted an opium license from the Burmese central government in Rangoon, the Yang syndicate remained an illicit opium franchise. To this day opium growing and trading have not been completely outlawed in Burma; competition over obtaining licenses is intense and allegedly the source of much corruption.

Consequently, throughout the 1950s, the Kokang Chinese were forced to smuggle their opium to the wealthy traders in the south who routinely obtained the government opium licenses through their special contacts in Rangoon. When opium prices took a sharp decline in the late 1950s, a small group of Kokang traders decided their only hope was to obtain a proper trading license that would also allow them to establish their own storage and refining facilities. For reasons that are little understood, the Burmese government still allows some licensed traders to operate like this; however, the government does acknowledge that most of the opium crop is lost to the illicit caravan trade.

In 1960 a group of Kokang traders along with the young Law Sik Han petitioned Yang Kyein Sein (Jimmy Yang), the brainy son of the original lord of the Kokang syndicate, to help them obtain an opium license. With a university education and natural political talents, Jimmy Yang had become a member of Parliament by virtue of holding a seat in the Shan State Council. Using his position, Yang went to the town of Taungyi and obtained a permit from the Minister of Customs, Sao Hkun Cho, for the Kokang traders to place their first legal shipment of opium. To save time, Yang also got access to an airplane from the minister of communications to have the opium flown from Kokang to the town of Lashio. Ironically, although Law got his start in the opium business through Jimmy Yang, not too many years thereafter a piece of political intrigue on the part of the Burmese government pitted Law against the Yang family in a bloody struggle for supremacy in the Kokang area.

The Burmese have always cast a suspicious eye toward remote Kokang in view of her many latent abilities for parleying opium, guns, and men into an independent power base. By mid-1963 the Burmese government under Premier Newin had taken steps to disrupt Kokangese unity by confiscating 12,000 viss of opium (one viss equals approximately 3.6 lbs.) belonging to Law's now growing enterprise. To regain his opium, Law was required to take leadership of a village militia force (called KwaKaYe or K.K.Y.) established by the Burmese government and then to declare war on Jimmy Yang, who had returned to Kokang following the dissolution of Parliament by General Newin in 1962. Although given no guns or formal aid by the Burmese government, Law and his followers would not go uncompensated as militiamen. With the removal of Jimmy Yang, the entire Kokang opium concession would become theirs, along with storage and transport facilities (from the Burmese army Eastern Command) and those unpurchasable laissez-faire conditions that nourish any young business. Since the Kokang and Wa states are among the richest opium-producing areas in the world, the reward was very great.

On 4 October 1963, Law finally agreed and made his intentions known to Jimmy Yang. Not wanting to see Kokangese fight Kokangese, and skeptical whether he could successfully take on Law with his Burmese backing, Jimmy Yang and his private army left Kokang State and eventually made their way to northern Thailand.

The Burmese government's choice of Law over Jimmy Yang was more than just a flip of the coin. As a member of Parliament, the outspoken Jimmy Yang had long argued for an autonomous Shan state and thus had become identified with the anti-Newin factions in Rangoon. Moreover, the Burmese were quite concerned that Jimmy Yang might use his wealth and political experience upon his return to Kokang State in 1962 to attempt an armed secessionist movement in that area. To the Burmese government the less-educated Law, in contrast, had demonstrated pecuniary rather than political instincts and thus seemed the more manageable of the two.

Although the Burmese would be content with their choice of Law for many years, they would seriously underestimate one important side of Law's career in Kokang State. From the earliest days, Law was able to gain strong popularity among the various ethnic groups in this difficult area. By establishing a reputation for fairness, Law utilized the stimulus from a growing and stable opium economy to forge a network of lasting relationships within the Chinese community and especially among the Wa tribesmen to the south and southwest of Kokang.

Once the Wa tribesmen began forming their own Burmese-sponsored militia units, Law would combine forces with them many times to guard opium caravans and fight rebels of the Burmese government. Later, when the communist party of Burma (C.P.B.) increased its activity around the Kokang and Wa states in the late 1960s, the Burmese regular army experienced a number of humiliating setbacks in trying to contain them. When the Burmese government was forced to turn to Law and his allied Wa units for help against the communists, they unavoidably acknowledged him as heading up the most effective military force in the area. In the same way that the Chinese KMT forces have been used in Thailand as an entrepreneurial army by the C.I.A. and Thai military, Law's mixed army would fight valiantly against the communists to protect their opium regime and retain the benevolent favors of the Burmese government.

Although no statistics are available, local sources feel that Law's opium-heroin profits never totaled more than $2 million over a ten-year period. This is a figure far lower than one would expect for a true opium king. In actuality, at least part of Law's "notorious reputation" was contrived by Thai narcotics agents to dramatize the significance of his arrest. United States narcotics circles were less hyperbolic and preferred to describe Law as "one of the four or five biggies" in the Golden Triangle. However, another important factor that reduced Law's profits stemmed from the organization of his opium regime.

The Joint Stock Opium Company

Given the sedentary and long-established nature of the Chinese community in Kokang, Law would have never been able to establish a "robber-baron" enterprise along the lines of the KMT smuggling operations in the Shan states and Thailand. Instead, as long as he remained around the Kokang area, Law was forced to follow more or less classic Chinese business rules using family connections and lineage loyalties to create a web of relationships that spread across a sizable population of relatives. Morever, by living close to the source of opium production, the ethnic highland villages, Law could ill afford to lose their cooperation through such coercion and gun-point sales as the ruthless KMT buyers have done on their periodic trips into the Shan states.

It is also reported that Law, for reasons of supply, had to open up his company to a large number of middle-level Wa and Chinese traders who scoured the hills in anticipation of each major opium shipment. These traders paid Law a tax for the use of storage, transport, and refining facilities; however, the overall dividends from Law's opium business were divided, in the estimate of the Shan State Army, in the following manner: 30 percent of the profits to Law, 10 percent to Law's extended family, and 60 percent to the middle-level traders.

Although this type of organization obstructed Law from garnering a personal fortune by international standards, those years of successfully running such a cooperative venture in the Kokang area left him with a solid reputation (ignominious as this may sound) among the many rebel groups and smugglers in the Shan states. Given the jealousy and internecine warfare that has plagued the Shan states, reputation and the ability to maintain alliances are still the rarest of resources in this naturally lush region.

However, no matter how ingeniously Law plied his trade among the local inhabitants of the Kokang-Wa area, an external threat in the form of Burmese communists would ultimately lead to Law's fall.

Communists in the Kokang and Wa States

As noted earlier, the Burmese communists were able to pose a strong threat in the Kokang region by the late 1960s. In

1968 a curious piece of historical irony would begin to haunt Law Sik Han. Four years after forcing Jimmy Yang out of Kokang State in 1963, Law was confronted by an expedition headed by Jimmy's younger brother, Francis Yang, who had returned to avenge his brother and fight Law's forces for Kokang supremacy. Heavy fighting is reported to have taken place for several months in 1967 before Francis Yang surrendered and returned to Thailand with only a handful of his original force. The remainder of his troops dispersed and settled in the Kokang area; however, a group of 200 men led by Phong Kya Sheng, a captain under Francis Yang, refused to surrender and went across to China to negotiate with the communist establishment. Six months later Phong returned with his men and began the first major communist offensive in the Kokang area. His attack on Kokang State was coordinated with a simultaneous communist offensive in the neighboring Kachin State led by the late Naw Seng, one of the greatest guerrilla fighters in Burma's history.

Phong Kya Sheng, along with his brother, Phong Kya Suh, chose the town of Kunchang in the northernmost part of Kokang State as their first major encounter with the Burmese army. During the long battle of Kunchang, the Burmese army suffered a serious water shortage and had to have ice air-dropped to their troops (previous attempts at dropping water containers ended in their smashing on contact with the ground). Burmese casualties eventually totaled over 140 men and they were finally forced to relinquish Kunchang to Phong's forces, giving the latter their first important foothold in Kokang.

Following this alarming setback, the Burmese turned to Law and his allied village defense units to take up the fight against the communists. Although no casualty figures are available, independent rebel groups often remark about the costly price in lives and wounded that both Law's militia units and Phong's communist units had to pay during their battle for Kokang State. However, working from his regional head-quarters in Lao Kai, Phong's well-disciplined troops had captured most of Kokang State by 1971, leaving Law a diminishing island of geography on which to maintain his opium regime.

Much of Phong's success in Kokang, and later in the Wa states, was related to his allegedly receiving arms and supplies from Red China. However, it is begrudgingly admitted by many of his adversaries that Phong is a brilliant leader and peculiarly dangerous for his refusal to wheel-and-deal with the petty warlords and drug entrepreneurs.

Phong's family, originally from Szechwan province in China, has lived in the Kokang area for four generations. Although his grandfather was purported to be wealthy, Phong's father squandered the family wealth through a number of poorly calculated business ventures. Many of Phong's adversaries point to his impoverished background as a key factor that enables him to maintain excellent relationships with the common people. However, Kokangese who know Phong claim he should be considered not so much as an ideological communist but as a singularly shrewd guerrilla fighter with a fanatical hatred of the Burmese. It is claimed that although he is officially under Burmese communist leadership he retains a considerable amount of independence.

By focusing his military efforts on the opium-producing areas, Phong's forces gradually dislodged both the militia opium lords and the many Shan rebel groups who indulged in small-time smuggling to buy arms. When Phong's men eventually gained control of the strategic nodes on Law's opium-marketing route, they ended an era of big-time operations in the Kokang district. Although the Burmese communists allow opium production to continue after they seize an area, they strictly outlaw local consumption of opium and immediately lay plans for a crop-substitution program. Though seldom acknowledged in official United States circles, the Burmese communists have been playing an important role in the suppression of narcotics in the Golden Triangle.

Law's Opium Refineries at Takilek
The effect of the communist advances in the Kokang-Wa states would have a great impact on Law's career. Before the communists effectively pushed him out of this area in 1971, it is reported that Law was only indirectly involved in the establishment of refining factories around the Takilek area to the south—preferring to remain in the north around Kokang. After

the communists' advances had considerably narrowed his territory, however, Law began to consider the dangerous move of becoming involved in the Takilek refineries, which by then were capable of producing no. 4, high-grade heroin.

Before his move to Takilek, Law was an important but still minor prince in the Golden Triangle dynasty in the eyes of Thai and United States narcotics experts. Veteran observers have speculated that had Law not gone to Takilek in 1971 but instead used his power and prestige to respond to the political situation among the rebel groups in the eastern Shan states, he probably would have experienced a different fate.

With his men, arms, and money, Law represented in 1971 the first leader since Chan Shee Fu powerful enough to create what one local source called the "steamroller effect" for squashing the internal differences among the Shan rebels and uniting them into a single force. Moreover, it should have been obvious to Law that by this time his usefulness as a village militia leader was being seriously questioned by the Burmese government. Thus, by avoiding the dangerous consequences of becoming associated with Takilek heroin, he could have pursued the well-worn strategy of building up a strong Shan rebel force and then secretly approaching the Thai government in a political role, promising to fight communists on Thailand's northwestern border in return for asylum in the northern Thai hills. This is exactly how the Chinese KMTs gained their entrée in 1961, and many feel Law could have swung such a deal in 1971.

However, the prince aspired to be a king. When Law went to Takilek to man his refining factories, his name moved up into that elite category of most-wanted drug traffickers. Apparently unknown to him, this stigma along with a heavy reward for his capture ended his chances of playing any future politics with the Thai authorities via Shan State Army connections.

The Burmese Army
During Law's heaviest involvement in Takilek heroin, he still remained an official militia leader under the Burmese government utilizing Burmese army facilities for his smuggling in return for helping them on missions against the communists. It was not until early 1973 when the Burmese government,

partly in response to United States antidrug pressure but
mostly in response to communist military successes over the
militia units, decided to disband all militia units in the Shan
states. The Burmese government set the deadline of 20 April
1973, for the dissolution of the militia system. For Law this
meant he must hand over all his arms and by default abdicate
the throne of his Takilek drug kingdom.

According to Shan rebel sources, Law was allegedly .
offered the rank of colonel in the Burmese army and many of
his Wa and Kokang leaders were to be given lower officer
grades in a new communist suppression system for the
Kokang-Wa region. It is claimed that Law greatly opposed
turning over weapons that he had privately purchased and
could only envision a dismally restricted future as a Burmese
army officer.

When Law declined the Burmese directive and offer, the
Burmese government lost its last moderately effective counterinsurgency force in the regions north of Takilek and Law was
forced to pack up his laboratory equipment and move out of the
Takilek region. However, when Law, the newly proclaimed
enemy of the Burmese government, began to move southwest
with his veteran troops, good arms, a surplus of opium, and his
laboratory equipment, he was still able to summon from the
desperate Shan revolutionaries the belief that he could be the
deciding factor in the long-awaited unification of the Shan
nationalist movement.

At this point, Law's presence clearly illuminated the
high-strung, quixotic tempo of the political maneuvering in the
Shan states. He was a man who privately built an empire out of
smuggling opium while a militia leader under agreement to
fight communists and rebels of the Burmese government. As
soon as he stepped out of this role, Law turned around and
was handed the Shan nationalists' banner and tentatively
began to help unite the Shan rebel groups into an organized
force against the Burmese government. The fact that an opium
magnate can overnight be transformed into a political-military
liberator underscores the political desperation that infects the
Shan states. A closer look at the political problems within the
Shan rebel community is needed to understand the frantic

negotiations that transpired between the Shan State Army and
Law Sik Han.

The Militia System, Shan Disunity, and Law

On the eve of Law's trek south into the lower Shan states,
the political lineup of the many Shan rebel groups still
mirrored a chronic disunity. Scholars and analysts have often
speculated why the Shans have never been able to organize
into larger, more integrated political groupings. Prior to 1973 a
major cause of Shan disunity had been the deliberately
devisive use of the militia system (KwaKaYe) by the Burmese
government. The Burmese government had employed this
system with Machiavellian cunning, always in an area where
Burmese army control was weak, where opium was plentiful,
and where enough rebel groups existed so that they could be
manipulated into cannibalizing one another over opium profits.

The Burmese government operated this system by going
into an area and offering one of the stronger rebel groups
militia status. As a militia force, a group was expected to fight
the other rebel groups in the name of the Burmese government.
Law had played this role for almost ten years. For cooperating
with the government, the militia force was allowed to use
government roads and various storage centers in different
towns for shipping its opium. Such a plan obviously benefited
the Burmese government in a number of ways. By getting a
group to accept militia status, the system in effect had rebel
group pitted against rebel group and thwarted the formation of
any broad alliances among the Shan rebels. Moreover, by
having militia troops engage the rebels, the Burmese regular
army troops were freed for other operations. And by getting
groups to accept militia status, the Burmese government made
allies with at least part of the Shan rebel community in an area
and achieved a semblance of control.

The calculated use of this militia system and the associated instability it created revealed some of the worst instincts
in the Burmese government's policies toward the minorities.
Rather than risk any unification among the Shan rebels, the
Burmese government has been content to allow, and indirectly
cooperate in, the growing and smuggling of opium in return for

the allegiance of certain Shan strongmen. Thus, the militia
system has affected internal Shan politics more than any other
single factor and by the close of 1968, ten years after rebellion
started, the militia system along with the greed and low
political consciousness of the Shan rebels had placed the Shan
movement at the lowest point in its history.

As one of the few Shan groups that neither accepted
militia status from the Burmese government nor delved too
deeply into opium smuggling, the SSA lay historical claim to
being descendants of the purest Shan nationalistic motives.
Composed mainly of outspoken and politically aware university
students, they were the most articulate spokesmen of Shan
grievances and revolutionary goals; they were and are also the
most broke and the most desperate.

Nonetheless, the SSA held together under three leaders:
Colonel Jao Nhu, Colonel Hsai Kiao, and Sao Chang. They
received a ray of hope when U Nu, the ex-premier of Burma,
arrived in Thailand as a political exile proclaiming he would
return to fight the Burmese government and proceeded to form
the Parliamentary Democracy Party (P.D.P.). However, primarily because of ethnic rivalry, the military arm of the PDP
was never successful. In December 1972, the SSA got another
shot in the arm when a large number of Red Lahus (an ethnic
not political label) under their Grand Prophet gave up militia
status and openly revolted against the Burmese government.
Although the SSA was not able to help them with arms, they
sent in small units to lend a hand against the Burmese army
and at least gained the trust of the Lahus.

By early 1973, however, the SSA was still a terribly weak
military organization. In trying to get arms and support, they
had gone with hat in hand to the Thai military, U Nu's
Parliamentary Democracy party, the Americans, and many
private sources in Bangkok. All to no avail. Because of the
KMT's heavy taxation program, they had been pushed out of
small-time opium smuggling, which at one time had allowed
them to buy limited numbers of arms in Laos. Their only
sources of revenue were the sporadic contributions they still
receive from the peasant supporters in the Shan states.

Law's Entrée

In May 1973, history therefore conspired to push the recently deposed opium king, Law Sik Han, onto the stage in a thoroughly new role—that of political unifier. Whether he was able to perceive the situation or not before leaving his temporary sanctuary in Lashio, by the time he reached the Kengtung area in the eastern Shan states he had received more overtures to become the patron of more rebel groups than any leader in Shan rebel history. Two factors created this political moment for Law: the recent military successes of Phong's communist forces, which sent many militia groups fleeing south, and the related decision of the Burmese to disband the militia units after observing their failures against the communists.

Law was not only wealthy and powerful but a proven anti-communist and a fresh enemy of the Burmese government. He thereby combined enough of the peculiar traits that the frustrated Shan nationalist revolutionaries needed in a leader. Law's biggest drawback was his international reputation as an opium smuggler; however, this was easily overlooked by the SSA leadership when they reviewed his military capabilities.

During the months before his arrest, Law had summoned under his command a number of ex-militia units who had gone over to the rebel cause. These included three units of the fierce Wa warriors, remnants of Shan units left leaderless through battle or capture, as well as Law's own ex-militia troop. In all these comprised about 3,000 men.

Moreover, Law had received strong overtures from Pu Chong Luang, the Grand Prophet of the Red Lahus who it is reported can muster 1,000 men and upwards of 7,000 if necessary. It should be noted that two of the Wa units had not yet rendezvoused with Law's troops, but were on their way to join him at the time of his arrest.

Overwhelmed by the importance of Law's combined military strength, the SSA decided to commit two units: the SSA troops under Colonel Hsai Kiao and the troops under Major Khamdeng recently pushed out of the Baet Kan area in the Shan states by the communists.

Besides the show of force that Law had already summoned, the SSA was also enthusiastic about Law's expertise at managing disparate groups and personalities. After years of practice and failure, the SSA leadership knew just what was needed to unify the rebels. The more stubborn characters, who out of greed and selfishness are afraid to be connected with a larger organization, must be tactfully but firmly intimidated. Following this, deals can be made and positions granted so that everyone is made happy again. The SSA claimed that no one does this more artfully than Law Sik Han.

Moreover, by bringing along his opium-processing equipment from Takilek, Law provided a factory in the jungle that the rebels claimed could have financed the biggest rebellion Burma has ever seen in the Shan states—leading, so the SSA hoped, to a full-scale revolution.

Law agreed to work closely with the SSA for one reason: they possessed the best relations with the Thai authorities. After becoming a nominal member of the SSA in June 1973, Law urged the SSA leaders to argue his case for political asylum within Thailand. They were to convince the Thai authorities that Law had only been in the opium-heroin business in order to buy guns to fight the communists for the Burmese government. Moreover, once the Thai government had been briefed on Law's military capabilities, they would surely see his relevance as a buffer force between them and the Burmese communists beginning to encroach on Thailand's northern border. Using such an approach the SSA rightly assumed that they would merely be trying to obtain the same agreement for Law that the Thai government has traditionally extended the Chinese KMTs.

At this point, the SSA and Law were using each other to play out what were ultimately two hopeless strategies. More than likely, Law never intended to seriously take up the Shan political cause. Relying on his armed strength, he viewed himself as stepping out of Burmese sponsorship in Takilek and turning his counterinsurgency services over to a new sponsor: the Thai government. This way he would be able to maintain his grip on what remained of his opium-heroin business and begin to build a new empire. He even encouraged the SSA leaders to forget their old differences with General Lao Ly of the KMTs and approach the latter to try and work out some sort of scheme for leaving each other alone in future smuggling operations.

Thus, Law would use the SSA to win the ear of the Thai government; however, he thoroughly underestimated his notoriety and the changing political atmosphere in Thailand and Burma. In the first place, Law's support among the rebels and revolutionary SSA was too great to allow Rangoon to sit by and watch him be given political asylum in Thailand. There are too many dissidents of the Burmese government in Thailand already. Nor would the United States narcotics people be enthusiastic about yet another irregular force with definite opium credentials being brought into Thailand as the KMT had been on the excuse they were needed to fight communists. Finally, the political significance of Law in the eyes of the Thai government had changed abruptly in the months preceding his arrest.

The latter was an important point, for at that time the Thai government under Thanom Kittikachorn and General Prapass—who would be deposed in October 1973—was sorely in need of a spectacular event to counter charges by many United States congressmen that the Thai government, if not directly participating in drug-trafficking themselves, at least was suspiciously slow in stemming the flow of narcotics leaving Thailand. Representative Lester Wolff of New York, an outspoken critic of the Thai government's handling of the drug traffic, announced he would visit Thailand on an investigative tour in August 1973. Many local observers claimed that the Thai government greatly feared the United States Congress might cut back on their foreign aid if they received a bleak report on the drug picture in Thailand. The sensational arrest of Law Sik Han the month before Representative Wolff arrived, some observers feel, was a necessary ploy to throw the snooping congressman off the track.

The SSA also had their own strategy for using Law. Once they had obtained political asylum in Thailand for Law, they would use his military might to begin to choke off KMT drug-trafficking in the Shan states. After proving themselves by crippling the Chinese KMT, they would turn to the United States narcotics people and offer their services for stopping all opium smuggling in the Shan states. The United States would respond, so they hoped, with a crop-substitution program and that much-needed world publicity for their political cause. They were confident that Law would eventually fit into such a political scheme because they would be offering him something more than a mere heroin concession—meaning a role in the eventual reconquest of the entire Shan states.

Law's Arrest

Sai Krue, a member of the SSA under Colonel Jao Nhu and fluent in Shan and Chinese, was used as an interpreter in SSA negotiations with Law. Thus, Law came to rely on him as a direct link to the SSA leadership, which was negotiating with the Thai authorities at this time. Someone, probably Thai narcotic agents, got to Sai Krue with a large bribe, and he agreed to dupe Law into believing that the Thai government was definitely interested in placing him and his troops in a counterinsurgency slot on Thailand's northwestern border. Sai Krue's duplicity was covered by arresting him along with Law and extraditing them both to Rangoon. A Thailand-based newspaper later announced that the Burmese had decided to give Sai Krue only a light sentence.

When Law accompanied Sai Krue to meet the Thai police he, like many kings in the past, erred by miscalculating his own value and thoroughly misreading the political forces that had marshaled against him.

One of these forces more than likely was the Chinese KMT. Shan rebels allege that once Law and his men entered the Mon Pan area of the Shan states, the KMTs began providing the Thai police with continual intelligence on Law's movements. Whether the KMT was directly involved in Law's arrest is difficult to prove; however, as the grand masters of the opium trade the KMT was once again able to witness the removal of another rebel strongman and major drug competitor in the Golden Triangle, while they still enjoy a mysterious security in the northern hills of Thailand.

Events Since Arrest

Law's arrest cut short his career as a political leader (at least temporarily) but the circumstances that led to his rise have not changed. While such political fragility exists in the Shan states, any one of many rebel leaders with the same combination of men, guns, money, and alliances may take the place of Law Sik Han. Chu Hong Chai, who heads the Ving Ngen ex-militia, was in fact alleged to have temporarily replaced Law as supreme rebel after his arrest. Although one opium king goes to jail, the political conditions that create opium kings have not been modified in the least.

However, the events that have transpired since Law's arrest may have hidden within them the answer for solving the political problems of the Shan states.

Following his arrest, the SSA felt betrayed by the Thai Border Patrol Police. One SSA officer said, "You have cut off the tiger's tail and let him go; it would have been smarter to kill him because now he may come back for you." His comment referred to two actions the Thai police had taken: the seizure of a shipment of arms on their way to the SSA and the arrest of Law. By hinting they would come back for the Thai police, the officer alluded to a possible rapprochement with the communists. What will happen to Law's other forces is anyone's guess, but now alienated from both the Thai and Burmese governments, the communists have a fair chance of recruiting them.

How long Law remains in a Burmese jail will be pretty much determined by the Burmese reaction to a possible rapprochement between the communists and the Shan rebels, especially Law's allied troops. As a fellow member of the socialist camp, the Burmese government may envision a diplomatic solution to their communist problem via Peking. However, if the Burmese communists appear too independent of Peking persuasion on this matter, some observers speculate that Law, the opium king, could be freed and returned to militia service. Although the United States narcotics people would pay heavily to see this not happen, the internal politics of the Shan states may finally convince the Americans that they cannot buy their way out of the opium-heroin problem, and the Burmese government that no payment is worth the danger of an enlarged communist threat.

From the point of view of world narcotics suppression, there is no doubt that the most practical solution for the Shan states (and the entire Golden Triangle) would be an eventual communist takeover. The communists already control large areas in the north and northeast of Burma and are reported to have launched a graduated offensive in the eastern Shan states on Kengtung itself. Moreover, as noted earlier, they have the cleanest record to date for controlling opium and replacing it with substitute crops.

However, whether the communists can provide the long-awaited political stability for the Shan states is another question. The communists, mainly composed of Wa, Chinese, Kachin, Igaw, and Lahu guerrillas, have yet to attract many recruits from the ethnic Shan population. At present, the Shans view them as foreign invaders who have severed the traditional ethnic and political boundaries especially in the lowland areas. One Shan rebel claimed that the communist party of Burma's refusal to form a Shan communist party reveals their true intentions of trying to Burmanize or Sinicize the Shan states rather than establish true autonomous ethnic zones as the communists have done in North Vietnam and southern China.

However, given the severe economic hardships within the Shan states in the last twenty years, any stable form of administration that can maintain public order and provide jobs and schools will inevitably gain popularity and support. Naturally, the Shan State Army and its political arm, the Shan State Progress party, would like to be that administration. However, given last year's [1973] catastrophe of trying to make it on the coattails of Law, the opium king, the SSA may finally be ready to consider different political alternatives for their homeland, the Shan states.

5

The Drug Addict as a Folk Devil *

David Downes

Drug addiction is, in many ways, a test case for a great deal of recent theory in criminology. Until very recently, it was possible to rest on the comfortable assumptions about the British "system" of treatment that were tied in with a detestation of the "criminalization" of addiction in America. This system has now been well and truly exposed as little more than masterly inactivity in the face of what was an almost nonexistent addiction problem. But at least its principle that addicts should be treated medically rather than outlawed was established and it is this that has led to the identification of the British "system" by some American reformers. But it is now impossible to say, as Edwin Schur did in his book *Narcotic Addiction in Britain and America* (and he was echoed by many

*Based on a talk delivered to the Central Council for Health Education's Conference on Dependence on Drugs and Alcohol, January 1968. Printed by permission of the author.

British criminologists, myself included), that the absence of a
black market, and the treatment instead of the punishment of
addicts, was enough to keep the drug problem at an insig-
nificant level.[1] If an embryonic black market now exists, it has
emerged *since* the alarming growth of addiction and dependency among adolescents and young adults, which is in turn
despite (or because of, according to the second Brain Committee Report) the availability of treatment by free prescription;
and if young addict subcultures (which a few years ago were
nonexistent) have emerged, it is again *despite* the legality of
treatment. So it is now the case that American proponents of
the so-called British system were hopelessly wrong and/or
misguided? I think not, for the following reasons:

(a) As David Ausubel has pointed out (though with the
intention of attacking the British system), "it is a fallacy . . .
to impute a causal connection between the method of control
currently employed and the relatively low rate of addiction"
(for example, in Britain a few years ago).[2] If that is the case,
one could argue that the fallacy applies to imputing a causal
connection between the method of control and the *rising* rate
of addiction in Britain today. The method of control has a
great deal of impact on the unwanted side effects of
addiction, on the life-style of the addict, on the mortality rate
of addicts, on the extent of drug orientation among addicts.
But arguably, it has little to do with the emergence of an
addiction problem that has to be accounted for by resort to
sociological and psychological factors quite distinct from the
method of control. The rate of growth of addiction therefore
(despite the Brain Committee) has a great deal to do with the
state of adolescence and perhaps the state of the nation in
the 1960s, with the *growing* competitiveness of the education
system and the efflorescence of a highly stylized teenage
culture, but having very little to do with the overprescribing
by individual doctors.[3] The trend of current American
theory is toward the view that most addicts go onto heroin
(as they will do with hallucinogenic or "soft" drugs) with
their eyes open. They may do so in the false belief that
addiction can be delayed, or modified, or reversed more
readily than they imagine at the outset; or they may do so in
a consciously self-destructive way, partly spurred by the

image of the addict as folk devil. The point is that they want the drugs and will obtain them from illicit sources if legal sources are unavailable. The question is *why*, not *how*, they begin to entertain the idea of themselves as addicts and progress from there to the *state* of addiction.

(b) The second reason why any move away from the principle at stake in the British system, so-called, should be vigorously resisted is that while the method of control cannot explain the growth of addiction, it *is* the major tool for minimizing the damage done once addiction is under way. Here, I am not thinking so much of the prospects of cure (though that must be in the forefront of medical and social policy) as of the implications for minimizing the unwanted side effects of the addict's way of life—damage to job prospects, family life, the need to resort to crime, and so on. And, contrary to some current thinking, the method of control can arguably *minimize* the rate of   growth of addiction (without necessarily preventing that growth from occurring at all) by lessening the distance between the addict and society, since the lesser the distance, the lesser the pressure to proselytize, to seek subcultural support of an intractably deviant nature. Peter Laurie has argued that the obverse occurs, and that, in America, a policy of repression has driven the addict underground into an intensive addict subculture intractable in nature but at least not growing in size.[4] On the last point, of size, I think that the American figures are still so suspect that no conclusion based on them can be sound, and there may well have been a hidden incidence of growth not amenable to police recording, especially among the middle class. But I would accept Laurie's conclusion that, even if a more tolerant policy leads to a larger number of addicts than would otherwise occur, but of a less intensive kind than under a system of punitive response to the addict, then we have gained in the long run.

This factor of subcultural withdrawal rests on the idea (which finds support in research on other kinds of deviance) that the more punitive the social reaction, the more society imposes a degraded status on the deviant, the greater the tendency for the deviant to withdraw into a tightly knit sub-culture in which he gains collective support from others sharing his situation. At present it seems to me that we have a system of treatment that is substantively tolerant and acceptive of the *addiction,* but emotionally and culturally harsh and condemnatory toward the *addict.* This gives the worst of both worlds, in that it couples that short-term escalation in individual dosage implicit in a tolerant ambulatory system with the pressures to subcultural withdrawal implicit in a generalized social hostility to the addict. Unlike the alcoholic, though, very much like the meths (methylated-spirits) drinker, the addict is treated as a folk devil, a presence to be exorcized rather than accommodated. Stan Cohen and Paul Rock have applied the term to the Teddy Boys, of the 1950s, and seek to explain the progressive fixation that impelled, toward the end of the 1950s large sections of English society to associate extreme delinquency with the slightest trace of Teddy Boy influence in dress.[5] They apply to the Teddy-Boy phenomenon Wilkins's theory of *deviation amplification*—this theory sees deviance as created more by social control than by any substantial inherent deviation.[6] The process begins when a new form of deviant behavior, or a form long in existence but put in the limelight by some quirk of fashion, is processed by the information media and presented as a potential or actual threat to valued standards; the community reacts punitively and stigmatizes the group as deviant; the group becomes more segregated and develops a deviant self-identity, and reinforces those aspects of its behavior appropriate to this identity; the community reacts more punitively still, and so the sequence leads on to either the annihilation of the group by imprisonment or some other form of social purgative, or the kind of explosion that has occurred between the races in America. At each state of the sequence, the game gets rougher for the deviant, and he either drops out and conforms or stays put *but* becomes more recalcitrant. As Laurie has stressed, after a time most stigmatized deviant groups eventually fade away for want of fresh recruits once the gap between the society and the minority has become alarmingly large, or, like the British Nazi party, ends up with very few but fanatical members. But this does not apply in all cases, particularly where the attributions of deviance are based on some unalterable or highly resistant characteristic, such as race. There is no changing a black skin, and if Negroes are treated as deviant, the amplification sequence spirals into major conflict. With Teddy Boys—and Mods and Rockers— society had it relatively easy: the deviance was *transient* and lacking in substance in the first place, and the absurdity was that society dealt with it in classical deterrence fashion only after a great deal of huffing and puffing and social damage. The costs involved seem quite disproportionate to the threat. Compare the crash programs of police mobilization and mechanization to deal with the descent of the Mods and Rockers on Hastings in 1964 with the current preparations for the treatment centers for addicts. Why can British society not mobilize as effectively for a crisis in social and medical provision as it can for keeping the Bank Holiday peace.

We should now see fairly clearly the dangers of the folk-devil syndrome applied to the problem of drug addiction. In the case of a punitive reaction by the community to most forms of deviance, there is a "tapering away" effect: at each twist of the spiral, some deviants adopt conformity, while a dwindling minority harden into recalcitrance. But, *by its nature*, this cannot happen with addiction. This is not to suggest that addiction is a physiologically irreversible state—far from it, the extend to which it is reversible should be more widely known. The damage done by chronic drug abuse is less than that initiated by chronic alcoholism. But it takes, as *is* well known, a great deal of medical, community, and economic support to provide the environment in which withdrawal is possible and likelihood of relapse is minimized: and in a hostile society, addicts are likely to avoid the commitment to withdrawal and are under stronger pressures to relapse. As Max Glatt has stressed, there are many addicts who, even in the present system, are reluctant to come forward through a fear of "registration"—fearing the stigma and sense of finality that they associate with the process.[7] It is on these kinds of fears that a black market can trade. Hence the deviation amplification sequence will not work with addiction, and may tilt many cases of dependency over into addiction proper. Because addiction is a *state*—not simply a role—it is not weakened by the phenomenon of *transience*: that is, the way in which many deviants are simply acting out a role they can shed if the costs outweigh the benefits. Hence any resort to the folk-devil syndrome in the case of addiction is likely to reinforce the very consequences it seeks to avert: that is, subcultural withdrawal, and proselytization in the search for group support. American experience seems to support this picture: what has been termed *retreatist*—that is, drug-using—groups have been found to be much more resistant to change than even the worst fighting gangs.

This is partly because, though the addict from illicit sources is under extreme social threat from the agencies of social control in America and, to a lesser extent, in England, illicit addiction inevitably draws some *cultural* support from the fact that drug dependence and therapeutic addiction are so widespread in our societies. Alcohol and the barbiturates—drawing from the same pharmacological base—support the middle aged, and the overlap between therapeutic and non-therapeutic drug dependence must sustain many people on the fringes of drug experimentation with the notion that they are doing nothing very deviant after all. This makes the case for educating the young to discriminate between types and uses of drugs even more drastic.

The most recent figures show a substantial rise in the proportion of all addicts known to the Home Office who are under twenty-one years of age—roughly a quarter of the total. This fact underlies a great deal of the anxiety felt by society about the addiction problem. But it also cautions to beware of the form that this anxiety can take, that is, the often well-intentioned, but invariably crude authoritarianism that fears the so-called irresponsibility and self-indulgence of youth (in ways that imply that adults are rarely, if ever, irresponsible and self-indulgent). In this view, adolescents are a separate species that is almost inherently deviant: combined with drug misuse or addiction, this section of the adult world sees a massive double threat to valued standards in the figure of the adolescent drug addict. As Terence Morris has stated: "Public attitudes toward the drugtaker are highly colored by the whole problem of generational conflict and the resentment of adults at the emergence of an adolescent culture that is reflected in a spectrum ranging from affluent pop singers to disorder on Bank Holiday beaches."[8] The work of Musgrove[9] and the Eppels[10] has shown the degree of hostility that a large proportion of adults display toward adolescents and the resentment of the false stereotype that many adults entertain of the standards and values of the young. The obvious danger is that drug misuse is *added* to this stereotype in blanket fashion, thus inhibiting communication between the generations even further. As Glatt has noted, even the older addicts who graduated during the 1950s are only too aware of the dangers of treatment of drug addiction becoming inextricably involved in the tensions between the generations: To quote George, who became addicted during the mid-1950s, and who has since died,

> They're [new type addict] just a drag, you know, because they don't take drugs because of some need or personal defect. It's just a case of pure exhibitionism with them, you know . . . . And, apart from the fact that it is making the whole thing, well, bringing the whole thing out into the public in a distorted way, you know, the junkie who does rely on his daily dose and causes nobody any trouble, he's the guy who eventually gets the kick up the backside; he's the one who's going to feel it because of these kids who are just rebelling against their mothers and fathers.[11]

In this passage, the negative description George gives to the new style of addict has a great deal to do with his romanticization of his own, older style of addiction. But the fears he expressed about the tightening up of the system due to public anxiety over the falling age of addiction have proved correct.

The conclusion for social policy is that things must not tighten up too much. There is the need to cut down on the pseudo-black market that originates in irresponsible overprescribing: but there is also the need to maximize contact with addicts, not to thrust them onto the black market proper by operating a policy of "less eligibility" in the forthcoming

treatment centers. When these arrive, and as yet the provision
falls way behind the Ministry of Health pronouncements, they
should be a vast improvement on the system until now:
nevertheless, there must be no insistence on uniformity of
provision. There must be diversity of provision. One lesson to
be learned from the American experience, as Dr. Griffith
Edwards had stressed, is "that patterns of drug use are not
static."[12] There is the danger that the British pattern of
addiction that so far seems to have appeared the most
psychologically valuable, comes to resemble the American
pattern of deprivation, and becomes part of the culture of
poverty of the city poor and ethnic minorities. The unpredictable fluctuations in prevalence, the possibilities of sudden
switches to different drugs, and the perennial danger of the
black market all point to the need for flexibility, experimentation, coordination in both contacting the drug-abuser and in
full-time access to treatment. With young addicts, for instance,
the scope for "unattached" social workers to seek addicts out
is obvious. The Soho Drug Group is a pioneer in this field, as
well as in the realm of a referral agency and a preventative
agency. There is a scope for incentives to be given to those G.P.s
who have worked effectively with addicts to be drawn into the
planning of the treatment centers. There is a need for some
full-time research units to look not only at narcotic addicts, but
at the whole spectrum of drug dependence as well. Above all,
there is the need for community services to be involved in the
care of addicts, particularly after attempts have been made at
withdrawal or transference to nonaddictive drugs. The cost of
expanding these services—which need expanding anyway,
irrespective of drug addiction—will be high, but far lower than
the costs of increased policies and political activity if a black
market in drugs becomes institutionalized. The dissemination
of accurate information on drugs is also essential: a start has
been made with the book by Glatt called *The Drug Scene*; the
one by Kenneth Leech and Brenda Jordan called *Drugs for
Young People: Their Use and Misuse,* which is appropriate for
use in liberal studies and secondary school discussion; and
Peter Laurie's Penguin Special on drugs.[13]

There is every possibility that, given the resources already provided by the ministry (and if it cannot make them available, it should reconsider its timing of its legislation coming into force in April [1968]) and the growth of an informed and compassionate climate of concern for the addict—that the British system will vindicate itself in the long term by comparison with the American system.

NOTES

1. Edwin M. Schur, *Narcotic Addiction in Britain and America: The Impact of Public Policy* (London: Tavistock, 1963).

2. David P. Ausubel, "Controversial Issues in the Management of Drug Addiction: Legalization, Ambulatory Treatment, and the British System," in *Narcotic Addiction*, edited by J. A. O'Donnell and J. C. Ball (New York: Harper and Row, 1966).

3. Reference here was to the Second Report of the Brain Committee, 1965.

4. Peter Laurie, *Drugs: Medical, Psychological, and Social Facts* (London: Penguin, 1967).

5. Stan Cohen and Paul E. Rock, "The Teddy Boy," in *The Age of Affluence*, edited by V. Bogdanor and R. Skidelsky (London: Macmillan, 1970).

6. Leslie Wilkins, *Social Deviance* (London: Tavistock, 1964).

7. Max Glatt, *The Drug Scene in Great Britain* (London: Arnold, 1967).

8. Terence P. Morris, "The Sociology of Crime," *New Society*, 29 April 1965, pp. 7-10.

9. F. Musgrove, *Youth and the Social Order* (London: Routledge, 1964).

10. E. and M. Eppel, *Adolescents and Morality* (London: Routledge, 1965).

11. Glatt.

12. Griffith Edwards, "Relevance of American Experience of Narcotic Addiction to the British Scene," *British Medical Journal* 3 (1967): 425-29.

13. Glatt; Kenneth Leech and Barbara Jordan, *Drugs for Young People: Their Use and Misuse* (London: Religious Education Press, 1967); Laurie.

6

The Police as Amplifiers of Deviancy*

Jock Young

I have evolved an explanatory framework for analyzing the moral career of the drugtaker. It is useful here, however, to examine a concrete instance in order to illustrate in detail the type of factors involved. I wish therefore to take as my example the position of the marihuana smoker in Notting Hill, an area of West London commonly frequented by the middle-class bohemian young. First, the area itself is remarkable in that it has a population that contains a large overrepresentation of young people and immigrants:

	Greater London	Pembridge Ward, Notting Hill
Ages: 20-29	13.5%	27.8%
Immigrants[1]	9.0%	29.2%
Rented private accommodation	32.0%	82.5%
Persons per acre	20.0	160.0[2]

*This work was compiled from various sections of The Drugtakers by Jock Young; reprinted with the permission of Granada Publishing Ltd., London, for MacGibbon and Kee.

The majority of its residents are overcrowded and poorly housed; they are also mixed to an extent unknown in other parts of London. Notting Hill is a series of communities and populations that, although living on each other's doorsteps, often have little contact with each other. There are the English working class, the bohemian young, the West Indians, the Irish, the middle-class professionals, and the Polish and East Europeans, to mention only the major groups represented. The large houses characteristic of Notting Hill were built around 1860 for prosperous middle-class families, who have long since gone; the houses were then subdivided and occupied by working-class families, and more recently subdivided even further to accommodate the young middle-class dropouts, students, and professionals who vie with the working class and immigrants for the area. Localities such as this, with a shifting, mixed population, are unable to control the activities of their members by the usual processes of informal social control. They *appear* tolerant and permissive to the extent that there is not—unlike in many areas of the city—a monolithic homogeneous population that can dictate patterns of behavior. It is in such a disunited community that one would expect bohemianism to be able to grow and flourish, and where social control is largely in the hands of formal agencies, chief among which is the police.

The theoretical orientation of this chapter centers around the premise that a situation defined as real in a society will be real in its consequences. In terms then of those individuals whom society defines as deviants, one would expect that the stereotypes that society holds of them would have very real consequences both to their future behavior and the way they perceive themselves. Thus Erving Goffman in *Asylums* charts what he calls the moral career of the mental patient, outlining the manner in which the particular images the hospital holds of the mentally ill are internalized and acted out by the patient.[3] In a similar vein I wish to describe the manner in which society's stereotypes of the drugtaker fundamentally alter and transform the social world of the marihuana smoker. To do this I draw from a participant-observation study of drugtaking in Notting Hill, which I carred out between 1967 and 1969. Moreover, I shall focus on the effect of the beliefs and stereotypes held by the police about the drugtaker, since it is a vitally important characteristic of society that there is an increasing segregation between social groups and that certain individuals are chosen to mediate between the community and deviant groups. Chief of these is the police and what I want to suggest is:

(a) That the policeman, because of his isolated position in the community, is peculiarly susceptible to the stereotypes, the fantasy notions that the mass media carry about the drugtaker.

(b) That in the process of police action—particularly in the arrest situation but continuing in the courts—the policeman, because of his position of power, inevitably finds himself negotiating the evidence, the reality of drugtaking, to fit these preconceived stereotypes.

(c) That in the process of police action against the drugtaker changes occur within drugtaking groups involving first an intensification of their deviance and in certain important aspects a self-fulfillment of these stereotypes. That is, there will be an amplification of deviance, and a translation of stereotypes into actuality, of fantasy into reality.

We are concerned here not with the origins of bohemian drugtaking, but with the social reaction against drug use. Now the position of the police is vital in this process, for they man the barricades that society sets up between itself and the deviant.

There are two interrelated factors necessary to explain the reaction of the policeman against the drugtaker: the motivations behind the conflict and the manner in which he perceives the typical drug user.

The Conflict between Police and Marihuana Smoker

It is essential to understand the basis of the conflict between police and drug user. It is not sufficient to maintain that the policeman arrests all those individuals in a community who commit illegalities, for if such a course of action were embarked upon the prisons would be filled many times over and a gigantic police force would become necessary. As

criminal acts occur widely throughout society, and the police
are a limited fluid resource, they must to some extent choose,
in terms of a hierarchy of priority, which groups warrant their
attention and concern. There are three major reasons why one
group should perceive another as a "social problem" necessi-
tating intervention.

1. Conflict of Interests

This is where either a deviant group is seen as threatening
the interests of powerful groups in society, or reaction against
the offenders is seen as advantageous in itself. The marihuana
smoker represents a threat to the police to the extent that, if
the occurrence of the habit becomes overlarge and its practise
unashamedly overt, considerable pressure will be put on them
by both local authorities and public opinion to halt its
progress, and in particular, to clean up the area in question.
At the same time marihuana smokers form a criminal group
that has the advantage as far as the policeman on the
beat—and more particularly members of the drug squads—is
concerned of providing a regular source of fairly easily
apprehendable villains. But to eliminate the problem—especially in areas such as Notting Hill where drugtaking is
widespread—would demand the deployment of considerable
forces and severely strain the capacity of the police to deal
with other more reprehensible forms of crime. It would also be
institutional suicide on the part of drug squads, and bureaucracies are not well known for their capacity to write
themselves out of existence. The solution therefore is to
contain the problem rather than to eliminate it. In this fashion
public concern is assuaged, regular contributions to the arrest
statistics are guaranteed, and the proportion of police time
channeled against the drugtaker is made commensurate with
the agreed gravity of the problem.

2. Moral Indignation

I have explained in part the way in which the bureaucratic interests of the police force shape their action against
the drugtaker, but I have not explored the degree of fervor

with which they embark on this project. To do this I must examine the moral indignation the policeman evidences toward the drugtaker.

A. K. Cohen writes of moral indignation:

> The dedicated pursuit of culturally approved goals, the eschewing of interdicted but tantalizing goals, the adherence to normatively sanctioned means—these imply a certain self-restraint, effort, discipline, inhibition. What is the effect of others who, though their activities do not manifestly damage our own interests, are morally undisciplined, who give themselves up to idleness, self-indulgence, or forbidden vices? What effect does the propinquity of the wicked have on the peace of mind of the virtuous? [4]

There is a very real conflict between the values of the police and those of the bohemian marihuana smoker, for whereas the policeman values upright masculinity, deferred gratification, sobriety, and respectability, the bohemian embraces values concerned with overt expressivity in behavior and clothes, and the pursuit of pleasure unrelated to—and indeed disdaining— work. The bohemian in fact threatens the *reality* of the policeman. He lives without work, he pursues pleasure without deferring gratification, he enters sexual relationships without undergoing the obligations of marriage, he dresses freely in a world where uniformity in clothing is seen as a mark of respectability and reliability.

At this point it is illuminating to consider the study made by R. Blum and associates of American policemen working in the narcotics field. When asked to describe the outstanding personal and social characteristics of the illicit drug user, the officers most frequently mentioned moral degeneracy, unwillingness to work, insecurity and instability, pleasure orientation, inability to cope with life problems, weakness, and inadequate personality. They rated marihuana users as being a greater community menace than the Mafia. The following quote by an intelligent and capable officer is illustrative:

> I tell you there's something about users that bugs me. I don't know what it is exactly. You want me to be frank? OK. Well, I can't stand them; I mean I *really* can't stand them.

Why? Because they bother me personally. They're *dirty*, that's what they are, filthy. They make my skin crawl.

It's funny but I don't get that reaction to ordinary criminals. You pinch a burglar or a pickpocket and you understand each other; you know how it is, you stand around yacking, maybe even crack a few jokes. But Jesus, these guys, they're a danger. You know what I mean, they're like Commies or some of those CORE people.

There are some people you can feel sorry for. You know, you go out and pick up some poor chump of a paper hanger [bad-check writer] and he's just a drunk and life's got him all bugged. You can understand a poor guy like that. It's different with anybody who'd use drugs. [5]

Similarly a British policeman—Detective Inspector Wyatt, formerly head of the Essex drugs squad—is quoted as saying about cannabis users: "Never in my experience have I met up with such filth and degradation which follows some people who are otherwise quite intelligent. You become a raving bloody idiot so that you can become more lovable." [6]

Thus the drug user evokes an immediate gut reaction, while most criminals are immediately understandable in both motives and life-style, for the criminal is merely cheating at the rules of a game that the policeman himself plays, whereas the bohemian is skeptical of the validity of the game itself and casts doubts on the world view of both policeman and criminal.

3. Humanitarianism

This occurs where a powerful group seeks to curb the activities of another group in their own better interests. They define them as a social problem and demand that action be taken to ameliorate their situation. This is complicated in the case of marihuana smoking, insofar as those individuals who make up the social problem would deny that any real problem exists at all.

I would argue that the humanitarian motive is exceedingly suspect, for it is often—though not necessarily—a rationalization behind which is concealed either a conflict of interests or moral indignation. For example, Alex Comfort in *The Anxiety Makers* has charted the way in which the medical profession have repeatedly translated their moral indignation over certain "abuses" into a clinically backed humanitarianism.[7] For example, masturbation was once seen as causing psychosis, listlessness, and impotence, and various barbaric clinical devices were evolved to prevent young people from touching their genital organs.

I suggest that there is a tendency in our society to cloak what amounts to moral or material conflicts behind the mantle of humanitarianism. This is because serious conflicts of interest are inadmissible in a political order that obtains its moral legitimacy by invoking the notion of a widespread consensus of opinion throughout all sections of the population. Moreover, in this century, because of a ubiquitous liberalism, we are loathe to condemn another man merely because he acts differently from us, providing that he does not harm others. Moral indignation, then, the intervention into the affairs of others because we think them wicked, must necessarily be replaced by humanitarianism, which, using the language of therapy and healing, intervenes in what it perceives as the best interests and well-being of the individuals involved. Heresy or ungodliness become personal or social pathology. With this in mind, humanitarianism justifies its position by invoking the notion of an in-built justice mechanism that automatically punishes the wrongdoer. Thus premarital intercourse is wrong because it leads to V.D., masturbation because it causes impotence, marihuana smoking because a few users will step unawares on the escalator that leads to heroin addiction.

The policeman, then, is motivated to proceed against the drugtaker in terms of his direct interests as a member of a public bureaucracy, he acts with a fervor rooted in moral indignation, and he is able to rationalize his conduct in terms of an ideology of humanitarianism.

The Marihuana Smoker as a Visible and Vulnerable Target

It is not sufficient to argue that the marihuana smoker is on paper a group with which the police are likely to conflict. Two intervening variables determine whether such a conflict will in actuality take place: namely, the visibility and vulnerability of the group.[8] The drugtaker, because of his long hair and—to the police—bizarre dress, is an exceedingly visible target of police action. The white, middle-class dropout creates for himself the stigmata out of which prejudice can be built, he voluntarily places himself in the position that the Negro unwittingly finds himself. Moreover, unlike in the middle-class neighborhoods where he comes from, and where he is to some extent protected by "good" family and low police vigilance, he moves to areas such as Notting Hill where he is particularly vulnerable to apprehension and arrest.

The Amplification of Deviancy

I have examined the reasons for police action against the drugtaker. We must now examine the manner in which this proceeds. It is not a question merely of the police reacting in terms of their stereotypes and the drug-using groups being buffeted once and for all by this reaction. The relationship between society and the deviant is more complex than this. It is a tight-knit interaction process that can be most easily understood in terms of myriad changes on the part of both police and drug user. Thus:

(a) the police act against the drug users in terms of their stereotypes;

(b) the drug-user group finds itself in a new situation, which it must interpret and adapt to in a changed manner;

(c) the police react in a slightly different fashion to the changed group;

(d) the drug users interpret and adapt to this new situation;

(e) the police react to these new changes; and so on.

One of the most common sequences of events in such a process is what has been termed *deviancy amplification*. The major exponent of this concept is the criminologist Leslie Wilkins, who notes how when society defines a group of people as deviant it tends to react against them so as to isolate and alienate them from the company of "normal" people. In this situation of isolation and alienation, the group—because of various reasons that I shall discuss later—tends to develop its own norms and values, which society perceives as even more deviant than before. As a consequence of this increase in deviancy, social reaction increases even further, the group is even more isolated and alienated, it acts even more deviantly, society acts increasingly strongly against it, and a spiral of deviancy ampiification occurs.[9]

Thus diagramatically:

Table 6-1

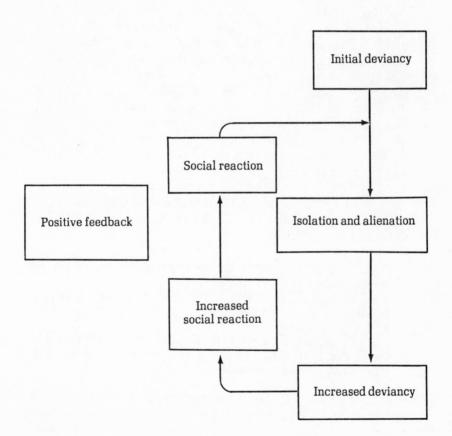

It should not be thought that the deviant group is, so to speak, a pinball inevitably propelled in a deviant direction, or that the police are the cushions of the machine that will inevitably reflex into a reaction triggered by the changing course of the deviant. To view human action in such a light would be to reduce it to the realm of the inanimate, the nonhuman. For although Leslie Wilkins himself uses a mechanistic model, there is no need for us to limit ourselves to such an interpretation. As David Matza has forcefully argued, the human condition is characterized by the ability of a person to stand outside the circumstances that surround him. "A subject actively addresses or encounters his circumstances; accordingly, his distinctive capacity is to reshape, strive toward creating, and actually *transcend* circumstances."[10] The drugtaking group creates its own circumstances to the extent that it interprets and makes meaningful the reactions of the police against it; both the police and the group evolve theories that attempt to explain each other and test them out in terms of the actual course of events: the arrest situation, encounters on the street, portrayals in the mass media, and conversations with friends. These hypotheses of the police about the nature of drug use and of the drugtaker about the mentality of the police, determine the direction and intensity of the deviancy amplification process.

Leslie Wilkins utilized this concept to explain the difference between the amount and nature of heroin addiction in the United States and Britain. He suggests that the following differences are critical:

(a) the heroin addict in Britain is perceived as sick, in the United States as a criminal;

(b) the addicts' perception of the police in America is as a hostile enemy, in England their perception ranges from helpful to neutral;

(c) the supply of heroin to an addict is absolutely illegal in the United States; in England it is freely available through legally designated channels.

In the United States, then, the addict is perceived as a criminal and his supply of heroin can only be obtained illegally. The junkie is isolated from society, he constantly faces the dangers of public and police reaction. He begins to accept the definition of his rejectors and perceives himself as a criminal, and this is confirmed as he is forced into crime in order to pay the high black-market prices that are his only source of supply. Society and the police are perceived as an enemy who stand between him and the drug. As a result a junkie subculture grows up that is criminal, predatory, and outlandish. Thus the brutal, obscene, and disgusting world that Burroughs so vividly portrays in *The Naked Lunch* is socially created. And the resulting deviance of the junkie only serves to continue the convictions of the public, societal reaction is maintained, and indeed increases and the junkie is placed beyond the bounds of society in an area where there is little hope of reentry. The junkie subculture becomes enmeshed with the underworld, its economic base is petty crime, and proselytization to juniors occurs in order to raise money. Thus addiction is both maintained and spread. In Britain, in contrast, Wilkins argues that the problem is held in check by the designation of the addict as sick and the legally available supplies of heroin.

What I wish to argue is that the marihuana smoker in Notting Hill has been subject over the last few years to a process of deviancy and amplification, milder it is true than that outlined by Wilkins of the American heroin addict, but nonetheless significant. Moreover, that is precisely the process that provides a meaningful understanding of the hypothetical escalation between marihuana and heroin.

Deviancy Amplification in Industrial Societies

To understand, then, the phenomenon of drugtaking in modern societies, the precise nature of deviancy amplification in such societies must be analyzed.

The determining factor as to treatment of individuals within society is the type of information we receive about them. Wilkins argues that in modern societies, compared to small rural communities, there is a significant information drop that leads to a qualitatively different mode of dealing with deviants. Whereas in all societies there is a variation in behavior, in small-scale societies there is much less chance of an individual or group being defined as deviant and being involved in a deviancy-amplification process. Wilkins distinguishes three variables in regard to the type of information available in a society with regard to the behavior of a particular individual or group within it. They are:

(a) the *channel* the information comes by;
(b) the *content* of the information;
(c) the *amount* of information.

Utilizing these three variables I have divided social systems into three types:

1 The small group or village community

(a) Channel: face-to-face contact;
(b) content: multidimensional;
(c) amount: large.

In a small society information is diffuse and available from face-to-face contact: the delinquent in a village is known not just for his delinquency, he is known in terms of his position in a kin network, he is known also in terms of a whole series of human attributes: the cheerful lad who delivers the papers, the boy who worked in his spare time in the village store, and—in terms of some understandable theory of why he stole—the boy whose mother showed him no affection and ran off with Jack the village postman!

All this information, rich and multidimensional, has important bearings on the group's actual behavior toward deviants. Dentler and Erikson in their study of small work groups have shown that the group permits a high degree of deviation within it and will indeed resist strongly any trend toward the alienation of an individual member.[11] Indeed, they suggest that deviants, by demarcating group boundaries, perform important functions in that group. It is only when the individual's behavior is perceived as extremely threatening to the group values that they will take the drastic measure of expelling him.

2 The metropolis: at the height of the industrial revolution: before the advent of the mass media

The prime characteristic of large urban societies is the extreme social segregation that occurs within them. It was in fact during the rapid growth of the towns during the industrial revolution that large-scale segregation in terms of class and ethnic groups occurred. Frank Musgrove notes what he calls the *Gresham's Law of Population Movement* within towns in which the "bad" population (in the sense of socially inferior) drives out the "good." This residential segregation is further reflected in terms of segregated schools, churches, clubs, and leisure activities. He writes of modern society:

> The suburban bureaucrat may live year in and year out without any but the most fleeting contact with anyone of a different level of occupation, education, or civilization from himself. His work is at the administrative headquarters remote from the factory operatives whose destinies he helps to shape; there he associates with others of like kind; he travels home, insulated by his motor-car from contact with any other order of being, to an area of social equals; his leisure is spent in a club with others of the same social standing. We have unthinkingly evolved, or deliberately fashioned, social concentration camps: places in which one social class is concentrated to the exclusion of others.[12]

Thus class is segregated from class, young people from old, rich people from poor, criminals from noncriminals, colored people from whites. This is precisely what Michael Harrington was referring to when he called the massive hidden poverty of America the *invisible land*.

In the metropolis of the industrial revolution we can say that, in terms of our three variables:

(a) channel: face-to-face contact for the small amount of the city that each group of people knew;

(b) content: either multidimensional for their own group or almost nonexistent for others;

(c) amount: small.

But the rise of the media has changed all this; social segregation remains and has indeed increased, but the *amount* of information we have about other groups within society has risen and is derived largely through the media of the newspapers, television, and radio. We come then to our third type of society.

3 Modern urban society

Studies of the mass media have almost universally shown that they have very little effect on changing attitudes where groups have actual empirical reference concerning the event, people, or group in question. If you are actually involved in a strike you will not be affected by the press even though it presents a uniform consensus of opinion opposing the strike. The only effect of the media, on a group who have actual empirical knowledge of a social event, is to reinforce preexisting attitudes. But the situation in a society of extreme social segregation is that there is widespread lack of direct information of one social group about another. It is in precisely this type of society that one would expect the media to provide a large amount of one's social knowledge. Now, the type of information that the mass media portrays is that which is *newsworthy*. In a sentence, it selects events that are *atypical*, presents them in a *stereotypical* fashion, and contrasts them against a backcloth of normality that is *overtypical*. The atypical is selected because the everyday or humdrum is not interesting to read or watch, it has little news value. As a result of this, if one had little face-to-face contact with young people one's total information about them would be in terms of extremes—drugtaking, sex, and wanton violence on one hand and Voluntary Services Overseas and Outward Bound courses on the other. But the statistically unusual alone is not sufficient to make news. The mass-circulation newspapers in particular have discovered that people avidly read news that titillates their sensibilities and confirms their prejudices. The ethos of "give the public what it wants" involves a constant play on the normative worries of large segments of the population; it utilizes outgroups as living Rorschach blots on to which collective fears and doubts are projected. The stereotypical distorted image of the deviant is then contrasted against the overtypical, hypothetical man-in-the-street, that persistent illusion of consensual sociology and politics. Out of this, simple moral directives are produced demanding that something must be done about it: the solitary deviant faces the wrath of all society, epitomized by its moral conscience, the popular newspaper. For instance, if we consider this headling in the People,[13] the atypical, the stereotypical, and the overtypical are fused into two magnificent sentences:

HIPPIE THUGS—THE SORDID TRUTH: Drugtaking, couples making love while others look on, rule by a heavy mob armed with iron bars, foul language, filth and stench, THAT is the scene inside the hippies' fortress in London's Piccadilly. These are not rumours but facts—sordid facts which will shock ordinary, decent, family-loving people.

Christopher Logue came nearest to describing the distortion of information by the mass media when he wrote:

Somehow, but how I am not sure, popular newspapers reflect the attitudes of those whose worst side they deepen and confirm. Pinning their influence exactly, by example or image, is difficult: they use common words cleverly; certain public figures nourish their vocabulary; in a few years we have seen "permissive" and "immigrant" gain new meanings.
One technique for worsening ourselves seems to go like this: Take a genuine doubt, formulate it as a question whose words emphasize its worst possible outcome, pop the question into print or into the mouths of respectable scaremongers as many times as you can, package this abstract with a few examples of judicial guilt; thus, when reiterated, the questions becomes an argument certifying the delusory aspect of the original, true doubt.[14]

What I am suggesting then is that the twin factors of social segregation and the mass media introduce into the relationship between deviant groups and society an important element of misperception, and that the deviancy amplification process is initiated, always in terms of, and often because of, incorrect perceptions.

Moreover, one of the characteristics of complex societies is that certain people are allocated special roles in the process of social control. These roles, such as that of the policeman, the magistrate, and the judge, tend to involve people who themselves exist in specially segregated parts of the system. What I want to suggest is that the particular individuals assigned to administrating the legal actions against deviants inhabit their own particular segregated spheres, and that the process of arrest, sentencing, and imprisonment takes place within the terms of their own particular misperceptions of deviancy.

Furthermore, our knowledge of deviants is not only stereotypical because of the distortions of the mass media, but is also, unlike in small-scale societies, one dimensional. That is, to take the methylated-spirits drinker as an example, we know very little of him as a person in terms of his individual characteristics, his kin, his way of life, and his attitudes to the world. We know him merely by the label *meths-drinker* and the hazy stereotype of activities that surrounds this phrase. Rarely—or not at all—have we even seen or talked to him in the church crypts of the East End or at Waterloo Station in the early hours of the morning. Similarly, the delinquent is known—for example—as someone who has stolen; we do not know him as the boy across the street, Jack's son, the budding young footballer, the boy with the cheerful smile. A little of this may be known to the courts through the advice of social workers and probation officers, but it is information that is sadly lacking when compared to the all-encompassing knowledge of villagers about their deviant members.

We are immensely aware of deviants in modern urban societies because of the constant bombardment of information via the mass media. Marshall McLuhan pictures the world as first expanding through the growth of the city and transport systems, and then *imploding* as the media bring the world close together again. "It is this implosive factor," he writes, "that alters the position of the Negro, the teenager, and some other groups. They can no longer be contained in the *political* sense of limited association. They are now *involved* in our lives as we [are] in theirs, through electric media." That is, in modern urban societies, compared with the metropolis that existed prior to the advent of the mass media, we can no longer have little knowledge of or at least conveniently forget the deviant. He is brought to our hearth by the television set, his picture is on our breakfast table with the morning paper. Moreover, the mass media do not purvey opinions on all deviant groups; they create a universe of discourse for our segregated social world in which many groups are ignored; they simply do not exist in the consciousness of most men. *Cathy Come Home* is shown on television and suddenly, dramatically, the public are aware of a new social problem. The "homeless" have become a problem to them. The methylated-spirit drinkers, however, although numerically quite a large population, are largely outside the universe of discourse of the mass media; they exist in a limbo outside the awareness of the vast majority of the population.

The media then—in a sense—can create social problems; they can present them dramatically and overwhelmingly, and, what is most important, they can do it suddenly. What I am suggesting is that the media can fan up very quickly and effectively public indignation concerning a particular deviant group. It is possible for them to engineer rapidly what one might call "a moral panic" about a certain type of deviancy. Indeed, because of the phenomenon of overexposure—the glut of information over a short space on a topic so that it becomes uninteresting—there is institutionalized into the media the need to create moral panics and issues that will seize the imagination of the public. For instance, we may chart the course of the great panic over drugs that occurred during 1967 by examining the amount of newspaper space devoted to this topic. Thus, the number of column inches in The (London) Times for the four-week period beginning 29 May was 37; this exploded because of the Mick Jagger (a rock star) trial to 709 in the period beginning 27 June; continued at a high level of 591 over the next four weeks; and then began to abate from the period 21 August onward, when the number of column inches was 107. Other examples, I suggest, are the skinheads in England, and Hell's Angels and the hippies in the United States.

To summarize, then, the crucial characteristics of the information in regard to deviants in modern societies are as follows:

(a) A gross misperception of deviants because of social segregation and the stereotyped information purveyed via the mass media. This leads to social reaction against deviants that is phrased in terms of stereotyped *fantasy* rather than an accurate empirical knowledge of the behavioral and attitudinal *reality* of their life-styles.

(b) A one-dimensional knowledge of the deviant in terms of the stereotyped *label* that we have fixed to him, leading to a low threshold over which we shall expel him from our society and commence a process of deviancy amplification. It is much more unlikely in a small-scale society with multidimensional knowledge of individual members that expulsion would occur.

(c) Instead of utilizing informal modes of social control, we have special roles manned by people who are often particularly segregated from the rest of society, and thus especially liable to misperception.

(d) Because of the *implosion* of the mass media we are greatly aware of the existence of deviants, and because the criterion of inclusion in the media is newsworthiness it is possible for moral panics over a particular type of deviancy to be created by the *sudden* dissemination of information about it.

So, when compared to other societies, the modern urban community has a peculiar aptitude to initiate deviancy-amplification processes, and to base this gradual expulsion of the deviant from the community on rank misperceptions.

The Position of the Policeman in a Segregated Society

The police occupy a particularly segregated part of the social structure. This is because of:

(a) A policy of limited isolation, based on the premise that if you become too friendly with the community you are liable to corruption.

(b) Public attitudes range from a ubiquitous suspicion to, in areas such as Notting Hill, downright hostility.

(c) In terms of actual contacts the Royal Commission Survey on the police found that just under a half of city police and three-quarters of country police thought that they would have had more friends if they had a different job. Two-thirds of all police thought their job adversely affected their outside friendships.

(d) A fair proportion of policemen are residentially segregated. Thus, a quarter of city police live in groups of six or more police houses.

(e) In the particular instance of middle-class drugtakers in Notting Hill, the police have very little direct knowledge outside the arrest situation of the normal behavior of middle-class youth.

The police, then, because of their segregation are particularly exposed to the stereotypical accounts of deviants prevalent in the mass media. They have, of course, by the very nature of their role a high degree of face-to-face contact with deviants, but these contacts as I shall argue later are of a type that, because of the policeman's position of power, make for a reinforcement rather than an elimination of mass-media stereotypes. In short, a person in a position of power vis-à-vis the deviant tends to negotiate reality so that it comes to fit his preconceptions. As a consequence of the isolation of the police and their awareness of public suspicion and hostility, there is a tendency for the police officer, in order to legitimize his role vis-à-vis the community, to envisage his role in terms of enacting the will of society, and representing the desires of a hypothesized "normal" decent citizen. In this vein, he is sensitive to the pressures of public opinion as represented in the media, and given that the police are grossly incapable because of their numbers of dealing with crime, he will focus his attention on those areas in which public indignation would seem to be greatest and which at the same time are in accord with his own preconceptions. He is thus a willing instrument—albeit unconsciously—of the type of moral panics about particular types of deviancy that are fanned up regularly by the mass media. The real conflict between police and drugtaker in terms of direct interests and moral indignation is thus confirmed, distorted, and structured by the specified images presented in the mass media.

The Fantasy and Reality of Drugtaking

I wish to describe the social world of the marihuana smoker in Notting Hill, as it was in 1967, contrasting it with the fantasy stereotype of the drugtaker available in the mass media.

It is a typical bohemian scene, that is, it is a highly organized community involving tightly interrelated friendship nets and especially intense patterns of visiting. The stereotype held in the mass media is that of the isolated drugtaker living in a socially disorganized area, or at best, a drifter existing in a loose conglomeration of misfits.

The values of the hippie marihuana smoker are relatively clear-cut and in opposition to the values of the wider society. The focal concerns of the culture are short-term hedonism, spontaneity, expressivity, disdain for work. The stereotype held is of a group of individuals who are essentially *asocial*, who lack values, rather than propound alternative values. They are prey to wicked pushers who play on their naivete and inexperience.

Drugtaking is—at least to start with—irregular. It is not an essential prerequisite of membership. Rather it is used instrumentally for hedonistic and expressive purposes and symbolically as a sign of the exotic "differentness" of the bohemian. Drugs are thus an important, although not central focus of such groups. Drugs hold a great fascination for the nondrugtaker, and in the stereotype drugs are held to be the primary—if not exclusive—concern of such groups. Thus a peripheral activity is misperceived as a central group activity.

The marihuana user and the marihuana seller are not, on the street level, fixed roles in the culture. At one time a person may sell marihuana, at another he may be buying it.[16] This is because at street level supply is irregular, and good "connections" appear and disappear rapidly. The supply of marihuana at that time derived from two major sources: tourists, returning from abroad, and hippie or immigrant entrepreneurs. The latter are unsystematic, deal in relatively small quantities, and make a restricted and irregular profit. The tourist's total contribution to the market is significant. Both tourists and entrepreneurs restrict their criminal activities to marihuana importation. The dealer in the street buys from these sources and sells in order to maintain himself in drugs and sustain subsistence living. He is well thought of by the group, is part of the hippie culture, and is not known as a "pusher." The criminal underworld has little interest in the entrepreneur, the tourist, or the dealer in the street. The stereotype, in contrast, is on the lines of the corruptor and the corrupted, that is the "pusher" and the "victim." The pusher is perceived as having close contacts with the criminal underworld and being part of a "drug pyramid."

The culture consists of largely psychologically stable individuals. The stereotype sees the drugtaker essentially as an immature, psychologically unstable young person corrupted by unscrupulous pushers.

The marihuana user has in fact a large measure of disdain for the heroin addict. There is an interesting parallel between the marihuana user's perception of the businessman and of the heroin addict. Both are considered to be hung up, obsessed, and dominated by money or heroin respectively. Hedonistic and expressive values are hardly likely to be realized by either, and their way of life has no strong attraction for the marihuana user. Escalation, then, from marihuana to heroin is a rare phenomenon that would involve a radical shift in values and life-style. In the stereotype the heroin addict and the marihuana user are often indistinguishable, the values of both are similar, and escalation is seen as part of a progressive search for more effective kicks.

The marihuana user is widely prevalent in Notting Hill; a high proportion of young people in the area have smoked it at some time or another. The stereotype based on numbers known to the police is small compared with the actual number of smokers, yet is perceived as far too large at that and increasing rapidly.

The effects of marihuana are mildly euphoric; psychotic effects are rare and only temporary.[17] The stereotypical effects of marihuana reflect the exaggerated ambivalence of the mass media toward drugs. Thus they hold promise of uninhibited pleasure, yet plummet the taker inevitably into unmitigated misery. So we have a distorted spectrum ranging from extreme sexuality, through aggressive criminality, to wildly psychotic episodes. The informed journalist, more recently, has found this model difficult to affix to marihuana usage. He has therefore switched gear and indicated how the innocuous pleasures of smoking are paid for by the sacrifical few who mysteriously escalate to the nightmares of heroin addiction.

The Policeman as a Negotiator of Reality

We live in a world that is, as I have suggested, segregated not so much in terms of distance but in terms of meaningful contact and empirical knowledge. The stereotype of the drug-taker-drugseller relationship is available to the public via the mass media. This stereotype is constructed according to a typical explanation of deviance derived from absolutist notions of society; namely, that the vast majority of individuals in society share common values and agree on what is conformist and what is deviant. In these terms the deviant is a fringe phenomenon consisting of psychologically inadequate individuals who live in socially disorganized or anomic areas. The emergence of large numbers of young people indulging in deviant activities such as drugtaking, in particular areas such as Notting Hill, would seem to clash with this notion, since it is impossible to postulate that all of them are psychologically inadequate and that their communities are completely socially disorganized. To circumvent this, absolutist theories invoke the notion of the corrupted and the corruptor. Healthy youngsters are being corrupted by a few psychologically disturbed and economically motivated individuals. Thus the legitimacy of alternative norms—in this case drugtaking—arising of their own accord in response to certain material and social pressures, is circumvented by the notion of the wicked drug pusher corrupting innocent youth. This allows conflicts of direct interest and moral indignation to be easily subsumed under humanitarianism. The policeman—like the rest of the public—shares this stereotype and his treatment of individuals suspected of drugtaking is couched in terms of this stereotype:

(a) The police, the courts, and the laws themselves distinguish between possession and sale of dangerous drugs.

(b) The individual found in possession of marihuana is often—and in Notting Hill frequently—ignored by the police. They are after the real enemy, the drug pusher. To achieve this aim they are willing to negotiate with the individual found in possession. Thus they will say, "we are not interested in you, you have just been stupid, we are interested in the person who sold you this stuff. Tell us about him and we will let you off lightly." Moreover, if the individual found in possession of marihuana actually finds himself in the courts, he will find himself in a difficult position, namely, that if he tells the truth and says that he smokes marihuana because he likes it, and because he believes that it does no harm and that therefore the law is wrong, he will receive a severe sentence. Whereas if he plays their game and conforms to their stereotype, namely, that he had got into bad company, that somebody (the pusher) offered to sell him the stuff, so he thought he would try it out, that he knows he was foolish and will not do it again, the court will let him off lightly. He is not then in their eyes the true deviant. He is not the dangerous individual whom the police and the courts are really after. Thus the fantasy stereotypes of drugtaking available to the police and the legal profession are reinforced and reenacted in the courts, in a process of negotiating between the accused and the accusers. The policeman continues then with evangelical zeal to seek the pusher, the forces of public opinion and the mass media firmly behind him. As a result the sentences for possession and for sale become increasingly disparate. In a recent case the buyer of marihuana received a fine of £5, while the seller received a five-year jail sentence. A year previously, the same individual who in this case was buying, was selling marihuana to the person who was sentenced in this case for selling.

The negotiation of reality by the policeman is exhibited in the widespread practice of perjury. This is not a function of the Machiavellianism of the police, but rather a product of their desire in the name of administrative efficiency to jump the gap between what I shall term *theoretical* and *empirical guilt.* For example, a West Indian who wears dark glasses, who has no regular employment, and who mixes with beatniks, would quite evidently satisfy their notion of a drug pusher. If he is arrested, then it is of no consequence that no marihuana is found in his flat, nor it is morally reprehensible to plant marihuana on his person. For all that is being done is aiding the cause of justice by providing the empirical evidence to substantiate the obvious theoretical guilt. That he might actually have only sold marihuana a few times in the past, that he mixes with hippies because he likes their company, and that he lives in fact from his National Assistance payments is ignored; the stereotype of the pusher is in evidence, and the reality is unconsciously negotiated to fit its requirements.

The Vested Interests of Police and Media

The police have a bureaucratic interst in apprehending the marihuana smoker to the extent that this avoids public recrimination of failing in their duty. They have also a certain moral indignation about drug use, for the hedonism and expressivity of bohemian drugtakers challenges the moral validity of their sense of the work ethic and just reward. They will tend in such circumstances to have an image of marihuana smoking as a pursuit that although pleasurable is dangerous and an appraisal of the bohemian way of life as being a miserable one compared to their own. Drug use is not freely chosen but a result of corruption of innocence. In this fashion they evolve a myth of the marihuana smoker that protects the validity of their own way of life. Their own role is immediately derived from such an ethos: they must save the innocent (that is, the drug user) in a humanitarian fashion and punish the wicked (that is, the drug pusher). The media have learned that the fanning up of moral indignation is a remarkable commercial success. They, therefore, play on and continue such distorted imagery. But the relationship between police and mass media is closer and more intricate than this, for a symbiotic relationship exists between the police and the crime reporter: the police providing information and the journalists holding back news in such a fashion as to aid police investigations. Precisely such a cooperative relationship exists over the control of drug use. Robert Traini, the chairman of the Crime Reporters Association, has indicated how the moral panic over drug use was initiated in Great Britain by the police approaching journalists and informing them that "the situation had got out of hand."[18] The mass media responded enthusiastically and police of all ranks become exposed to a playback and subsequent elaboration of their prejudices.

The mass media representing a reified public opinion was a major pressure on the police. The moral panic that evolved in the middle 1960s soon got firmly on its way.

The Amplification of Deviance and the Translation of Fantasy into Reality

With time the effect of police action on the marihuana smoker in Notting Hill results in:

(a) the intensification of the deviancy of the marihuana user; that is, the consolidation and accentuation of his deviant values in the process of deviancy amplification.

(b) a change in the life-style and reality of marihuana use so that certain facets of the stereotype become actuality. In short, a translation of fantasy into reality.

I wish to consider the various aspects of the social world of the marihuana user that I outlined earlier and note the cumulative effective of intensive police action:

(a) Intensive police action serves to increase the organization and cohesion of the drugtaking community, uniting its members in a sense of injustice felt at harsh sentences and mass-media distortions. The severity of the conflict compels bohemian groups to evolve theories to explain the nature of their position in society, thereby heightening their consciousness of themselves as a group with definite interests over and against those of the wider society. Conflict welds an introspective community into a political faction with a critical ideology, and deviancy amplification results.

(b) A rise in police action increases the necessity for the drugtaker to segregate himself from the wider society of nondrugtakers. The greater his isolation the less chance there is that the informal face-to-face forces of social control will come into operation, and the higher his potentiality for further deviant behavior. At the same time the creation by the bohemian of social worlds centering around hedonism, expressivity, and drug use makes it necessary for the nondrugtaker, the "straight" person, to be excluded not only for reasons of security but also to maintain definitions of reality unchallenged by the outside world. Thus after a point in the process of exclusion of the deviant by society, the deviant himself will cooperate in the policy of separation.

(c) The further the drugtaker evolves deviant norms, the less change there is of his reentering the wider society. Regular drug use, bizarre dress, long hair, and lack of a workaday sense of time, money, rationality, and rewards, all militate against his reentry into regular employment. To do so after a point would demand a complete change of identity; besides modern record systems would make apparent any gaps that have occurred in his employment or scholastic records, and these might be seen to indicate a personality that is essentially shiftless and incorrigible. Once he is out of the system and labeled by the system in this manner, it is very difficult for the penitent deviant to reenter it, especially at the level of jobs previously open to him. There is a point therefore beyond which an ossification of deviancy can be said to occur.[19]

(d) As police concern with drugtaking increases, drugtaking becomes more and more a secret activity. Because of this, drugtaking in itself becomes of greater value to the group as a symbol of their difference, and of their defiance of perceived social injustices. That is, marihuana comes to be consumed not only for its euphoric effects but as a symbol of bohemianism and rebellion against the unjust system. Drugtaking and trafficking thus move from being peripheral activities of the groups, a mere vehicle for the better realization of hedonistic, expressive goals, to become a central activity of great importance. The stereotype begins to be realized, and fantasy is translated into reality.

(e) As police activity increases, the price of marihuana rises. This, together with the increase in the size of the market, makes the business more attractive both for the professional importer and the full-time pusher. The small dealer, motivated by social and subsistence living considerations, does not disappear but he becomes more of a rarity and his career is considerably shortened, for it is the street-level pusher who fits the model of marihuana selling held by the police. His long hair and lack of economic or criminal rationality make him an easy target. He is subject to a process of deviancy amplification and—because he is the focus of police attention in his corruptor role—takes the main brunt of harassment. Intrinsically part of the subculture, his imprisonment represents to heads (drug users) the most overt example of social injustice. As risk increases, large profits are more likely to motivate people to enter marihuana distribution than the lure of a prestigious community job or the ideology of turning people on. Hippie, West Indian, and Pakistani entrepreneurs become more systematic: the business becomes economically rational. Small-time criminals, previously peripherally involved, are more likely to see it as a possible full-time occupation. Elaborate organizations begin to evolve. At this point, significant external events have intervened and hastened this process; for the Nixon Administration's Operation Intercept, which attempted to cut supplies of marihuana entering the United States from Mexico, had the effect of increasing the consumption of hashish in North America.[20] The resin is easier to smuggle and derives from the Far East, the Middle East, and North Africa. London became, as one perceptive underground commentator on the drug scene pointed out, "a major staging post in the world's drug traffic: every day large amounts of hash are smuggled direct[ly] from London to the U.S.A. . . .as much as half of the hash arriving in London is forwarded direct[ly] to the U.S.A. where shit [hash] fetches between 4 and 4½ times its London price."[21] The augmented national organization meshes with international networks that stretch from Pakistan to San Francisco. Not that this is centralized *to any extent* like the heroin market, but it is considerably more organized and professional than before. Violence and rumors of violence emerge; an embryonic drug pyramid begins to settle out of the confused sporadic market of the rest. At the same time, increased customs vigilance reduces the proportion of marihuana (usually "grass") brought in by amateurs largely for their own consumption. Grass becomes less available and hashish the staple form of marihuana. As the organization of smuggling becomes more complex, in order to meet the demands of an international market with high risks, the number of hands through which the resin passes increases. Profit maximization involves the progressive dilution of the resin. These impurities lead to hangovers (although of a mild and soporific nature), which rarely occurred with hashish and grass previously available. Once again, on several scores, the fantasy stereotype begins to be translated into reality.

(f) The marihuana user becomes increasingly secretive and suspicious of those around him. How does he know that his activities are not being observed by the police? How does he know that seeming friends are not police informers? Ugly rumors fly around about treatment of suspects by the police, long terms of imprisonment, planting, and general social stigmatization. The effects of drugs are undoubtedly related to the cultural milieu in which drugs are taken: a Welsh rugby club drinks to the point of aggression, an all-night party to the point of libidinousness, an academic sherry party unveils the pointed gossip of competitiveness lurking under the mask of a community of scholars. Similarly, the effects of marihuana being smoked in the context of police persecution invite feelings of paranoia and semipsychotic episodes. As Allen Ginsberg astutely notes:

> It is no wonder . . . that most people who have smoked marihuana in America often experience a state of anxiety, of threat, of paranoia in fact, which may lead to trembling or hysteria, at the microscopic awareness that they are breaking a Law, that thousands of Investigators all over the country are trained and paid to smoke them out and jail them, that thousands of their community are in jail, that inevitably a few friends are "busted" with all the hypocrisy and expense and anxiety of that trial and perhaps punishment—jail and victimage by the bureaucracy that made, propagandized, administers, and profits from such a monstrous law.
>
> From my own experience and the experience of others I have concluded that most of the horrific effects and disorders described as characteristic of marihuana "intoxication" by the U.S. Federal Treasury Department's Bureau of Narcotics are quite the reverse, precisely traceable back to the effects on consciousness not of the narcotic but of the

law and the threatening activities of the U.S. Bureau of Narcotics itself. Thus, as Buddha said to a lady who offered him a curse, the gift is returned to the giver when it is not accepted.[22]

This relates to Tigani el Mahi's hypothesis that making a drug illegal, and failing to institutionalize its use through controls and sanctions, produces adverse psychic effects and bizarre behavior when the drug is taken. Thus stereotypical effects become in part reality.[23]

(g) As police activity increases, the marihuana user and the heroin addict begin to feel some identity as joint victims of police persecution. Interaction between heroin addicts and marihuana users increases. The general social feeling against all drugs creates a stricter control of the supply of heroin to the addict. He is legally bound to obtain his supplies from one of the properly authorized clinics. Lack of personnel who are properly trained, or who even have an adequate theoretical knowledge of dealing with the withdrawal problems of the heroin addict, results in the alienation of many from the clinics. The addict who does attend either is kept on maintenance doses or else has his supply gradually cut. Either way euphoria becomes more difficult to obtain from the restricted supply, and the "grey market" of surplus National Health heroin, which previously catered for addicts who required extra or illicit supplies, disappears. In its place a black market springs up, often consisting of Chinese heroin diluted with adulterants. This provides a tentative basis for criminal underworld involvement in drug selling and has the consequence of increasing the risks of ovedosage (because the strength is unknown) and infection (because of the adulterants). But the supply of black-market heroin alone is inadequate. Other drugs are turned to in order to make up the scarcity; the precise drugs varying with their availability, and the ability of legislation to catch up with this phenomenon of drugs displacement. Chief of these are methadone, a drug addictive in its own right, which is used to wean addicts off heroin, and freely prescribed barbiturates. As a result of displacement, a body of methadone and barbiturate addicts emerges, the barbiturates being probably more dangerous than heroin and cause even greater

withdrawal problems. For a while the overprescription by
doctors creates, as once occurred with heroin, an ample grey
market of methadone and barbiturates. But the pressure on the
doctors restricts at least the availability of methadone, and the
ranks of salable black-market drugs are increased in the
process. Because many junkies share some common bohemian
traditions with hippies (they often live in the same areas, smoke
pot [marihuana], and affect the same style of dress), the black
market of heroin, methadone, barbiturates, and marihuana
will overlap. The heroin addict seeking money in order to maintain his habit at a desirable level and the enterprising drug
seller may find it profitable to make these drugs available to
marihuana smokers. Some marihuana users will pass on to
these hard drugs, but let me emphasize *some*, because in
general, heavy use of such drugs is incompatible with hippie
values, for full-blown physical addiction involves being at a
certain place at a certain time every day; it involves an obsession with one substance to the exclusion of all other interests;
it is anathema to the values of hedonic expressivity and
autonomy. But the number of known heroin addicts in Britain is
comparatively small (only 1,555 in 1971), while the estimates of
the marihuana-smoking population range up to one million and
beyond. Thus it would need only a minute proportion of marihuana smokers to escalate for the heroin figures to rise
rapidly. Besides, the availability of methadone and barbiturates
gives rise to alternative avenues of escalation. Methadone,
once a palliative for heroin addicts, becomes a drug of
addiction for individuals who have never used heroin. To this
extent increased social reaction against the drugtaker would
make real the stereotype held by the public about escalation.
But the transmission of addiction, unlike the transmission of
disease, is not a matter of contact, it is a process that is
dictated by the social situation and values of the person who is
in contact with the addict. The values of marihuana smokers
and the achievement of subterranean goals are not met by
intensive heroin use. Escalation to heroin (or methadone and
the barbiturates) will occur only in atypical cases where the
structural position of the marihuana user changes sufficiently
to necessitate the evolution of values compatible with heroin

use as solutions to his newly emergent problems. Availablity of a drug alone is insufficient to precipitate addiction, there has to be a meaningful reason for its use. At the moment, the widespread structural unemployment in Britain may provide— along American lines—precisely such a cause. Increased availability *plus* the desperation associated with exclusion from the means of earning a living is the sort of combination that might spell a serious heroin problem in the future. The irony is that if it comes it will strike hardest among the lower-class youth on the edge of the drug culture. The middle-class marihuana smoker will have a degree of immunity to the solution heroin offers.

(h) As the mass media fan public indignation over marihuana use, pressure on the police increases; the public demands that they solve the drug problem. The number of marihuana users known to the police is a mere tip of the iceberg of actual smokers. Given their desire to behave in accordance with public opinion and to legitimize their position, the police will act with great vigilance and arrest more offenders. All that happens is that they dig deeper into the undetected part of the iceberg; the statistics for marihuana offenders soar; the public, the press, and the magistrates view the new figures with even greater alarm. Increased pressure is put on the police, the latter dig even deeper into the iceberg, the figures increase once again, and public concern becomes even greater. We have entered a fantasy crime wave, where the supposed statistical increase in marihuana use bears little relationship to the actual rate of increase. Because of the publicity, however, the notion of marihuana smoking occurs for the first time to a larger number of people, and through their desire to experiment there will be some real increase in the rate of smoking. We must not overlook here the fact that moral panic over drugtaking results in the setting up of drug squads that by their very bureaucratic creation will ensure a regular contribution to the offense figures that had never been evidenced before.

Police action, then, has not only a deviancy-amplification effect in the formal sense of the unintended consequences of the exclusion of the marihuana smoker from "normal" society, but it also has an effect on the content of the bohemian culture within which marihuana smoking takes place.

I have discussed a process that has been going on over the last three years, to some extent accentuating the contrasts in an ideal typical fashion in order to make more explicit the change. The important feature to note is that there has been change, and that this has been in part the product of social reaction. For many social commentators and policymakers, however, this change has merely been indicative of their initial presumption about the essential nature of the drugtaker. That is, that a minority are individuals with new psychopathic personalities having weak superegos, unrealistic egos, and inadequate masculine identification. Inevitably these people, it is suggested, will pass on to heroin, and lo and behold the figures show that this has actually occurred. Similarly, the police, convinced that drug use is a function of a few pushers, will view the deviancy amplification of the bohemian and the emergence of a drug pyramid as a substantiation of their theories that we have been too permissive all along. Thus false theories are evolved and acted upon in terms of a social reaction, the result of which are changes, which, although merely a *product* of these theories, are taken by many to be a proof of their initial presumptions. Similarly, the drugtaker, evolving theories as to the repressive nature of the police, finds them progressively proven as the gravity of the situation escalates (shown diagrammatically in Table 6.2).

That is, the spiral of theoretical misperceptions and empirical confirmations can occur, very similar to the spiral of interpersonal misperceptions described by Laing, Phillipson, and Lee in *Interpersonal Perception*.[24]

What must be stressed is that we are dealing with a delicately balanced system of relationships among groups, and among values and social situations, which can be put out of gear by the overreaction of public and police. It is my contention that the tendency for unnecessary overreaction is part and parcel of the nature of modern large-scale urban societies, and that a proper understanding of the nature of deviancy amplification and the moral panic is a necessary foundation for the basis of

Table 6-2

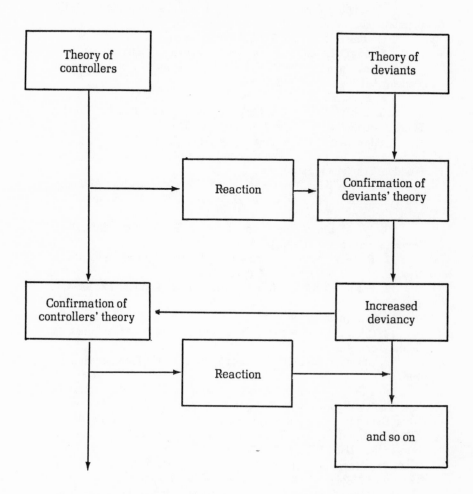

rational social action. My feeling, here, is that we could quite easily launch ourselves, through faulty mismanagement of the control of drugtaking, in England into a situation that would increasingly resemble that obtaining in the United States.

NOTES

1. Excluding Irish who are a fairly substantial part of the population of Notting Hill.

2. Notting Hill Summer Project, 1967.

3. Erving Goffman, *Asylums* (London: Penguin, 1968).

4. A.K. Cohen, "The Sociology of the Deviant Act," *American Sociological Review* 30 (1965): 5-14.

5. R. Blum, ed., *Utopiates* (London: Tavistock, 1965).

6. T. Devlin, "Drug Talk Makes Sixth Formers Queasy," *London Times Educational Supplement*, 30 January 1970.

7. Alex Comfort, *The Anxiety Makers* (London: Nelson, 1967).

8. See D. Chapman, *Sociology and the Stereotype of the Criminal* (London: Travistock, 1968).

9. Leslie Wilkins, "Some Sociological Factors in Drug Addiction Control," in *Narcotics*, edited by D. Wilner and G. Kassebaum (New York: McGraw-Hill, 1965).

10. David Matza, *Becoming Deviant* (Englewood Cliffs, New Jersey: Prentice-Hall, 1969), p. 93.

11. R. Dentler and K. Erikson, "The Function of Deviance in Groups," *Social Problems*, no. 7, pp. 98-107.

12. Frank Musgrove, *The Migratory Elite* (London: Heinemann, 1963).

13. 21 September 1969.

14. C. Logue, "A Feir Feld Ful of Folks," *The* (London) *Times*, 13 September 1969.

15. Marshall McLuhan, *Understanding Media* (London: Sphere, 1967).

16. This observation is in accord with international information: The Wootten Report, *Cannabis: Report by the Advisory Committee on Drug Dependence* (London: H.M.S.O., 1968), p. 21; *Le Dain Report* (Ottawa, Canada: Interim Report of the Commission of Inquiry into the Nonmedical Use of Drugs, 1970), pp. 318-19; Erich Goode, "How the American Marihuana Market Works," *New Society*, no. 402, 11 June 1970, pp. 922-24 (a survey of the New York marihuana scene).

17. Howard Becker has charted how the incidence of psychosis caused by marihuana smoking declined as the American subculture grew; see "Social Bases of Drug-Induced Experiences," *Journal of Health and Social Behavior*, no. 8 (1967), pp. 163-76.

18. Robert Traini, *The Work of the Crime Reporters Association* (paper read at the eighth National Deviancy Symposium, University of York, 10-11, July 1971).

19. For a discussion of the deviancy amplification of bohemians, see J. Young, "The Hippie Solution," *The Politics of Deviancy*, edited by I. Taylor and L. Taylor (Harmondsworth, England: Penguin, 1973).

20. The *Le Dain Report* (pp. 315-17) notes that grass (marihuana), long the staple of the Canadian subculture, is now being replaced by hashish because of Operation Intercept, the greater smuggling possibilities of the resin, and the larger profits involved. Concomitant with this is the increasing organization of the distribution network.

21. "Pharmaceuticals: Is London a Dealer's Heaven?", *Friends*, 15 May 1970, p. 5.

22. Allen Ginsberg, "First Manifesto to End the Bringdown," in *The Marihuana Papers*, edited by D. Soloman (New York: Signet Books, 1968), p. 242.

23. Tigani El Mahi, "The Use and Abuse of Drugs," *W.H.O. Reg. Off. Eastern Mediterranean*, EM/RC 12/6XVI (1962).

24. R. Laing, H. Phillipson, and A. Lee, *Interpersonal Perception* (London: Tavistock, 1966).

7

Methadone's Rise and Fall *

Andrew Moss

Methadone is a synthetic narcotic developed in Germany during World War II, and "methadone maintenance" means giving methadone to heroin addicts as a substitute for heroin. The maintenance of heroin addicts on heroin itself has been illegal in the United States since 1924, when the maintenance clinics set up under the Harrison Act of 1914 were closed down in the belief that they had generated a black-market epidemic of opiates. Forty years later it was demonstrated in New York that methadone could successfully be given to addicts in place of heroin, and that addicts who had been switched to methadone could be rehabilitated in comparatively large numbers.

Methadone maintenance emerged as policy as the Nixon Administration's response to the heroin epidemic of the late

*Printed with the permission of the author.

sixties. It remained the main component of the federal strategy for dealing with heroin until 1974. Sometime in 1974, the policy was reversed. Though heroin use remained widespread, it appeared that addicts were no longer coming forward for methadone treatment. The massive growth in the number of clients in programs had in fact flattened out in 1973, and in New York City, which accounts for about half of all methadone-maintenance clients, the number in treatment had actually dropped between 1973 and 1974.[1]

On the providers' side, the federal government began quietly to relegate methadone to second or third place as a method for dealing with heroin addicts. The 1974 federal strategy projected the percentage of drug-treatment clients in maintenance, as opposed to drug-free programs, as falling to a quarter of all clients by 1976, or to less than half the 1974 percentage.[2] This withdrawal, which appears to have been partly motivated by the growth of a methadone black market, marked the end of the largest experiment in drug treatment in half a century.

Methadone was probably doomed as a treatment by the illusions that were necessary to sell it as a policy. Fear of heroin has persisted in the United States since the closing of the Harrison Act clinics, and when the New York experiments demonstrated that methadone maintenance could rehabilitate addicts, it was necessary to publicize them in a way that distinguished methadone from heroin. Methadone was sold as a "cure" for heroin addiction, a description that made it appear far more effective than it turned out to be when it was spread across the nation. Then, in the late sixties, the panic reaction to the nationwide heroin epidemic—the "epidemic of concern," as it has been called—meant that something had to be sold as the answer to drug-related crime. Methadone was the answer. This idea, along with the belief that methadone "cured" drug addiction, generated false hopes for methadone that were based on persistent uncertainties about how the policy was supposed to work—about who methadone was supposed to help, how it was supposed to help them, and what would be reasonable measures of success. These questions were overshadowed by methadone's apparent success between 1969 and 1973, when the number of clients in treatment rose exponentially and addicts were queuing up for admission, and now they are obscured by methadone's apparent failure. To disentangle them it is necessary to go back to the Dole and Nyswander program in New York City, in which methadone first emerged as a successful treatment for addiction.

Dole and Nyswander Program

The Dole and Nyswander program began in the mid-sixties, when, according to a study by Amitai Etzioni and Richard Remp, "the health professional elite in New York State, seeking to effect substantive change in the social management of narcotic addiction, were able to recruit and establish two knowledge-producing units which took the study and treatment of narcotic addiction out of the sole domain of the Public Health Service . . . . These studies mark a deliberate attempt to extend the boundaries of medical-scientific control in an area previously controlled by the bureaucratic elite."[3] They also mark a kind of nodal point in the tortuous passage of drug management away from the influence of the Bureau of Narcotics and Dangerous Drugs, which had adamantly opposed maintenance programs for addicts. One of the two programs set up by the "health professional elite" evolved into the Dole and Nyswander program at Beth Israel Hospital.

Etzioni and Remp suggest that Dr. Dole's prestige as a distinguished biochemist and member of the Rockefeller Institute was an important asset in steering the program through the waters of professional distrust and B.N.D.D. (Bureau of Narcotics and Dangerous Drugs) opposition. The BNDD apparently "put pressure on the associate hospitals to shadow research people, to obtain records, to seize methadone prescriptions and to threaten the pharmacists who filled the prescriptions."[4] However, the program grew from a handful of clients in the mid-sixties to some 1,900 in 1969, and it reported consistent success on three dimensions, which became the standard criteria for evaluating methadone-maintenance programs—retention of clients in the program, number of clients in employment, and reduction in criminal activity. These findings were reported first at a conference in 1968—at which methadone received a rather cautious endorsement, stressing its suitability for older addicts—and then at successive annual methadone-treatment conferences.

The Dole and Nyswander program gained added credibility from a series of independent evaluations carried out by the Methadone Evaluation Unit of the Columbia School of Public Health, under the direction of Dr. Frances Gearing. Dr. Gearing reported retention rates of eighty percent or more clients up to two years in the program, measures of successful employment status ("employed," "in school," or "homemaker") rising to ninety percent or so of clients remaining in the program, and arrest records falling to levels comparable with the general population.[5] These figures presented the program as successfully rehabilitating the great majority of its clients.

Dr. Gearing's authority overshadowed the rather less impressive findings of some other early programs. At the press conference following the 1969 Methadone Maintenance Conference, the chairman, Dr. Arthur Zitrin, summarized the papers presented as showing that methadone-maintenance programs were effective for fifty to eighty percent of the "patients" admitted. A questioner followed up the remark:

> Question: Dr. Gearing, can you give us any clues on the basis of your evaluation here and your hearing from the reports of other cities why your rates of success vary so much?
>
> Dr. Gearing: On the contrary, I was impressed with the fact that their rates of success were so similar, with one minor exception. . . .
>
> Question: Then Dr. Zitrin misled us.[6]

The Gearing evaluation reports became the source documents for advocates of methadone maintenance. They are quoted extensively by the Ford Foundation report on drug abuse published in 1972 and by the influential study published by the Consumers' Union in the same year. Largely on the basis of these evaluations, Edward Brecher, the author of the Consumers' Union report, made the very strong recommendation that "methadone maintenance promptly be made available under medical auspices to every narcotics addict who applies for it."[7]

A second legacy of the Dole and Nyswander era was persistently misleading press coverage of methadone. In the early years of the program (and in fact well up into the great expansion of methadone programs under the Nixon administration), press reports of methadone programs avoided describing methadone as a narcotic and took the line that it was a "cure for addiction," with the strong implied suggestion that methadone was a transient stage on the way to drug-free status. One of the charges laid against the Dole and Nyswander program by the BNDD was that it had generated such misleading publicity. Etzioni and Remp, who find some substance in this charge, suggest that the way in which the press covered the methadone program reflected "at least in part the way in which Drs. Dole and Nyswander themselves conceptualized and presented their work, perhaps to avoid arousing the full range of emotional connotation associated with narcotic maintenance."[8] They quote Dr. Dole, in a *New York Times* article, as referring to the substitution of "painkilling methadone" for the "crippling addiction to heroin," and comment that such value-laden statements seem to be essentially attempts to legitimize methadone, presumably in the face of BNDD opposition.[9] As a result of such hazy press coverage, a cloud of misleading ideas was to follow along behind the methadone expansion of the next five years, the most damaging of which was the idea that most methadone users would eventually become drug free. This myth seems to have persisted essentially because authorities in the field did not overtly deny it.

In fact neither the Dole and Nyswander program nor any other maintenance program has ever pushed a substantial proportion of its clients through to long-run abstinence from methadone, and in the case of the Dole and Nyswander program the idea seems to be contradicted by the theory on which the program was based. According to this theory, heroin addiction stems from a metabolic disorder that produces a biological need for the drug. The need can be met with methadone, which is a quite addictive narcotic, but which was originally thought to have the desirable properties of not producing euphoria and of "blockading" the action of heroin (so that if a client shot up with heroin on top of his methadone dose, he would not get high). Neither of these last two properties turned out to be the case—methadone, when taken intravenously, does produce euphoria, and many clients continue to shoot heroin while in methadone-maintenance programs. In fact, while methadone is a medicine from the practitioner's point of view, from the street addict's point of view it seems to be just a different kind of junk. However, the metabolic theory provided the medical underpinning for a successful program, and it accorded well with the very high success rates in the program—confirming the idea that heroin addiction could be switched off by applying the correct medical procedure. This idea persisted into the great expansion of programs during the Nixon administration, along with press coverage that said methadone was a way station to abstinence, and with the belief that methadone programs could rehabilitate a very high proportion of their clients.

Federal Adoption

In retrospect, the great expansion of methadone programs between 1969 and 1973 seems inevitable. The incoming Nixon administration had chosen to make "crime in the streets" its main election issue, and crime was increasingly associated in the public mind with heroin addiction. The 1960s epidemic was then at or approaching its peak (in terms of incidence of new addiction), and the current estimates of the number of addicts were of the order of 300,000. In about 1970 the first addicted veterans began to return from Vietnam, raising the specter of several hundred thousand new addicts on top of the domestic epidemic. Heroin addiction, in 1970, was a kind of national metaphor for social disruption, in much the same way that environmental pollution is today. Given this situation, the incoming Nixon administration identified heroin addiction as Public Enemy Number One in its war on crime and began a major move to expand treatment capacity and shift control of drug-related funds into the hands of the medical profession. Dr. Jerome Jaffe, who had been director of the Illinois Drug Abuse Program, was brought into the White House as a special consultant on drug abuse, and shortly thereafter became head of the new

Special Action Office for Drug Abuse Problems (S.A.O.D.A.P.), the coordinating body for drug policy. Jaffe was an advocate of mixed modality programs, offering both maintenance and drug-free treatment, but he clearly believed strongly in methadone. At the 1969 conference, when asked what would be the most effective way to spend money allocated for drug programs, he had said:

> I now feel that if I had a limited number of dollars to spread around in Chicago . . . we would be expanding our methadone program without any question . . . .
> When money becomes a problem, I will tell you now that on the basis of our information to date, it will go into the provision of adequate amounts of drugs rather than elaborate rehabilitation programs.[10]

In 1971 the drug-treatment policy of the premethadone era, the civil-commitment policy initiated by the Narcotic Addict Rehabilitation Act (N.A.R.A.) of 1966 was officially laid to rest in a series of hearings on amendments to the Act, and methadone maintenance, to be administered largely through the Department of Health, Education, and Welfare, was inaugurated as the main component of the new federal strategy.[11] Jaffe and the other expert witnesses called to testify were cautious about methadone, but it is clear from the discussion that the new legislation was being set up primarily to legalize and expand maintenance programs. The process by which methadone became the administration's main heroin-abuse strategy has not been documented yet, but the experience of the Washington, D.C., program seems to have been extremely influential. Edward Jay Epstein, in a highly critical article, quotes Egil Krogh, who had been White House liaison for the District of Columbia, at a 1971 press conference:

> We found there was a cause-and-effect relationship fairly clear between heroin addiction and the need to commit crimes to support the habit, so we felt we greatly needed to expand the capability of the District of Columbia to deal with the problem . . . . After a year we found that those addicts in high dosage methadone had a marked decline in criminal

recidivism . . . . We would like to expand that treatment across the country.[12]

Expand it they did. The number of federally funded drug-treatment programs rose from sixteen at the beginning of 1969 to 926 in 1974, with the biggest increase coming at the beginning of SAODAP's operations in 1971. During the same five-year period, federal expenditures on drug treatment and enforcement rose from about eighty million dollars annually to about eight hundred million, with the amount spent on treatment rising gradually to two-thirds of the total. The number of clients in federally funded programs rose to eighty thousand, of whom more than half were in methadone-maintenance programs.[13] The federal funding of drug abuse programs triggered a parallel state and local boom, so that by 1973, according to a SAODAP survey, there were some 73,000 clients in methadone maintenance programs.[14] Given the retention rates of the new mass-produced programs, probably an equal number of people had passed through the program by this point, which suggests that by 1973 something like 150,000 heroin users had come in contact with methadone maintenance.

As methadone programs expanded, the various bureaucratic critics of maintenance fell reluctantly into line. The BNDD, which could legitimately have prosecuted doctors in the early programs under the Harrison Act, began to reverse its traditional antimaintenance policy in 1969, when a study group recognized that "research in the development of methadone-maintenance therapy . . . has indicated promise in the rehabilitation and management of certain narcotic drug-dependent persons." In a realistic qualification, the study group added that "the most important single advantage of supplying methadone to addicts . . . is that it brings the patient in daily contact with a therapeutic effort, and gives the program director the leverage needed to apply rehabilitative techniques."[15]

In 1971 the American Medical Association (A.M.A.) followed suit with a set of guidelines sanctioning maintenance programs under fairly stringent conditions. Like the Bureau, the AMA took a realistic view of the limitations of maintenance programs, acknowledging in its guidelines that clients might remain in the maintenance program "for an indefinite period."[16] The Food and Drug Administration (F.D.A.), the last of the bureaucratic footdraggers, removed methadone from Investigational New Drug (I.N.D.) status in 1972. Until this point, doctors running methadone programs had been obliged to pretend that their primary interest was research. The FDA was unwilling to shift methadone directly to New Drug Applications (N.D.A.) status and created an unprecedented joint IND-NDA category that allowed the administration to maintain some control over programs while still legitimizing methadone use.[17] The caution in these endorsements provides an interesting contrast to the White House policy of extending drug treatment, with methadone maintenance the major form of treatment, to the whole heroin-using population of the country.

In practice, as it turned out, the caution was well justified. Methadone applied across the board by a network of local treatment agencies turned out to be a different animal from methadone in the Dole and Nyswander program in New York City.

Truth of Methadone Treatment Emerges

Probably the first casualty of the widespread distribution of methadone was the metabolic theory of addiction. In 1972, at the fourth Methadone Treatment Conference, Dr. Avram Goldstein, director of the Addiction Research Laboratory at Stanford, pointed out that the by-then well-known phenomenon of addicts continuing heroin use while on methadone contradicted the metabolic theory. Goldstein's own research demonstrated that this phenomenon could not be caused by inadequate doses of methadone; he had demonstrated, in blind dose comparisons, that dosage was largely irrelevant to success in treatment as measured by any of the usual variables. Goldstein put forward a different theory to explain how methadone works:

An addict who enters a methadone program is motivated, however ambivalently, to give up heroin. By establishing a tolerant-dependent state, methadone *permits* the ambulatory addict, despite the availability of heroin, to discontinue its use without becoming sick . . . .

The dependence produced by methadone has another important advantage—it brings the patient into the clinic daily, ensuring regular contact with the clinic staff, and introducing a degree of regularity into his disordered life . . . .

Methadone cannot magically prevent heroin use in a patient who wants to use heroin; it can only facilitate a behavior change in people who have made a conscious decision to change. Thus the paramount feature of a successful methadone program is what it does in ways *other than chemical* to help the patient rehabilitate himself.[18]

Goldstein's theory corresponds quite closely to what the BNDD study group had said in 1969, and probably to what most practitioners in the field believed about methadone. It leads to a kind of social-welfare approach to the rehabilitation of heroin addicts in which methadone plays the role of a chemical hook—what Edward Jay Epstein calls "methadone as chemical parole."[19] The argument also suggests that the success of a methadone program may be more dependent on the quality of the rehabilitative services it provides—therapy, job finding, long-term follow-up, and so forth—than on the methadone itself. This line of reasoning strikes directly at the main advantages of methadone programs over their drug-free competitors—their low cost and ease of organization.

The second casualty of mass distribution of methadone was the idea that success rates would normally be high. Reliable information about the success of methadone programs is difficult to obtain, partly because evaluation and follow-up are themselves expensive activities and partly because of the anxieties that developed inside methadone programs as opposition to methadone grew. However, a study by the Johns Hopkins School of Public Health, published in 1974, gives some idea of what may be expected from a local treatment program. The study examined ten programs outside the New York area and compared maintenance programs with drug-free programs. Maintenance programs were found to retain 63 percent of their clients for six months and 34 percent for twelve months. The mean length of stay in a program was six months. The comparable figures for nonmaintenance programs were 44 percent and 20 percent, and 3.7 months. Heroin use and illegal activity were found to decline by about 50 percent for the maintenance clients and there was a gain in employment of about 23 percent. (Figures for the nonmaintenance programs were rather better but were not thought to be comparable since many more of the patients in these programs entered treatment under some form of legal pressure.) The methadone programs cost about one-third as much as the nonmaintenance programs per episode of treatment.[20]

These figures should be compared with those cited above from the Gearing evaluations of the Dole and Nyswander program. Clearly they present a much less optimistic picture of methadone maintenance.

The third casualty of expansion seems to have been clarity about program objectives. The idea that maintenance should lead to abstinence, for example, persisted widely among programs even though no evidence was produced to show it could be achieved. Staff in many programs were still working on the assumption that "tapering off" should be the normal goal of treatment in 1972. And in fact, abstinence remained official federal policy as late as 1973,[21] which seems plainly ridiculous in the face of an average stay in treatment of six months.

One suspects that both treatment-program staff and government officials were reluctant to face up to the implications of mass distribution of methadone under the conditions that appeared to obtain in practice—a rapid turnover of clients in programs and a general difficulty in weaning clients away from methadone. These conditions might be expected to lead to the development of a massive street market in methadone—in effect to methadone becoming a new drug of abuse—and in fact such a street market was already visible in 1971. In 1972, at the fourth Methadone Treatment Conference, J. A. Newmeyer reported that about one in six of the clients entering the Haight-Ashbury Medical Clinic said they had been using street methadone in attempts to kick, and a small percentage said they had been using intravenous methadone for pleasure.[22] Similar evidence was available in the death statistics. In New York City there were 368 "methadone-associated user deaths" in 1971, or about a quarter of all addict deaths.[23] These figures, it should be remembered, precede the great expansion in methadone programs.

Finally, a certain amount of paranoia developed in some methadone programs as it became apparent that methadone was not a panacea and critics of maintenance—many of them black or latino, and many of them associated with therapeutic community programs—began to attack local maintenance programs. The main arguments used against methadone seem to have been that maintenance acts as a control technique, neutralizing the clients politically; that maintenance is really substituting one addiction for another and does not touch the social causes of heroin use; and that maintenance just displaces the addiction problem, pushing former heroin users into heavy consumption of even more dangerous substances such as barbiturates or alcohol.[24] While there is a certain amount of truth in these arguments, critics of methadone suffered from the lack of. any successful alternative programs to point to. Therapeutic community programs, on the Synanon model, are notoriously short on evaluation, but during the period of debate, between say 1971 and 1974, they were not generally thought to be effective for more than a small proportion of addicts. (Brecher, in the Consumers' Union Study, quotes a statement by Chuck Dederick, founder of Synanon, that relapse rates among Synanon graduates were of the order of ninety percent.[25]) Since addicts were queuing up to get into methadone programs, and since no reliable information was available about what might be called the *social* side effects of methadone, such as the black market, the debate succeeded mainly in polarizing the supporters of the different programs and producing walls of suspicion that made it difficult to find out how well *any* program was functioning. Often the debate got fairly hostile. Dr. Goldstein published an open letter to critics of his own program that said, in part:

I can't help wondering where the strong antimethadone campaign really comes from. I don't doubt the sincerity of people who pick up and pass on the antimethadone slogans. But I judge actions by their consequences. Who really profits from the antimethadone propaganda? Here we have a fantastically lucrative big business—heroin . . . . . What happens to the profits when methadone programs grow large enough to cut significantly into the heroin trade? Who gains from scaring people away from methadone?[26]

Dr. Goldstein's argument depends on the proposition that methadone-maintenance programs were effectively cutting into the demand for heroin without methadone itself becoming a major street drug. (Presumably a heroin dealer would just as soon sell methadone as heroin if there was a market for it.) This argument was weakened as better data on the impact of methadone programs became available, beginning with a kind of rewriting of the evaluations of the Dole and Nyswander program.

Reevaluations
In 1972, James F. Maddux and Charles L. Bowden pointed out that the frequency of employment and frequency of arrest calculations in Dr. Gearing's evaluations were based on shrinking samples, as were the calculations in many other program reports. In these reports, clients who dropped out of methadone programs were simply not included in the base figures from which employment and arrest rates were drawn. Since those who drop out are likely to be those who are having trouble, the employment and arrest records are biased in a favorable direction. Recalculating the employment figures for five program reports, Maddux and Bowden showed a general drop in the employment figure from somewhere in the region of eighty percent to somewhere in the region of fifty percent. They also pointed out that the arrest figures were inflated by Dr. Gearing's method of reporting the number of arrests per 100 man-years in the program, a method that overweights the successful records of a relatively small number of long-term clients. On the basis of their recalculations, Maddux and Bowden reached the conclusion that "reports of success with methadone-maintenance programs appear both ambiguous and exaggerated."[27]

These conclusions were confirmed by a series of studies by the Addiction Research and Treatment Corporation (A.R.T.C.) in New York City, in which retention rates, employment rates, and crime-reduction rates for addicts in ARTC's own programs were analyzed very closely. These studies showed that methadone programs tended to lose younger addicts and those with relatively high arrest rates and relatively more unstable backgrounds, and to hang on to older addicts who were in the process of maturing out of the street scene. In summarizing these studies in 1973, Dr. Irving Lukoff, director of the ARTC evaluation team, concluded that "it is necessary to entertain the view that much of the improvement is a function of age, with the changes wrought by maturation playing a significant role."[28]

There was a substantial decline in the arrest rate for addicts entering the ARTC programs, but on examination it turned out that most of the decline in the first year of treatment was due to a drop in the number of drug charges. In the second year of treatment, though assaultive crimes, felonies, petty misdemeanors, and larceny dropped somewhat, the major decline was again in drug-related charges. Furthermore these declines were measured against rates reported during the year prior to entrance to the program. When crime rates after treatment were compared with crime rates reported for the whole period of addiction, only drug charges showed a drop. Lukoff concluded: "The crimes that most concern the community require a prolonged investment in treatment before they begin to show a substantial decline relative to crime rates based on the full period of drug use."[29]

If the ARTC conclusions hold for methadone programs in general, and if the usual lengths of stay in programs are of the order of the six months reported in the Johns Hopkins study, then methadone-maintenance programs cannot be expected to have a significant effect on crime rates. Furthermore if it is true that methadone programs succeed mainly with older addicts who are in the process of giving up the hustling lifestyle, they cannot be expected to have a significant effect on the spread of epidemics either. What little is known about the spread of heroin use suggests that it is primarily younger users who spread addiction, and that most recruitment happens in the first year or so of an addict's career.

Conclusion

The heroin epidemic of the late sixties, to which methadone was a response, seems to have peaked of its own accord in the early seventies. The epidemic among Vietnam veterans never materialized. These two facts alone should promote a major rethinking of the assumptions on which the federal drug-treatment strategy is based. However, heroin use remains at a high level and new epidemics appear to be threatening. According to a recent statement by Dr. Robert Dupont, Jaffe's successor at SAODAP, there is a secondary epidemic going on in smaller towns at the moment, and a new nationwide epidemic, generated by an increase in the supply of Mexican heroin, is likely.[30]

So far as I know, no attempt has been made to relate the local rise and fall in heroin use to the establishment of methadone programs, or of drug programs in general. Dr. Dupont reported at the 1973 methadone-treatment conference that the epidemic in Washington, D.C., has been successfully controlled, but as he pointed out, the effects of the Washington drug-treatment program cannot be separated from the effects of a concurrent law-enforcement attack on heroin, or from the effects of long-run changes in attitudes toward the drug.[31] Edward Jay Epstein observed that the decline in crime in Washington began before the drug-treatment program was large enough to make much difference.[32]

Methadone clearly became a major street drug. Recent figures published by the Drug Enforcement Administration (D.E.A.) (figures that should perhaps be treated with some caution since the DEA is the historical successor to the BNDD, the traditional opponent of maintenance programs) suggest that methadone is now responsible for nearly as many addict deaths as heroin. According to the DEA figures, out of 1,093 drug-related deaths in 24 cities during the period from January 1974 to March 1974, 336 were related to heroin or morphine and 252 were related to methadone. While the proportion of heroin- and morphine-related deaths appears to be relatively stable, the proportion associated with methadone is rising rapidly—up from 69 out of a total of 789 drug-related deaths in the same three months of 1973. The rise in total drug-related deaths over the year appears to be mainly due to methadone (it is worth noting that barbiturates have consistently accounted for about the same number of deaths as heroin and morphine).[33] The DEA report also observes that about half the total number of methadone users arrested (the figures in this case were from the summer of 1973) were in treatment programs, and half were not, suggesting that the street market in methadone is now of the same order of magnitude as the treatment market.

The DEA figures are fairly sobering and may account for the backing away from methadone that is visible in the 1974 federal drug strategy. While the policy document itself is somewhat inconsistent—it talks about the orderly expansion of methadone programs on one page but shows a projected decline in the number of methadone clients on another—it appears to be the government's policy to expand drug-free treatment programs over the next two years, while allowing methadone-maintenance programs to shrink gradually away.[34] Methadone appears to be coming to the end of its ten-year run.

Methadone maintenance did not end heroin addiction in the United States, did not end drug-related crime, and unfortunately did create a black market in methadone. However, methadone proved useful in rehabilitating certain kinds of drug users, which is as much as can be said for any other kind of treatment program at the moment. (Methadone maintenance certainly succeeded in what might be thought of as its covert objective—legitimizing treatment for drug users.) There is no systematic evidence to suggest that any other kind of program, or even the treatment approach to drug use in general, can seriously cut down on mass heroin use. One hopes, therefore, that methadone's failure to live up to its advertising as a panacea does not mean that methadone-maintenance programs (and maintenance programs in general, since heroin maintenance is likely to be considered guilty by association) will die out. It may be that methadone, if used with less illusions and more controls, can function successfully as a treatment for older heroin users without creating a massive black market.

Enough evidence has probably accumulated over the last few years to answer such questions as who should be given methadone and who should not, and how methadone should be administered to control diversion into the black market. One suspects, however, that many of the questions about methadone will not be answered publicly without some kind of independent investigation into how methadone programs and the other programs of the great expansion of treatment have functioned. There is a precedent for such an investigation in a General Accounting Office investigation into the NARA civil-commitment policy of 1966, which was published in the 1971 Congressional hearings.[35] This investigation laid the groundwork for the great expansion of drug-treatment programs under the Nixon administration. Failing such an investigation, methadone maintenance may be swept quietly under the rug as a panacea that failed. If so, we may meet the next heroin epidemic with illusions about maintenance as misleading as those with which we met the epidemic of the sixties.

NOTES

1. *New York Times,* 10 November 1974.

2. *Federal Strategy for Drug Abuse and Drug Traffic Prevention 1974* (Washington, D.C.: U.S. Government Printing Office, 1974), p. 27.

3. Amitai Etzioni and Richard Remp, *Technological Shortcuts to Social Change* (New York: Russel Sage Foundation, 1973), p. 39.

4. Ibid., p. 44.

5. F. R. Gearing, "Evaluation of Methadone Maintenance Treatment Program," in *Methadone Maintenance,* papers presented at the Second National Methadone Maintenance Conference, edited by Stanley Einstein (New York: Marcel Dekker, 1971). Also F. R. Gearing, "Methadone Maintenance Treatment Programs in New York City and Westchester County. Progress Report for 1971—The Year of Expansion," paper submitted to the New York State Narcotics Addiction Control Commission, 1972.

6. Einstein, p. 222.

7. E. M. Brecher and the Editors of Consumer Reports, *Licit and Illicit Drugs* (Boston: Little, Brown, 1972), p. 530, also ch. 15.

8. Einstein, p. 222.

9. Etzioni and Remp, p. 45.

10. Einstein, p. 41.

152   DRUGS AND POLITICS

11. "Treatment and Rehabilitation of Narcotics Addicts," *Hearings before Subcommittee No. 4 of the Committee on the Judiciary*," U.S. House of Representatives, 92d Cong., 1t sess., 1971.

12. Quoted in E. J. Epstein, "Methadone, the Forlorn Hope," *The Public Interest* (Summer 1974).

13. *Federal Strategy for Drug Abuse and Drug Traffic Prevention 1974*, pp. 16, 22, 23.

14. *Federal Strategy for Drug Abuse and Drug Traffic Prevention 1973* (Washington, D.C.: U.S. Government Printing Office, 1973) p. 83.

15. G. Haislip and E. Lewis, *Recommendations of the Bureau of Narcotics and Dangerous Drugs Study Group on Methadone Maintenance Research 2* (unpublished, 1969), quoted in M. X. Morrell, "Maintenance of Opiate Dependent Persons in the United States: A Legal-Medical History," in *Drug Use in America*, the Technical Papers of the Second Report of the National Commission on Marihuana and Drug Abuse (Washington, D.C.: U.S. Government Printing Office, 1973), p. 538.

16. American Medical Association Council on Mental Health and AMA Committee on Alcoholism and Drug Dependence, "Oral Methadone-Maintenance Techniques in the Management of Morphine Type Dependence," *Journal of the American Medical Association* 219 (March 1971): 1,618. Quoted in Morell, p. 542.

17. Morell, p. 543.

18. Avram Goldstein, "The Pharmacological Basis of Methadone Treatment," in Fourth National Conference on Methadone Treatment, *Proceedings* (New York: National Association for the Prevention of Addiction to Narcotics, 1972), p. 31.

19. Epstein, p. 16.

20. Interdrug Final Report, *An Evaluation of Treatment Programs for Drug Abusers*, Volume 1 (Baltimore: Johns Hopkins School of Hygiene and Public Health, 1974): 1, 8, 10.

21. *Federal Strategy, 1973*, p. 25.

22. J. A. Newmeyer, G. R. Gay, R. Corn, and D. Smith, "Methadone for Kicking and for Kicks," in Fourth National Conference on Methadone Treatment, *Proceedings*, p. 461.

23. J. Nadler, F. Fumia, and C. Cherubin, "Deaths of Narcotic Addicts in New York City in 1971: Those Reported to be Using Methadone," in Fifth National Conference on Methadone Treatment, *Proceedings*, p. 324.

24. See, for example, R. Bayer, "The Radical Critique of Methadone Maintenance, a Radical Response," in Fourth National Conference on Methadone Treatment, *Proceedings*, p. 359.

25. Brecher, p. 78, also see ch. 10.

26. Mimeographed letter.

27. James F. Maddux and Charles L. Bowden, "Critique of Success with Methadone Maintenance," *American Journal of Psychiatry* 129, no. 4 (October 1972): 100.

28. Irving F. Lukoff, "Issues in the Evaluation of Heroin Treatment," paper presented to the Epidemiology of Drug Use Conference, Puerto Rico, February 1973, p. 16.

29. Ibid., p. 34.

30. Robert L. Dupont, statement at the North American Congress on Alcohol and Drugs, San Francisco, December 1974.

31. Robert L. Dupont and M. H. Green, "The Decline of Heroin Addiction in the District of Columbia," in Fifth National Conference on Methadone Treatment, *Proceedings,* p. 1,474.

32. Epstein, p. 24.

33. "Methadone, A Review of Current Information," Report of the Statistical and Data Services Division, Office of Administration and Management, Drug Enforcement Administration, December 1973 (revised 1974).

34. *Federal Strategy for Drug Abuse and Drug Prevention 1974,* pp. 22, 24, 27.

35. "Treatment and Rehabilitation of Narcotics Addicts," p. 199.

8

The Politics of Drugs *

Irving Louis Horowitz

Drug analysis, like drug addiction, has come of age. Now
that heroin addiction is reported to have reached epidemic
proportions among American troops in Vietnam, marihuana
has become nearly as common as cigarettes on campuses, and
LSD is an entrenched household staple, the search for cures
looms everywhere. The study of drugs was pioneered by the
social scientists; medical research has in the past been more
concerned with alcoholism and chemical equivalents to harmful drugs. But now medical, pharmaceutical, and biological
researchers have emerged in full force—creating a literature
that catalogues each of the hundred strains of marihuana,
proposes methadone-treatment centers in every major city,
assures us that heroin kills far fewer people than the
unsanitary injections used to introduce it into the body, and

*This work originally appeared in *Social Policy*, July-August 1972.
Reprinted by permission.

explains the physical effect of every drug. We have manuals of drug symptoms, dictionaries of drug slang, and self-help programs ranging from government reports to privately sponsored treatment centers. Yet with all this investment of numbers, time, energy, money, research, and the panoply of professionally responsible agencies, the use of drugs in American society continues to increase dramatically.

It is estimated that between six and seven million people suffer from alcohol-induced problems. Estimates of the number of people addicted to drugs are not so easily obtained, but on the basis of less than perfect information, the number of drug users can hardly be much below six to seven million. For example, 30 percent of college students—roughly two and a half million—reportedly use marihuana. And a recently concluded New York State Narcotic Addiction Control Commission report estimated 525,000 users of minor tranquilizers in New York; 487,000 users of marihuana; 361,000 users of barbiturates; 409,000 users of seda-hypnotics and diet pills; 157,000 users of heroin; and 181,000 users of pep pills and minor tranquilizers. There are an additional 100,000 users of LSD, methadone, morphine, and cocaine. What complicates these figures is that many people are using more than one drug, so one cannot simply assume one user for each kind of drug used. Nonetheless, on the basis of the New York data alone, it would seem likely that about ten million people use, without direct supervision, some form of drug that is either casually prescribed or illegal.

Since this is an area of vast underreporting, for obvious legal reasons, drugs are undoubtedly even more widely used. Whether the actual figure is ten million or twenty million, we are dealing here not simply with acts of personal deviance, but rather with a normative framework in which drug use not only is rising, but is also considered quite within the pale of respectable behavior.

If one were to define drug abusers by their inability to maintain a job, or by their involvement in petty theft or grand larceny, then the figures cited above would be lowered dramatically. Generally in this country the official response to drug use has been universal condemnation. There has been little attempt to determine the degree to which individuals are incapacitated by particular drugs. The exception is advocacy of methadone treatment as a counter to heroin addiction; indeed, it is argued that such treatment is consonant with the ability to do a day's work. Therefore, while methadone is addictive in its own right, its users could be omitted from any estimates of the social costs of drug addiction. Methadone therapy encourages the recognition that a statistic based on socioeconomic cost may be far more meaningful than one based on the sheer numbers of drug users. It thus represents a considerable improvement in the humanity as well as the methodology of those in charge of distinguishing drug usages from drug problems.

Drug conferences are themselves a by-product of drug traffic and drug use. Few occur in areas where there is no perceived problem (if any such places still exist). Drug conferences, which have occurred throughout America on many campuses, do not anticipate an emerging problem, but more often respond to an ongoing situation. Young people come to such conferences in order to rationalize certain kinds of behavior; in effect, to find out why they behave the way they do. Young people are not going to change as a result. The interests of the young are often legal rather than medical in character. Young people want an advocacy model that can provide arguments to legitimate their deviant behavior.

At a time when considerable attention is focused on the issue of drug use and drug abuse as a result of the hearings recently conducted by the National Commission on Marihuana and Drug Abuse, it is appropriate to examine the political parameters fairly and squarely. Amid the welter of practical recommendations, including compulsory elementary-school instruction on the dangers of drug abuse, the outright legalization of marihuana, the appropriation of government funds to research projects for safe mind-altering drugs, it becomes apparent that the schism is not so much between medical opinion (although there are differences of opinion at this level) as between social classes. Middle-class users complain that the very severity of antidrug laws makes enforcement impossible, and hence makes a mockery out of law itself. In contrast, working-class nonusers, or at least their legislative supporters, believe that any change of status would serve notice on the public that marihuana use was being mildly encouraged and sanctioned.

The same class contradictions are exhibited at the law-enforcement level. The most dramatic illustration of this is the data released by two divisions of the Department of Justice. The Bureau of Narcotics and Dangerous Drugs, in its current release, celebrates 1971 as a banner year for seizures of heroin and other drugs—up 138 percent between 1970 and 1971. At the same time, in the Justice Department's U.S. crime reports, comparing 1961, 1970, and 1971, one notes an unmistakable trend upward in all crimes that are drug related or drug induced. The categories of robbery and burglary, for instance, are up more than 200 percent over the decade, thus offsetting any possible advantages of increased caches uncovered by the narcotics squad.

Whatever the validity of the analogue between alcohol and drug usage, the consequences of the present differential treatment are notorious and dangerous. Legalized drug use does not mean the celebration of such use. It means changing the terms of the dialogue on drugs from medical and therapeutic terms to political and ethnic terms—where it should be anyhow, and where it ultimately will move to.

The ominous alternative to legalized and regularized drug usage is not only learning to live with intolerably high rates of crime (which itself serves to frustrate the right to life, liberty, and the pursuit of happiness), but also an ever increasing degree of harassment and limitation of basic civil rights. The brief UPI dispatch in the 11 March 1972 issue of the New York Times tells the story in blunt terms: "Central State University announced that it would begin testing students for possible drug use when they register for the spring quarter. . . .The school said it had started the testing program because of a wave of campus crimes that it said were drug related." The next step would be universal testing for drug use as a requirement for employment, rental, and travel.

Medical arguments on drugs continually revolve around the health-hazard aspects of drug use. An enormous literature concerns the effects of each drug at the level of biology and human physiology. Most of this literature is intended to advise agencies that are handling problems of addiction. As a result it offers little of value to those people who use drugs. It is not that medical and biological explanation is without merit. Few serious people oppose research on the effects of drugs, despite the fact that we still do not have an operational definition of the term *drug*. But such research is simply not a fruitful means to explain the widening and deepening use of special sorts of chemicals that endanger the body and damage the mind. A whole range of biological and medical literature explains the hazards of drugtaking. The difficulty is that this literature has no apparent demythologizing effect on users. Although there is a range of literature on whether marihuana is addictive or nonaddictive, whether LSD will create certain problems in adolescents or pregnant mothers, such medical literature quite clearly has not been an effective deterrent. It has not led to an adequate distinction between drug use and drug problems.

Whatever the physical and psychological effects of an illegal drug may be, the social and political consequences loom far larger as dangers. Many identify the drug culture as middle class, link it to the culture of students and minorities, connect it to the demimonde of rock and jazz music, and view it as the rallying cry and unifying point for many political protest rallies and massive rock festivals. In a sense those who adhere to a strictly legal view that abolition is warranted on the grounds of the unworkability of present laws are on thin ice—since many laws related to race relations could be contested on similar grounds of pragmatism. Therefore, if we have a cardinal need to get beyond the medical haze, there is a parallel need to get beyond the juridical maze.

A range of soft and hard drugs are used with medical prescriptions and are, in point of fact, sanctioned as usable. Thus it is not the drug itself that creates the problem, but the legitimation of its use. The use of a large number of chemicals is punishable not because of the intrinsic medical merits or demerits of the particular drug, but rather because of the extrinsic importance of who prescribes or who denies the use of that drug—which is, of course, an extremely important distinction. Law and jurisprudence in America create the impression that punishment is for taking drugs, but in point of fact the punitive action is for taking drugs without legitimation and without the kind of prognosis that presumably is a prerequisite for drug intake.

The world of the young, which admittedly contains a disproportionately high number of users, is not uniquely predicated on long-range moral considerations or long-range assumptions about life and death, but immediate, sensuous, existential, and concrete assumptions about pleasure and pain. In other words, the drug environment is a world of pleasure and pain; whereas the medical, biological, and chemical literature is a world of life and death. Thus the ideology of drug users and drug exposers are like two ships in the night. Often the physical and biological literature fails to address itself to the social aspects and the social base of the entire drug culture.

An interesting illustration that much fright literature on drugs has badly missed the point is the case of an Irish Catholic girl recently reported in the New York Times. A student at the University of Buffalo, she described her condition to an encounter group there. "I went to Boston for the funeral; there was just me and his girl friend and we both felt alone and terrible. I snorted cocaine." A male student from Detroit gave the obvious and appropriate response: "We're all whacked out of our heads, but you are something special. Like I've dealt and I've tasted, but you go up there and stare at the cold corpse of this friend that took the trip and then you go snort." The point is not whether the encounter therapy is sound, or whether the girl is "strange" (as she says of herself). Rather, that the threat mechanism, even in the harshest and most direct form of a corpse, did not serve as a deterrent to her addiction. This would indicate the decisional nature of the problem; that is, the decision that short-run "highs" are worth more than long-run "happiness."

As Joel Fort pointed out in his critique of the American Medical Association report on "Marihuana and Society": "Although spelled out as a basic goal in our Declaration of Independence, the pursuit of happiness is somehow looked upon as immoral and unacceptable by a considerable number of Americans who are able to rationalize alcohol and tobacco use, television watching, and extramarital sex so as not to be uncomfortable." Furthermore, as such inside legal critics of present drug laws as John Kaplan have repeatedly noted, the medical literature concerning which drug is more risky or whether alcohol is less harmful to the body than drugs entirely misses the point. The point is not biological in character, but distinctly political: alcohol is legal; marihuana and heavier forms of drug addiction are illegal. In that very fact forms of social solidarity, such as those described by David Smith in his work with the San Francisco drug clinics, can emerge as countercultural norms. In relation to drugs as a generational phenomenon, this period in American society has relied much more heavily on notions of experience than it has on faith in reason. What has happened at the level of world politics is related to the rise of a drug counterculture. There is a persistent feeling of impotence and unrequited rage at what goes on in the larger world, a sense of disconnection and anomie with respect to the political life in Washington, or what goes on in foreign capitals, or even what goes on in the state capitals or municipalities. And the response is often self-change, inner-directed forms of protest.

There are then transcendent questions that go far beyond chemistry, biology, medicine, or, for that matter, law; questions about what might be called the *political dimensions* of drugtaking. By looking at the individual drug user instead of the collective drug subculture, we have overlooked the most profound difference between current users and the considerable numbers of past users: civil liberties. What distinguishes the present mode of narcotization from that of previous years is its public character. What now exists is a demand for the use of drugs as a right rather than as something done surreptitiously or privately. Leaving aside moral judgments, one would have to say that this is the most revolutionary aspect of the current drug scene. The idea of turning policemen onto drugs, or the public use in public places of different kinds of nonsanctioned drugs, is distinctly innovative; although in a nonpolitical context this was also done during the prohibition era. Such acts are an open affront and challenge to the legal system. In effect the drug culture claims that the public morality itself sanctions drugtaking rather than inhibits or prevents wide usage.

There are unanticipated consequences of this redefinition of social morality. Not only is the drug culture public rather than private, but it is also public in the sense of communal in a way that the liquor culture is not. Most alcoholics are closet alcoholics. They are private drinkers who are not known as alcoholics, and who do not perceive themselves as alcoholics. They do not view themselves as sick or as part of a viable subculture with shared values. They rarely have a civil libertarian view of the right to have alcohol, despite the repeal of prohibition. The drug culture, in the very act of passing a marihuana joint around, and collectivizing the use of drugs in relation to rock or folk music, has made the drug act not only public but also communal.

The communal use of drugs coincided with the rise of new subcultures and deviant cultures. There is a close relationship between deviant life-styles and marginal political styles. The drug scene has introduced a note of ambiguity into what constitutes marginality in political life and what constitutes deviation in life-style. When a life-style is deviant and people do things surreptitiously and out of fear, then they are implicitly acknowledging that the act performed is illegal and punishable, and even ought to be punished. But when one acts on the basis of civil liberties, in terms of the right of marginal groups to engage in drug use of certain kinds, then drug use becomes a political fact; and it becomes possible to be a part of the political scene in terms of legislation, candidates, and the stand of political parties on various issues. The likelihood is that there will be all kinds of legal reforms of the drug laws because most students in law school are drugtakers. At the political level, as a consequence of the widespread use of drugs, there are now new political issues and new interest groups. These correlate with the emergence of youths themselves as an interest group. Therefore, the drug issue has a political validity that derives from the penetration of the young into mass politics.

And if we move briefly from the problem of drugs in relation to politics to the generational aspect of drugtaking, it becomes evident that drugs serve to define a generation in relation to and in contradistinction to alcohol. Every generation has its form of self-inflicted narcotic addiction. Special habits, normative for the subculture, but deviant to the larger society, define membership in important ways. This is the case whatever the character of the addiction process. Drug use is a definition of membership. The failure to use drugs is a statement of nonmembership in a culture, in a generation, or in a peer group. Drugs make one a member in a group that is illegal, distinct from the parental world, and at the same time create a common bond among people who in fact have few other expressions of common linkage and common cause. The search for the social bond through drugs and among different stratification lines, upper and lower class, black and white, civilian and military, is itself a cardinal aspect of high drug use among American youth.

Drugs like heroin, opium, and, to a lesser degree, marihuana preparations serve as psychic depressants; whereas most forms of alcohol intoxication serve as psychic stimulants. There are "uppers" as well as "downers," but for the most part, drugs link up better with the idea of being cool, being relaxed, being psychologically in a state that is acquiescent and accepting of all kinds of differences of opinion, differences of behavior, and differences of belief. What has often been described as the democratic spirit of the young may in part be a reflection of a drug-induced state of benign neglect—or what is termed *being mellow*. Alcohol, for its part, links up with a hot culture; the idea of getting hot in turn relates to the value of intensity and involvement—at least at the emotive level. The relationship between drug use and alcohol use and cool and hot generations—the adjective *cool* is regarded as favorable, and the adjective *hot* as unfavorable—has a great deal to do not just with the cultural milieu of drug addiction, but with the psychological condition that alcohol yields. The notion of coolness in relation to a series of political, sociological, and technical problems has created a serious gap between the drug culture and the political culture—at least in the obvious sense of these terms.

This distinction between drugs and alcohol, or cool and hot styles, should not be taken as absolute. In point of fact many young drug users combine their marihuana intake with wine, beer, and liquor. For experienced drug users such combinations are as carefully diagnosed for their effects as linkages between two drugs. At the other end of the age spectrum many adults are now using drugs that not long ago were considered the private possession of the youth culture; and they take up their new drug habit without necessarily relinquishing any affinity for alcohol. While it still seems useful to make broad cultural distinctions, they ought not to be employed heuristically; that is, with the intention of demonstrating that the legality of alcohol is somehow sanctioned by its effects on the user, in contrast to the illegality of the drug use on account of its presumed effects. For it is precisely such legalistic usages of cultural differentiation that create rather than relieve the problem of drug definition and treatment. The very illegality of drugs is of exceptional importance as a social bond between young people dedicated, whether drugs are pleasurable or painful, to defining themselves against existing mores.

Indeed, the solutions to drug abuse and addiction that have been developed by the young themselves are much more potent and viable than the heavy-handed negativism that one hears on television, reads in the press, or sees in Synanon, Odyssey House, and other agencies. Rather than isolation from society, these approaches promulgate a counterculture in a society—a counter-drug culture that in effect has arisen in different forms for different groups. Health exercises, natural foods, Yoga and Indian religion, the rise of militant black cultural nationalism that explicitly repudiates drugs on political grounds, all of these positive responses represent a much greater and more eloquent force for the reduction of drug-taking than the proposed solutions thus far brought to bear on the subject by physicians and psychiatrists.

The revolution of the present period has been an experiential revolution. It has taken the form of a bodily revolution. There is a persistent emphasis that the political revolution begins with the private body. An individual wakes up in the morning and does or fails to do certain things. One either processes his hair or wears a natural hair style. One either lets his hair grow long or cuts it short. One either wears a white shirt or wears a polo shirt. One either puts on a tie or does not put on a tie. All of these "trivial" decisions are somehow real. They are not made in Washington; but they manage to make Washingtonians uptight. In other words, stylistic considerations have become politically substantial. They are politically important because symbols are never just stylistic in nature. Symbols represent certain keynote values, certain moral statements about the nature of being, about what is a political soul, about who is a social animal. These symbolic notations are tremendously important in stimulating a drug subculture, because it is uniquely fitted to the politics of experience. Like dress, like sexuality, and like modes of biological behavior in general, the drug scene ultimately is what one does to oneself. Drug intake is not something done abstractly or by indirection.

Drug use, and participation in a drug culture, is an activity that reflects itself in behavior and demeanor, that is, what one considers to be a proper life-style. In the drug act, therefore, the youth culture connects up with an experiential revolution. It is a revolution that assumes that all change begins with the "mind" or "self" rather than with the external social world. There are undoubtedly weaknesses and problems in this kind of implicit idealistic epistemology. Exploitation is, after all, an objective process. Negative events and processes go on in the world whether one takes drugs or not. Nonetheless, it does seem extremely cogent to explain the rise of the drug culture and of an experientially grounded revolution in the divorce of mass man from policymaking.

If we are going to talk seriously about solutions, we must deal with the fact that a strong counterculture is being created and encouraged that is viable and visible enough to offset the obvious effects of drugs. Clearly many of these kinds of movements—the Jesus-freak movement, the natural food movement, the Yoga movement, the Indian religion movement—have an enormously exaggerated manneristic and theatrical quality. They reveal a painful naivete in the way they are presented. But when we keep in mind the potency and the power of the drug culture and subculture, the need to have a relatively simplistic model to counter the impact of drugs as a cultural force is manifest. If there is going to be any kind of serious attention given to the drug problem, the answer is not going to be found in the morning methadone lineup. This only leads to a search for a new legitimate "high"—one that does have the merit at least of permitting the individual a working life. Indeed, "legalized" drugs are simply incorporated into the larger demimonde of the "illegal" drug scene. This is not going to be a way out of this problem, because legal drugs fail to create a climate of any higher consciousness. The chemistry industry is partially the source of the problem, and it takes a good deal of imagination to believe that it is going to be the source of the solution.

There is a growing awareness, especially among those sectors of the medical and legal professions most directly responsible, that drug problems are social problems more than chemical problems. A primary reason for the huge gap between users and warners is that the medical, chemical, and biological writings on drugs are political, resting on an assumption that life, individual life, is an ultimate good. This belief in the supremacy of life over other values seriously challenges the political images and the moral imperatives of many young people who are primary users of the drug culture. The differences between the view that life itself may be curbed at any given moment, by hydrogen bombs, by World War III, or any other objective and impersonal source of military or technological destruction, and the argument that individual life must be preserved at all costs represent two sets of assumptions about the value of personal life that highlight the political and social generational conflict in our society. The drug culture is a symbol of that, no matter how acute and poignant its manifestations.

9

Knowledge, Power, and Drug Effects

Howard S. Becker

Scientists no longer believe that a drug has a simple physiological action, essentially the same in all humans. Experimental, anthropological, and sociological evidence have convinced most observers that drug effects vary greatly, depending on variations in the physiology and psychology of the persons taking them, on the state the person is in when he ingests the drug, and on the social situation in which drug ingestion occurs. We can understand the social context of drug experiences better by showing how their character depends on the amount and kind of knowledge available to the person taking the drug. Since distribution of knowledge is a function of the social organization of the groups in which drugs are used, drug experiences vary with variations in social organization. I

*This work originally appeared in an abridged version as "Consciousness, Power, and Drug Effects," in *Transaction/Society* 10, no. 4 (May-June 1973): 26-31.

explore that possibility in three quite different settings of drug use: the illegal use of drugs for pleasure, the use of medically prescribed drugs by doctors' patients, and the involuntary ingestion of drugs by victims of chemical warfare.

Drug effects have a protean character, varying from person to person and place to place. They can vary in that fashion because drugs almost always have more than one effect on the organism. People may conventionally focus on and recognize only one or a few of these effects, and ignore all others as irrelevant. Most people think the effect of aspirin is to control pain; some know that it also reduces fever; few think of gastric irritation as a typical effect, though it is. The example suggests that users focus on "beneficial" effects and ignore those irrelevant to the benefit they seek. Because drugs have so many effects, the effects can be interpreted variously and thus reflect extremely subtle contextual influences.

Drug Effects, Knowledge, and Social Structure

When a person ingests a drug his subsequent experience is influenced by his ideas and beliefs about that drug (Becker 1967). What he knows about the drug influences the way he uses it, the way he interprets its manifold effects and responds to them, and the way he deals with the sequelae of the experience. Conversely, what he does not know affects his experience, also, making certain interpretations impossible, as well as actions based on that missing knowledge. I use the term *knowledge* in an extended sense, to refer to any ideas or beliefs about the drug that any of the actors in the drug-use network (for example, illicit drug sellers, physicians, researchers, or lay drug users) believe have been tested against experience and thus carry more warrant than mere assertions of faith. All people are probably especially likely to take knowledge they believe to have been tested against experience as a guide to their own interpretations and actions. Members of contemporary Western societies who accept the value of science and scientific knowledge so uncritically must be doubly so.

Dosage

Many drug effects are dose related. The drug has one set

of effects if you take x amount and quite different effects if you take five x. Similarly, drugs have different effects when taken orally, by inhalation, intramuscularly, or intravenously. How much of the drug you take and how you take it depend on what you understand to be the proper amount and route of use. Those understandings depend on what you have learned from sources you consider knowledgeable and trustworthy.

If I have a headache and ask how many aspirin I should take, almost anyone will tell me two; that knowledge is widely available both on the package and in lay medical folklore. It will also be understood that I should swallow the aspirin rather than dissolving them in water and injecting them. Most people, however, have no knowledge readily available about the use of a large variety of drugs, either those medically prescribed (for instance, cortisone) or those used without benefit of medical advice (for example, LSD). To use them, would-be users develop some notions about how much to take and how to take it, either by trial-and-error experimentation or by adopting the ideas suggested by sources they consider reliable (scientists, physicians, or more experienced drug users). Those sources usually have recommendations about drug use. They can tell the prospective user how much he should take and how he should take it in order to cure his cold, control his blood-clotting time, have a mystical experience, get high, or whatever other effect he may desire. They can also tell him how much will be too much, producing unwanted effects of overdose. They may tell him to take four pills of the kind the druggist will sell him, one after each meal, and one before retiring; they may give more elaborate instructions, such as those given diabetics about controlling their metabolic balance with food and insulin; they may formally suggest that the novice has probably smoked enough hashish and ought to stop until it takes effect; or tell him that most people find 500 micrograms of "good acid" enough to induce an adequate amount of consciousness expansion.

Using these acquired understandings, the user takes an amount whose effect he can more or less accurately predict. He usually finds his prediction confirmed, though the accuracy of conventional knowledge (as opposed to its confirmation by a retrospective adjustment of expectations) needs to be known.

In this way, his access to knowledge exerts a direct influence on his experience, allowing him to control the physiological input to that experience.

This analysis supposes that the user has complete control over the amount he takes, any variation being due to variations in his understanding of the consequences of taking different doses or taking the drug in different ways. But drug availability is often regulated by law, so that the user can take only what he can get under given conditions of supply. I might want to take large amounts of cortisone, but I am restricted to what a doctor will prescribe aɴd a pharmacist will sell. Except in hospitals, doctors ordinarily prescribe and pharmacists sell amounts larger than recommended for one time use, so that a user can take more than he is "supposed to," as sometimes occurs with prescriptions for barbiturates. I can also purchase drugs illicitly or semilicitly (for example, from a friendly neighborhood pharmacist) and so evade medical control of dosage.

A user also loses control over the amount he takes when someone more powerful than he forces him to take more than he wants or, indeed, to take a drug he does not want to take at all. This occurs commonly in pediatric medicine, in mental hospitals, and, in tuberculosis hospitals when patients are given drugs whose taste or effects they dislike; in chemical and biological warfare; and in the addition of chlorine or fluorides to city water supplies. In these cases, the relevant knowledge for an understanding of the drug's effects, insofar as they depend on dosage, is the knowledge held by the powerful person or organization that can force the user to ingest the drug.

Main effects

Social scientists have shown how the definitions drug users apply to their experience affect that experience. Persons suffering opiate withdrawal will respond as "typical" addicts if they interpret their distress as opiate withdrawal, but not if they blame the pain on some other cause (for instance, recovery from surgery). Marihuana users must learn to interpret its subtle effects as being different from ordinary experience and as pleasurable before they "get high" (Becker 1953). Indians and Caucasians interpret peyote experiences differently (Aberle 1966) and LSD "trips" have been experienced as consciousness expansion, transcendental religious experience, mock psychosis, or being high (Blum 1964).

The user brings to bear, in interpreting his experience, knowledge and definitions derived from participation in particular social groups. Indian culture teaches those who acquire it a different view of the peyote experience than is available to non-Indians. Marihuana users learn to experience the drug's effects from more experienced users. LSD trips are interpreted according to the understandings available in the various settings in which it is taken.

The process has been studied largely in connection with nonmedical drug use, but presumably occurs in medical use, also. Here the chief source of authoritative interpretations is the physician who prescribes the drug, and for many people the pharmacist. Patients on maintenance regimes of a drug for a chronic disease like diabetes, epilepsy, or gout, might develop a user's "drug culture," trading information and generalizing from their common experiences, but this has not been extensively studied.

In both cases, the knowledge acquired from authoritative sources lets the user identify the drug's main effect, know when it is occurring, and thus decide that what is occurring, even when it seems undesirable or frightening, is really acceptable, if only because expected.

Side effects

Side effects are not a medically or pharmacologically distinct category of reactions to drugs. Rather, they are effects desired by either the user or the person administering the drug. Both side effects and main effects are thus socially defined categories. What is a side effect or a main effect will thus vary according to the perspective applied; mental disorientation might be an unwanted side effect to a physician, but a desired main effect for an illicit drug user.

A drug user's knowledge, if adequate, lets him identify unwanted side effects and deal with them in a way satisfactory to him. A user concentrating on a desired main effect (relief from a headache) may not observe an unpleasant side effect (gastric irritation) or may not connect it with his use of aspirin. He interprets his experience most adequately if those who prepare him for the drug's main effects likewise teach him the likely side effects and how to deal with them. Illicit drug users typically teach novices the side effects to look out for, give reassurance about their seriousness, and give instruction in ways to avoid or overcome them; this mechanism probably prevents a great deal of potential pathology, though it can only operate when drug users are adequately connected in networks through which the information can pass. Many LSD users became expert at "talking down" people experiencing "bad trips," and marihuana users habitually teach novices what to do if they get "too high." Physicians probably vary in the degree to which they teach patients the potential side effects of the drugs they prescribe. Patients for whom physicians prescribe drugs seldom share a user culture. Since their medication produces potent side effects, they can experience profound effects without knowing their prescribed drug is responsible, should the physician fail to inform them. The physician himself may not know, since the drug may have become available before the effects had been discovered; this seems to have happened when oral contraceptives were introduced and many women experienced edema, depression, vascular difficulties, and other undesired effects that no one, at the time, attributed to The Pill (Seaman 1969).

Research and communication

Knowledge, and the social channels through which it flows, affect the interpretations and responses a drug user makes to the experience the drug produces. How is that knowledge produced? We can call its production *research*, using their term in the extended way I have been speaking of knowledge. Research, so conceived, consists of the accumulation of ideas tested more or less systematically against experience of the empirical world. Researchers may use elaborate techniques and equipment or rely on simple devices and modes of analysis. At one extreme, the research pharmacologist systematically tests the effects of a drug on a wide variety of organ systems; at the other, a casual experimenter with a drug he thinks will get him high takes it over a period of weeks, noting his own reactions, and possibly comparing them with those of others experimenting with the same drug.

Research, especially that concerning subjective experiences produced by drugs, relies heavily on conventionally accepted rules of logic, inference, and common-sense and scientific reasoning. Those rules help people decide when they have "experienced" something and what has produced the experience. Even when a variation from the ordinary that might be due to ingestion of a drug is identified, drug users often have to decide whether it is an ordinarily uncommon event or something special that might be due to the drug. Marihuana users, for instance, experience considerable hunger and must decide whether it is ordinary hunger or drug induced. In deciding such questions, users make use of such common-sense notions as that antecedents produce consequences, lay versions of such scientific procedures as Mills's method of difference.

This goes to the question of whether drug effects are entirely mental constructs or whether they are in some way constrained by physiological events in the body. To what degree can people have, as research on placebo effects suggests, "drug experiences" that have no physiological base? Experimental work (Schacter and Singer 1962) suggests that there must be some physiological basis for the experience. Without arguing the matter here, I believe that there must be some physiological event to be intepreted, but that it need not be drug caused. Human beings experience a variety of physiological events all the time; when one is properly alerted, those ordinary events can be interpreted as drug caused, as can events that in fact are drug caused.

In any event, anyone who wishes to demonstrate to himself and others that he is experiencing a "drug effect" is constrained by the rules of common sense and folk or professional science. He cannot convince himself of the validity of his experience unless he can manipulate some actual experience according to those rules to produce an acceptable conclusion. (To the degree that other systems of producing knowledge are employed—for instance, divination —users appeal to their rules for validation.)

The kind of research done on a drug depends on the facilities, technical skills, and motivations available to those who do it. I describe varieties of social structures producing research later, so I shall not go into them here. Similarly, whatever knowledge has been accumulated may or may not be available to the ultimate user of the drug, depending on the constraints on communication in the organizations drug use occurs in.

We can distinguish three major social structures in which drug use occurs of the drug exercise over their own drugtaking and especially over the production and distribution of drug-relevant knowledge. In one variety users retain control; the major empirical case is illicit drug use for pleasure, though the use of patent medicines provides an interesting comparison. In a second variety, the user delegates control to an agent presumed to act on his behalf; the major empirical case is modern medical practice, though the use of drugs for religious purposes is also relevant. Finally, in some cases, chemical warfare being the most prominent, the user has no control over his ingestion of the drug or over the production and dis-tribution of knowledge associated with use of the drug.

User Control
In a situation of user control, such as the illicit use of drugs for pleasure, the user takes as much as he wants on whatever schedule he wants; his dosage is self-initiated and self-regulated. He relies on knowledge generated in user groups to organize his drugtaking activities and interpret his drug experiences. He may feel substantial pressure from drug-using peers with whom he associates, but his use is voluntary and under his control in that no one has issued him anything as authoritative as a medical order and no one has forced the drug on him over his objections, as occurs in chemical warfare and forced medication.

Users generate knowledge about the drugs that interest them largely by their own research, though that may include consulting such scientific and medical sources as pharmacology texts or the *Physician's Desk Reference*. They use the lay techniques available to them, largely self-experimentation and introspective observation. These methods are particularly appropriate when the effects to be investigated consist largely of subjective experiences difficult to tap by other means. While such methods are unreliable in individual cases, they are less likely to be influenced by idiosyncratic errors when a large number of users pool their observations and produce generalizations consonant with their collective experience. The reliability of generalizations so constructed depends on the efficiency of the communication channels through which information moves-and the adequacy of the mechanism for collating it.

Ordinarily, information about a drug illicitly used accumulates slowly, often over many years, in the pooled experience of users, who compare notes on their own experiences and those of others they have heard about. Insofar as users are connected, even though very indirectly, over a long time a large number of experiences circulate through the connected system and produce what can be called a *drug culture* (not the melange of political and cultural attitudes the term is often applied to, but rather a set of common understandings about the drug, its characteristics, and the way it can best be used). The development of knowledge about marihuana probably best approximates this model, many years of extensive marihuana use in the United States having produced a vast body of lore that does not vary much by region or social group.

Other methods of cumulating and collating knowledge occasionally occur. The drug known as STP underwent a hip equivalent of the mass testing of polio vaccines when thousands of pills containing it were thrown from the stage at a be-in. Though no one knew what they were, thousands apparently took them and within a few days most interested people had heard something about their effects. Information piled up at the Haight-Ashbury Free Medical Clinic and other places where people suffering adverse reactions were likely to go. In a short time, the major effects, appropriate dosages, likely side effects, and effective antidotes were well known.

Knowledge produced this way has certain defects. It cannot discover anything not capable of being discovered by the simple techniques known to a mass population of users. If, as alleged, LSD damages chromosomes and thus produces birth defects in offspring even after drug use ceases, typical styles of user research could not discover it, for that kind of knowledge requires more sophisticated equipment and techniques of analysis than users have available. Further, any unwanted effects whose onset is delayed are likely to be missed by user research, which relies on simple and immediate cause-effect relations; if the effect occurs a year after use begins, the user population may not discover the connection. (If, however, the user population includes well-trained scientists, as was always the case with LSD and is increasingly true with respect to all psychedelic drugs, this problem can be overcome.) Finally, the effectiveness of the research is limited by the connectedness of the user network. The operation depends on redundancy for the reliability of the knowledge produced and disconnected networks may gather insufficient data to overcome the unreliability of the individual datum. The underground news media might help with this difficulty; insofar as they are widely read, they can provide an otherwise nonexistent link between isolated users or user groups.

But knowledge produced by user research has the great virtue of being directed precisely to the questions the user is interested in having answered. If he wants to know whether the drug will make him high, the available research, conducted by people who share his interest, will give him an answer. In this it differs from research done for medical purposes, which is typically directed to questions raised by scientists or physicians, not by the ultimate user of the drug.

Users thus have available, under optimal conditions of knowledge production, relatively reliable and accurate guides to the questions about the drug they use to which they want answers. They use this to maximize the benefits they desire from use of the drug, whatever those benefits might be, and to minimize side effects. Often, because they participate in user groups, when a question arises whose answer they do not know, someone who does know it is readily available. This is particularly important in dealing with potentially dangerous or disturbing side effects. Naturally, the optimal circumstances seldom obtain; when knowledge is incomplete, inaccurate, or unavailable, users will have predictable troubles. This is particularly obvious when a drug first appears and knowledge has not yet been produced and disseminated.

If we switch to another instance of user control—the use of patent medicines—we see the importance of the character of user networks. (I rely here on informal observation and speculation.) If my speculations are correct, people produce knowledge about patent-medicine effects either on their own or in small family groups. Take the case of laxatives. The constipation they are used for is presumably not widely discussed among people suffering from it. Users cannot easily identify one another as fellow sufferers and thus as potential sources of information. Parents may share the results of their own experiments with their children, as may spouses with one another, but one can imagine that the knowledge would not move much beyond that. Specialized groups (for example, fellow inmates of an old people's home) might share such information, but in general, knowledge probably would not cumulate, except perhaps in families (perhaps descending, like toilet words, in the female line); each new user or small group would have to rediscover it. My speculations may be incorrect, but they highlight the importance of communication channels in understanding the experiences of users who control their own drug use.

Control by the User's Agent

When the user delegates control to an agent, interesting variations in the production and distribution of knowledge occur, with equally interesting variations in the kinds of experiences users have. The major empirical case is that of the physician prescribing medication for his patient (though an interesting variation is provided by the religious use of drugs, as evidenced in the relation between Don Juan and his pupil Carlos Castaneda [1968]). Here the user takes the drug the doctor prescribes for him, in the amounts and on the schedule the doctor recommends. The doctor's prescription reflects what the doctor wants to accomplish, rather than what the patient wants; their desires may coincide, but need not and in many cases do not.

The doctor uses at least two criteria in evaluating drugs. He wants to alleviate some dangerous or unpleasant condition the patient is suffering from, in a way clearly visible both to him and to his patient. The drug effect that most interests the doctor is one that produces demonstrable (in the best case, visible to the patient's naked eye) improvement. But the doctor also uses a second criterion: he does not want the drug to interfere with his control over the patient. The rationale for that desire is well known: since (the rationale goes) the doctor knows what will help the patient better than the patient himself, the patient must surrender himself to the physician to achieve maximum results; if the patient rejects the physician's advice, his health may be impaired. While I do not believe the rationale is factually correct, it is unnecessary to demonstrate that to observe that doctors believe they have a legitimate interest in maintaining what Eliot Freidson (1961, 1970a, 1970b) has usefully labeled *professional dominance*.

The patient usually relies on the physician for his knowledge about dosage, main effects, and side effects of the drug prescribed. But the physician may not give the patient all the knowledge that is available to him, because he does not want the patient to use that knowledge as a basis for disobeying medical orders (see Lennard, et al. 1972). Henry Lennard has given me a telling example. Certain of the tranquilizing drugs sometimes produce an unusual effect on male sexual functioning: while the man experiences orgasm, no ejaculation occurs. This naturally causes those who have the experience some anxiety. Since these drugs are given to relieve anxiety, Lennard asked psychiatrists why they did not tell patients that this might occur. "If I did that," ran the typical answer, "the patient might not take the drug and, *in my judgment*, he should run the risk of that anxiety in order to protect himself from his basic anxieties." (Physicians also withhold information about side effects because suggestible patients often experience effects they have been told about, even when there is no physiological basis for the experience. They believe that this risk outweighs the risk of morbidity associated with lack of information, but I know of no definitive data on the matter.)

Sometimes the physician does not give the patient adequate information about the experience the drug will produce because he does not have the knowledge himself. Research on drugs for medical use is organized quite differently than user's research, and its organization creates substantial barriers to a free flow of information. Drug research is a highly specialized discipline, with its own journals, professional societies, and scientific world to which the physician does not belong. He does not follow the latest developments in pharmacology, read its journals, or attend meetings of its scientific organizations. So he depends for his knowledge of drug effects on such general medical literature as he keeps up with, on his immediate colleagues, and on the knowledge provided by pharmaceutical companies through their literature and salesmen (Coleman, et al. 1966). Most of his knowledge, especially of new drugs, probably comes from the last source. (Some physicians, especially those in specialized practices who see many cases of the same disease, may engage in casual experimentation similar to that done by illicit drug users, trying different dosages and treatments on different patients. They may then pool their observations with like-minded specialists and generate knowledge similar to that contained in drug-user cultures, with the same advantages and drawbacks.)

Another serious barrier to the practicing physician's acquisition of knowledge about the drugs he prescribes arises from the organization of pharmaceutical research and manufacture. While pharmaceutical companies, the scientists who work for them, and the physicians who participate in their drug-testing programs all no doubt want to produce medically valuable drugs that will help physicians combat disease, they are also interested, as congressional investigations have shown, in profits (Harris 1964). They design their research to produce profitably marketable products that can be sold, via physicians' prescriptions, to the public, and that will also pass government tests of purity, efficacy, and lack of dangerous side effects. They look primarily for drugs that will produce (or seem to produce) effects on diseased patients, of the kind physicians want, or can be persuaded to want, to produce.

They appear to investigate possible side effects as congressional investigations have shown, so far as required by prudence and the law. (We have no studies of the organization of pharmaceutical research laboratories, their characteristic patterns of investigation, their reward structures, and the relations between the two, so I have relied on more public sources, for example, House Government Operations Committee 1971.)

Pharmaceutical research thus produces knowledge about the main effect a doctor might need to treat a patient. That is what the companies' advertising communicates to the physician. If he looks carefully, he can find material on side effects and contraindications, but it is not pressed on him. In general, companies do not seek or force on the practicing physician information that would lessen the profitability of a drug they believe has good commercial possibilities.

The physician, then, may not know that the drug has some effects it in fact has, or he may not choose to tell the patient when he does know. When, for either reason, the patient the drug is prescribed for does not know what it may do, he runs two risks. He may have experiences that are quite pronounced, extremely unpleasant, and even dangerous, but not realize that they result from his medication. As a consequence, he may continue to take the drug that produces the unwanted side effect. For instance, certain commonly prescribed antihistamines occasionally produce urethral stricture; allergic patients who take large quantities may experience this but never report it to the allergist because it does not seem to be in his department. If the condition becomes severe they consult a urologist. He may discover they are taking large doses of antihistamine and cure the difficulty by recommending one that does not have this side effect. But not all physicians know of the connection, and failure of the patient to report or the physicians to make the connection can lead to serious difficulty.

The patient may also experience symptoms that have an insidious and gradual onset, and never recognize that there is any change in his condition that requires explanation. This was apparently the experience of many women who took birth-control pills (Seaman 1969). They suffered serious and continuing depression, but it appeared gradually and seemed nothing out of the ordinary, so that they did not realize anything had occurred that might be attributable to the hormone. It is probably especially true of drugs taken for medical purposes that the mood changes they produce will be so gradual so as not to be noticed or will be attributed to psychological difficulties, changes in social relationships, or other causes unrelated to the medication. Thus, the physician whose patient begins to experience mood changes may be treated as a neurotic, and the difficulty, when the user does become aware of it, will not only be undiagnosed but also misdiagnosed. This must have happened frequently among early users of oral contraceptives, especially unmarried women whom physicians often consider especially prone to neurotic symptoms (Seaman 1969).

In either case, the drug experience is amplified and the chance of serious pathology increases because the doctor has insufficient knowledge of the drug's effects to warn the patient, or because he chooses not to warn him. The patient, not knowing what is likely to happen, cannot recognize the event when it occurs and cannot respond adequately himself or present his problem to an expert who can provide an adequate response.

As we have seen, knowledge accumulates in illicit drug-using groups when users are in touch with one another and communicate the results of their personal research to one another freely. Though the medical and scientific professions are organized in a way that ought to promote full communication to practicing physicians of adverse drug reactions, a recent study suggests obstacles that impede that communication (Koch-Weser, et al. 1969). Hospital physicians were asked to report all adverse drug reactions and, simultaneously, clinical phramacologists made independent checks. From two-thirds to three-quarters of the adverse reactions to prescribed drugs verified by the pharmacologists were *not* reported by the physicians. Physicians tended to report those adverse reactions in which morbidity and danger were high, and in which the connection between the drug and the reaction was already well known. This means that the system works poorly to accumulate new information, although it is relatively efficient in reconfirming what is already known. Add to this the probability that patients are probably less likely than illicit drug users to compare experiences on a large scale. There is then a substantial risk that adverse information will never be accumulated so that it can be passed on to the drug's ultimate user for him to use in interpreting such events as occur subsequent to drug use.

Many of the user's difficulties in interpreting his experience will result from the stage of development of knowledge about the drug. I have argued elsewhere that adverse reactions to illicitly used drugs decline as their use increases and a fund of knowledge grows among communicating users, allowing them to use that accumulated wisdom to regulate dosage and deal with adverse effects (Becker 1967). A similar natural history may occur with the use of drugs in medical practice. Doctors seek drugs that will make a decisive and noticeable improvement in a patient's condition. Pharmaceutical companies and researchers attempt to produce such drugs. In the effort to produce a *noticeable* improvement, company recommendations, insufficient research, and physician inclinations combine to produce a tendency to prescribe dosages larger than required for the desired medical effect, large enough to produce serious side effects. Because the research done prior to use on patients has not looked thoroughly into possible side effects, no one connects these occurrences with the new medication. Where the drug is potentially profitable, as in the case of antibiotics, adrenocortical steroids, or oral contraceptives, its use will be heavily promoted and widely publicized, so that physicians will feel pressure both from patients and the example of their more innovative peers to begin prescribing the new drug. Massive use, combined with a tendency to overdose, will produce enough adverse reactions that someone will eventually investigate and establish the connection. More such reactions will occur before the information filters through the barriers already discussed, but eventually conventional dosages will be lowered and the incidence of adverse reactions will decline.

When they occur, furthermore, they will be recognized and treated more effectively. Eventually, presumably, the numbr of adverse reactions will reach a minimum based on the number of physicians who are either ignorant of their character or who do not communicate their knowledge to patients so that the reactions can be recognized, reported, and treated.

The introduction of oral contraceptives appears to embody this natural history. When first introduced, both the manufacturers and prescribing physicians were determined to use sufficiently large doses that they would not have to face the wrath of a pregnant woman who had been assured that *that* could not happen. The large doses produced serious side effects in a variety of organ systems, as well as severe psychological depressions. As knowledge of these effects became more widespread, many physicians (and others) did not wish to publicize them, since women who know of them might refuse to take the pills. Eventually, doctors discovered that one-tenth the conventional dose was sufficient to produce effective contraception, with many fewer adverse reactions. With both physicians and users alerted by massive publicity, adverse reactions were more quickly reported and dealt with.

To what degree does the process I described occur because the investigation and production of medically prescribed drugs is carried on by profit-making corporations in a capitalist economy? Obviously, those elements of the process that reflect marketing strategies designed to maximize profits —focusing research on products likely to produce high sales at low costs and a relative neglect of potential side effects— would not occur in a noncapitalist economy. On the other hand, most of the other elements, reflecting as they do the interests of an organized medical profession as distinct from the interests of patients, would presumably occur in any developed society that contains such a group. The desire of physicians to achieve discernible results and to maintain control over patients would probably continue to influence the dissemination of knowledge from researchers to physicians to patients and, consequently, the kinds of experiences medical patients have as a result of using prescribed drugs.

Carlos Castaneda's account (1968) of his instruction in the use of psychedelic substances by Don Juan is the only one I know of with the delegation of control to a religious, rather than a medical, agent. The relationship between the two, and its effect on Castaneda's drug experiences, appears similar to the medical model. Don Juan often gave Castaneda insufficient information with which to interpret his experiences and avoid unpleasant panics, because he felt Castaneda's inexperience (for which read "lack of professional training") would make it impossible for him to understand, because he wished to retain control over his student's progress, and because he wanted his pedagogy to turn out the result he sought, even though the experience might be unpleasant or frightening for Castaneda in the short run and the result might ultimately be failure. The disparity between teacher and student goals parallels the disparity between physician and patient interests and goals, and some of the resulting experiences of the user who has delegated control appear similar.

Control by External Agents
People sometimes find themselves required to ingest drugs involuntarily, the whole process under the control of an independent agent who administers the drugs for his own purposes. The external agent's purposes sometimes conflict directly with those of the user, as when people find themselves the victim of chemical warfare (Hersh 1968) in the form of a poison-gas attack or a contaminated water supply. In other cases, the agent administers the drug because he believes it is in the best interest of the community to do so, as when people with tuberculosis or leprosy are medicated to prevent them infecting others (Roth 1963). In such cases (and in such similar instances as the forced medication of mental hospital inmates and the administration of amphetamines to allegedly hyper-kinetic school children) those administering the drug frequently insist, and believe, that the medication serves the ultimate interest of the user as well, however much he may wish to avoid it. In both chemical warfare and forced medication, the characteristic features of a serious disagreement about the legitimacy of the drug's administration and the

consequent necessity of coercion to effect that administration appear. The crucial feature of the social structure in which the drugs are used, then, consists of an imbalance in power between those administering the drug and those to whom it is administered such that drug ingestion is forced on unwilling users.

Those administering the drug usually have goals quite divorced from anything the user might desire. Although physicians in ordinary medical practice have goals somewhat divergent from those of their patients, they must nevertheless take realistic account of the possibility that patients will cease coming to them unless the treatment proves satisfactory. When the one administering the drug has sufficient control that the user cannot escape, he can safely ignore the other's interests altogether, so that his actions can be designed solely to serve his own interests, personal or (more likely) organizational.

The emphasis on the interests of the person administering the drug shows up in the calculation of dosage. In contrast to the careful self-regulation characteristic of user-controlled drugs, and the attempt to prescribe a dose that will produce a result satisfactory to the user for whom one is acting as agent characteristic of agent control, external agents usually look for a maximum dose, one that will not fail to produce the result they seek. In the case of chemical warfare, they seek to kill or incapacitate those to whom the drug is administered, so they look for dosages in the range of the LD50 (the dose at which fifty percent of those dosed will die). In the case of mass administrations of tranquilizers in mental hospitals, they look for a dose that will allow patients to continue to take care of themselves but render them incapable of violence and totally suppress psychotic symptoms that interfere with hospital routine. In general, dosages are higher than in medically prescribed or self-regulated use, because they are meant to kill, disable, or control the target population, rather than cure their diseases or give them pleasure.

Since goals are set unilaterally, those administering the drug must use coercive measures to insure that the desired dose gets into its target. As the divergence in goals between

the two parties increases, the difficulty of administration
increases proportionally. Physicians often worry that patients
will suspect that their prescription is not good for them and
thus not take their medicine. Where the divergence is
relatively great and obvious, as it is in tuberculosis and mental
hospitals, hospital personnel usually supervise patients' ingestion of medication very closely; even so, inmates often discover
ingenious ways of evading forced medication.

In chemical warfare, where the interests of the parties
are diametrically opposed, the problem of an "effective
delivery system" becomes extremely important, thus highlight-
ing the degree to which other forms of drug ingestion rely on
the voluntary cooperation of the user. Chemical warfare
agencies concern themselves with foolproof means of dosing
entire populations, and so work on such devices as aerosols,
which guarantee ingestion by saturating the air everyone must
breathe, or methods of contaminating urban water supplies. In
their zeal to dose all members of the target population, they
create for themselves a problem that does not bother those
who administer drugs in a more selective way that requires
user cooperation. A homely example is the policeman who,
attempting to squirt a political demonstrator with Mace,
neglects to allow for the wind blowing toward him and gets a
faceful of his own medicine.

Those who administer drugs to involuntary users are
either indifferent about providing those who get the drug with
any knowledge about it or actively attempt to prevent them
from getting that knowledge. Hospital personnel seldom inform
inmates receiving forced medication about main or side effects
or how they can be interpreted. They must suggest that "this
pill will make you feel better" or that "the doctor thinks this
will make you feel better" or that "the doctor thinks this will
help your condition," but seldom give more detailed information. The difficulties occasioned by lack of knowledge already
discussed can thus arise, though thay may be counteracted by
the development of a user's culture among people who are
confined in total institutions and subject to the same drug
regimen.

Where destruction or incapacitation of the target population is the aim, those who administer the drug may wish to

prevent any knowledge that the drug is being administered, or of its effects, from reaching those who ingest it. In this way, they hope to prevent the taking of countermeasures and, by preventing the use of available knowledge to reach an understanding of what is happening, create, in addition to the drug's specific physiological effects, panic at the onslaught of the unknown. It was just this phenomenon that both Army chemical warriors and those of the psychedelic left hoped to exploit by putting LSD into urban water supplies. Not only, they hoped, would the drug interfere with people's normal functioning by causing them to misperceive and hallucinate, but also the people would not even know that they had been given a drug that was causing these difficulties and so would be frightened as well. (As it turns out, Mayor Daley need not have worried about Yippies putting LSD into the Chicago water supply during the 1968 Democratic Convention. As Army Chemical and Biological Warfare investigators had already discovered, LSD breaks down rapidly in the presence of chlorine, and the Chicago water supply usually contains enough chlorine that one can easily taste it. This defect in LSD as a chemical warfare agent has led the Army to an attempt to produce a water soluble version of the T.H.C. [tetrahydracannabinol, one of the active agents in marihuana], which otherwise is most easily ingested in smoke.)

Conclusion

If drug experiences somehow reflect or are related to social settings, we must specify the settings in which drugs are taken and the specific effect of those settings on the experiences of participants in them. This analysis suggests that it is useful to look at the role of power and knowledge in those settings, knowledge of how to take the drug and what to expect when one does, and power over distribution of the drug, knowledge about it, and over the decision to take or not to take it. These vary greatly, depending on the character of the organization within which the drugs are used. In illicit drug use, the effects of the drug experience depend on the social links and cultural understandings that grow up among those who use the drug. In the use of medically prescribed drugs, the effects reflect the profit orientation of pharmaceutical manu-

facturers and the characteristic professional dominance exer-
cised by physicians. Where drug use is forced on people, the
results reflect the unilateral exercise of power in the interest
of the stronger party.

Naturally, these are pure types and many of the situations
we observe in contemporary society are mixtures of them.
Many people, for instance, originally begin taking a drug
because a physician has prescribed it for them, but then
continue to get supplies of it in illicit or semilicit ways; their
use probably contains features of both user control and control
by the user's agent. Folk medicine probably consists of a
similar mixture, since folk curers may not have professional
interests that diverge from those of their patients to the same
degree that the modern physician does; then again, they may. I
do not suggest that empirical cases will fall neatly into one or
another of these categories, but rather that the pure categories I have discussed show most clearly how knowledge and
power can influence the experience of a drug user. Much more
needs to be known about the pure types I have described (for it
may turn out that my analyses are one-sided and incomplete),
as well as about the numerous marginal types that exist.

In the course of writing this, I became conscious of the
ambiguity of the very idea of a *drug*. Much of what I have said
about use enforced by a powerful external agent could be
applied without much change to our daily ingestion of the
pollutants in air, water, and food. Is smog a drug? Why not?
Many people consider the fluoridation of city water supplies
an instance of chemical warfare against them, sometimes
going so far as to attribute the action to a foreign enemy. Are
fluorides drugs? Clearly, we label as *drugs* a somewhat
arbitrary selection of the materials we routinely ingest. It
might be useful to look at the entire common-sense classification of ingested substances to see how we decide to call some
things *foods*, others *drugs*, still others *pollutants*, and what-
every other categories people use. We could then ask what the
consequences of such differential labeling are. We take
different kinds of regulatory actions with respect to foods,
drugs, and pollutants. What are the differences and how do
these affect the distribution of knowledge and power with

respect to ingestion of these materials and, therefore, the distribution of various kinds of experiences among those ingesting them. By extending the analysis I have begun here with respect to drugs, we might gain greater understanding of such diverse phenomena as smog poisoning, malnutrition, and indigestion.

The analysis might similarly be extended, in another direction, from consideration of chemically induced physical and psychological experiences to those produced by diseases of various kinds. We can investigate, for example, the way information about the effects of diseases is generated—what kind of research? done by whom? with what ends in mind?— and how it is communicated—in what social channels? with what barriers to overcome? We can then see how the resultant distribution of knowledge affects people's responses to their symptoms.

Beyond that, and I believe of more general import, we can investigate the sociology of normal physiological functioning. Consider that medical symptoms exhibit themselves as departure from normal function: breath that is "shorter" than normal, appetite that is "less" than normal, pain that is beyond normal expectation, bowel movements that are "unusual," and so on. What is the folk wisdom with respect to "normal functioning"? How is it taught and learned? How does it vary from group to group?

References

Aberle, David F. 1966. *The Peyote Religion among the Navaho.* Chicago: Aldine.

Becker, Howard S. 1953. "Becoming a Marihuana User." *American Journal of Sociology* 59 (November): 235-43.

———. 1967. "History, Culture, and Subjective Experience." *Journal of Health and Social Behavior* 8 (September): 163-76.

Blum, Richard, and Associates. 1964. *Utopiates.* New York: Atherton.

Castaneda, Carlos. 1968. *The Teachings of Don Juan.* Berkeley and Los Angeles: University of California Press.

Coleman, James S., et al. 1966. *Medical Innovation*. Indianapolis: Bobbs-Merrill.

Freidson, Eliot L. 1961. *Patients' Views of Medical Practice*. New York: Russell Sage Foundation.

_____. 1970a. *The Profession of Medicine*. New York: Dodd, Mead.

_____. 1970b. *Professional Dominance*. New York: Aldine-Atherton.

Harris, Richard. 1964. *The Real Voice*. New York: Macmillan.

Hersh, Seymour. 1968. *Chemical and Biological Warfare: America's Hidden Arsenal*. Indianapolis: Bobbs-Merrill.

House Government Operations Committee. 1971. *Hearings* (May 3-5, May 26). Washington, D.C.: Government Printing Office.

Koch-Weser, Jan, et al. 1969. "Factors Determining Physician Reporting of Adverse Drug Reactions." *New England Journal of Medicine* 280 (January 2): 20-26.

Lennard, Henry L., et al. 1972. *Mystification and Drug Misuse*. New York: Harper and Row.

Roth, Julius. 1963. *Timetables*. Indianapolis: Bobbs-Merrill.

Schater, Stanley, and Singer, Jerome. 1962. "Cognitive, Social, and Physiological Determinants of Emotional State." *Psychological Review* 69 (September): 377-99.

Seaman, Barbara. 1969. *The Doctor's Case Against the Pill*. New York: Peter H. Wyden.

10

Playing a Cold Game:
Phases of a Ghetto Career*

Alan G. Sutter

This chapter describes some aspects of drug involvement as it is woven into a career line emerging out of the urban ghetto. The initial source of evidence for my account was gathered in the course of ethnographic fieldwork as part of a larger study of youthful drug use in predominantly black ghettos of the San Francisco Bay Area.[1] Apart from numerous informal conversations, extensive participant observation and life-history interviews with key informants, central figures, those who were recognized by their peers as most knowledgeable about their world, were brought together in "panel sessions." As panel members gathered for group discussion

*This work originally appeared in Urban Life and Culture 1, no. 1 (April 1972): 77-91, a Sage Publication; and as chapter 16, "Phases of a Ghetto Career," in The Dream Sellers, by Richard H. Blum and Associates (1972), Jossey-Bass. Reprinted with the permission of Russell Sage Publications and Jossey-Bass Inc., Publishers.

and critically examined each other's experience, it was possible for me to separate individual experiences from those more collective in nature and to check the validity of my own observations.

The following account suggests a few important lines of inquiry and does not represent an exhaustive study of drug involvement per se. It explicates a career line of a black ghetto-raised youth who becomes (or fails to become) a hustler who may eventually deal in hard drugs. The notion of a career line refers to the changing perspective in which a person orients himself with reference to others, to the patterned sequence of positions he comes to occupy within a social network, and to a person's developing sense of identity that symbolically emerges in the course of shifting group affiliations.

Wanting to be the "Baddest"

Little tiny "dudes," six to eleven years old, engage in the earliest form of drug involvement as they play near the ramshackle, scrawl-covered buildings of housing projects, near empty lots and playgrounds, and around commercial establishments in the urban ghetto. Here they will confront a world of spontaneous play-groups and alliances. In seeking fun, partnership, and adventure, they swarm over the streets from nearby city blocks. The patterns of play activity are differentiated by the emergence of a distinctive set of especially bold and nervy little dudes who begin to develop a reputation for being "bad." Having fun is often contingent on risk-taking behavior, and things like glue, paint thinner, gasoline, or anything that can be manufactured on the spur of the moment become agents for distinguishing the bold and fearless from the timid and frightened. When drug-use practices occur, they are usually woven into the embryonic posture of being bad:

We'd go on a Saturday and see who could sniff the most tubes of glue, man. This one dude, you know, he was about fourteen and we were about ten, and he was high, and we were all laughing in the park. We had our little bottle of whiskey with us, you know. Didn't even know what to do, dump the glue in a sock, and you know, roll it, and after you start sniffing, it's just something new and you flash. Throw the whisky bottle away. I'm bad now! You go around with the other little cats.

This set of particularly bold little dudes is already prepared at this early age to engage in petty stealing, vandalism, and fighting. Physical assaults are woven into their daily routine as part of the spirit of play. Their high tolerance for aggression heightens a sensitivity to danger and awakens the need for self-defense. To wander along the street alone, to ride a bicycle, or to walk home after school can become an obstacle course. Lurking in the atmosphere is an ever-present tension, a sense of fear that cramps the stomach with butterfly twitters. It becomes essential that a little dude meet violence by defending himself or engaging in fights to assert himself: "You got to be a rough little dude when you're coming up. You got to be to survive, man." The elevation of toughness to a supreme virtue is symbolized by bravery in the face of danger and the demeanor of a hard character.

This generalized sensitivity to danger does not mean that all children living under ghetto conditions are "belligerent little bastards"—on the contrary. As particular play-groups are differentiated from the mainstream of children by their "nervy" and often public displays of aggression, they are in turn shunned and set apart by childhood associates. Despite a world with a high tolerance for violence and a threatening atmosphere, most children stay clear of rowdy little dudes who "think they're bad" and gradually form their own friendships and alliances:

There was this certain little group that were my age, but they was doing different things than I was doing. I was going to school and playing ball, pretty good little kid until I hit junior high, but they were running around fighting and sniffing glue and shit like that.

It is typical among the nervy little dudes to "act big" and to cultivate a reputation as "the baddest." Taking on the expressive patterns of fear-inspiring older dudes, lured by legendary tales of ferocious exploits, they strut about with a posture of arrogance and gradually set themselves apart from more conforming children whom they regard as "punks."

> You just want to be bad, man; it's in the air. . . . The little dudes around the block, they want to act older than they are, think it's all big and bad to beat up some kid on the street. . . . Fuck it, man! Everybody was a mess-up, all the kids in West Oakland. 'Cause when I was small, it was me and my cousin. We're the same age, and we were going to elementary school together, and all the thought on my mind was just rule the school, man, rule the school. When I get in sixth grade I'm gonna rule the school, man, and that was my highest desire. I didn't care about nobody, and that's what I did. I ruled the school. I thought that was the greatest in the world. As far as we were concerned we were the baddest, and I thought that was boss [great].

Drug involvement provides a mixture of fear, pleasure, and confident hope in the face of new and unfamiliar sources of fun. Adventuring with aggression and techniques for altering consciousness and mood have an explosive potential that is deliberately sought out and cultivated among these little dudes. The potential dangers of solvent inhalation combine with the possibility of discovery and punishment, tending to heighten and intensify the intrigue associated with fun and being the baddest.

Associated with the quest for fun is an early awareness of "messing-up"; for messing-up can become a mark of distinction, and the attendant risk of "getting into trouble" is thrilling. Encounters with "adults," especially school authorities, increase steadily; these "children" are openly defiant, and their drug-use practices are highly visible. Yet, the little dudes rarely even imagine themselves as using real drugs, and there is no commitment to their use. Drugtaking is fluid and unstructured, occurring on the spur of the moment during play. Through a process of exploration, different meanings are imputed to their tentative experimentation, altering mood states are discerned, and different sensations are grasped symbolically. This process of exploration is part of the initial phase in the developing experience with illegal drugs; while the cultivation of a bold and nervy character will lay the basis for becoming a cold dude.

As these bold little dudes pass through early adolescence, from around twelve to fifteen years old, they will form new partnerships and alliances. If they continue along the same course, directly expressing the spirit of masculine aggression, they will move into a genuinely "rowdy" stage, and being bad takes on new meaning. From the spirit of play in limited, spur-of-the-moment situations, being bad develops into a central image and leads to a more serious and sustained belligerency in a wider range of situations. Progressive involvement with police also enters into the definition of being bad.[2]

"Low-Riders" and "Fuck-ups"
"The Low-Riding Bag"

Rowdy life, the "low-riding bag" is impulsive and unrestrained with a readiness, almost an urge, to throw yourself into anything exciting. Attempts are made to "terrorize" and elicit fear while in the presence of others. Boisterous and audacious conduct increases, and criminal activity takes on a violent, even vicious character. It is well known that in some neighborhoods, a rowdy group will simply convert the street corners and alleys into a restricted domain. It is best to be ready to run wherever you are going. When you leave, be in a car or expect to get brutalized. Fighting is sought out, violence is courted in a deliberate attempt to create hazardous situations; a worthy character is a bad character, and to be bad at this time means to be rowdy, almost "crazy." The dudes who enter into the low-riding bag are often considered "crazy" in that they "don't give a shit about nothin' and no-body," even their selves:

> You know, fuck it, man! You want to fight, man, and you want to drink, and you want to fuck, and you want to steal, man. You gotta be bad, man, 'cause if you're not bad you ain't shit.

Over time, this set of early-adolescent youth becomes the main representative of physical prowess, eventually becoming known as the "badder crowd" in selected junior-high schools, "hoods," and "thugs," in the eyes of upper- and middle-class high-school youth, and as "little gangsters" in the eyes of older dudes in the "fast life."

These are the types of dudes that when they are not even loaded [under the influence of a drug], they're vicious and sort of unruly, rowdy, you know. They carry it over when they are loaded. Go outside and yell in the street, pick on people that's passing by. You can be right there walking along with 'em, you know, and all of a sudden they'll say, "Let's go rip up that dude's suit, or let's go rip off that house right now, man," and they'll be in the house, and pretty soon they're coming out with radios and tape recorders, you know. These are the cats who go out for terrorizing, just stone little gangsters. They take you off into another dimension somewhere.

There is a readiness to consume a wide variety of intoxicant substances. Although liquor, mainly wine, is the favored and most often used drug, almost anything is likely to be seized. Sniffing volatile organic solvents is fairly common; the use of barbiturates (such as reds, yellows, blues, rainbows, christmas trees) other hypnotics, and amphetamine compounds take on a patterned character; smoking marihuana, although less frequent than the use of other drugs, does enter into the repertoire of rowdy youth. There is also a growing competition between close associates with frequent struggles to achieve the most exotic experience or to act in the most outrageous and bizarre manner after consuming whatever substance is known to alter consciousness and mood. The competitive character of drug use sets the stage for thrilling episodes that are later recounted in gossip sessions, where romantic tales of prowess are exchanged, and new reputations are built.

It's like you always got to be one step bigger than anybody else, you know. Like if everybody's drinking beer you goin' out and get some whiskey. So he's drinking wine and you go out and drop some pills. You always hassling just to show everybody what you can do.

Rowdy dudes seldom have the chance to use marihuana on a regular basis. Even though youngsters in junior-high school often "claim" proudly that they "get loaded," that they're "wasted," or "ripped," on grass, and may even act out imagined roles, close examination reveals that marihuana use is episodic and relatively unsystematic. When on occasions marihuana becomes available, the pattern of use takes on the same characteristics as the use of alcohol and other intoxicating drugs:

> Grass really sparks you, man. I mean I think the trip is out of sight. I can get loaded, man, but there's a dude that's sitting right there I don't like. I hate his mother-fucking guts, man, and if he says anything wrong, when I'm loaded, man, I can get up and hit him and think nothing about it.

The impending prospect of "getting busted" becomes an integral part of the world of rowdy dudes and enters into their conception of being bad at this stage. Low-riders begin to feel they are the targets of a massive conspiracy of school, police, probation, and even recreation authorities: "Everybody's down on me, man; they're messing with me; always on my case," expresses for many a proud realization that one is "bad" enough to be "wanted." The theme of "fucking-up" expresses a mood of resignation to the fate of always "blowing it," always "getting busted," or ending up in jail. Being "wasted," the routine experience of inebriation on a wide variety of chemical agents, provides a convenient justification for having "fucked-up" and also fits the attitude of careless bravado in the face of danger.

To be sure, the impulsive, violent, and careless behavior occurring in groups of rowdy dudes has a marked impact on how they are treated by others, and, in turn, how they define their sphere of life. Partnerships, cliques, and circles in the low-riding set definitely move in the direction of a segregated collective experience inside the ghetto community. They form a distinctive world of social practice and belief and remain on the periphery of the illegal drug market. Their dangerous and conspicuous behavior, coupled with their tendency toward violence, is a warning signal to experienced drug users and dealers. Reckless and irresponsible conduct is too great a hazard to those who deal drugs in the illicit marketplace and to most of the youth who consume drugs obtained through this market. Thus, before a dude who is in the low-riding bag can really get into the drug market, he has to "mellow off." He must learn to "maintain his cool," otherwise he remains a "chump" who never listens, who never learns, who cannot wake up to what is happening. He will be "iced" (kept at a safe distance and ignored) or downgraded by most of the dudes on the set:

> The rowdy dude won't listen; he's too busy droppin' his low-ridin' hand; he won't look around and see what's happening. There's a lot of people that I wouldn't accept; they live in this world, and they don't know a damn thing about it, you know; they don't understand nothing; they don't know how to act around women; they don't know how to make money; they don't know what's the value of money; they don't know nothin' about nothin'. When I can detect this in a dude, you know, fuck him. I tell him after a while, "Say, ah, man, lookee here, you not righteous you know. You ignorant, you know. You a damn fool. So just make it, man. I don't even want to talk to you!"

"Fuck-ups"

The rowdy dudes who fail to "lighten up" join the ranks of "fuck-ups," those who are recognized in later life as having been "raised by the state." They are taken out of circulation through death or incarceration and seem to "vanish" from the street scene by the time they reach their sixteenth birthday. As fuck-ups, they derive their primary identity from prison rituals and cliques where legends of great escapes are manufactured and elaborated in gossip sessions. During their prison experience, they become what is known as "jailhouse slick," slick in the sense of learning all the hustling games from those who have failed. When they are released, they try to apply their jailhouse knowledge, usually "blow it," and return to the jailhouse. The fuck-up, as a social type, does not seem to care whether he lives, dies, or remains in jail.[3]

Most dudes will "grow out" of the low-riding bag before joining the ranks of "chumps" and fuck-ups. They either identify themselves with militant political activists, enter into a genuine spirit of sociability and party life, settle into fairly conventional school routines, or advance themselves in a variety of hustling games. Among those who continue their violent practices into later life, some will begin to develop a certain amount of discipline and self-control. They will "mellow off" or "lighten up," if for no other reason than to remain out of jail.

"Mellowing Off"

A more sociable pattern of life comes into being at a time when little dudes get interested in girls, develop a concern for their own appearance, and attempt to imitate the expressive styles of older cats on the set. By the time a rowdy dude moves into high school, an awareness of his exclusion from the mainstream of group life will usually force him to reflect on the consequences of his activity. Girls begin to "shine him on," ignore him, or rank him for not dressing right, not talking right, and not acting right. Among the more thoughtful rowdy dudes, there is an increasing concern that friends and acquaintances are getting killed, going to jail, or getting nowhere with their escapades of "terrorism"; while older cats are "getting high" and enjoying themselves. Thus, during the latter part of junior-high school, and especially upon entrance into high school, there is a general movement toward cool sociability.

Passing from a low-riding bag into a cool round of life has a marked impact on drug-use practices. There is a dramatic shift to smoking marihuana, since grass comes to symbolize a more refined and sophisticated style that is opposed to aggressive conduct. There is a concerted attempt to remain casual and composed, to cultivate poise and unruffled emotions.

See, people I know, after they got hip to weed, they just climbed out of that rowdy trip. They squared off completely, you know. Wanted to jump sharp, enjoy themselves, and be mellow instead of getting all brutalized. That is definitely true. You don't hear much about gang fighting anymore even. People getting hip to weed.

The early outlines of a primitive system of drug distribution begins to emerge among the group of "cooler little dudes" around eleven or twelve years of age; however, the main source of marihuana comes from older relatives and friends in the neighborhood. Once in a while, a youngster will have access to an ounce of marihuana, which he distributes among his friends, but, for the most part, continuous access to marihuana symbolizes the *coming of age* in ghetto. That is, a little dude "grows up" when he can "get loaded on weed" at will and participate in the round of life typical of older cats. If he is "fortunate" enough to have a "cool" older brother, he will be introduced to marihuana early in the game. Older dudes often "turn on" their younger brothers to prevent them from being arrested. The following comments by a seventeen-year-old dude illustrate the therapeutic value of marihuana in the "treatment" of glue sniffing and rowdy conduct:

> I found out a lot about my little brother sniffing glue, and I used to whip on him thinking he'll hang it up, man. You know, he got busted three times behind glue, and I couldn't reason with him at all, 'cause behind my back he would go sniffing glue with his younger partners who were all in that bag. So I says, if there's anything gonna make him grow up and see the light, it's weed. If he gets loaded, he'll stop sniffing glue and be more cautious. Start the time machine going, see, 'cause if you smoke grass you're bound to be with people that are older and more cool. So I started getting him loaded, and he's never sniffed glue since then, and he's never been busted again.

Drug-use practices among older dudes tend to filter down into the ranks of the emerging cool little dudes, and this diffusion process generates a give-and-take bartering system. Most of the time, a youngster will simply "run across" a "matchbox" (one fifth of an ounce) of marihuana for no more than $5 and more often for nothing, simply as a favor. (This condition is, of course, contingent on the general supply of weed in the area.) He will learn how to clean the contents from seeds and twigs and roll about fifteen "joints." Then he can pass around joints as an expression of friendship and trust, or he can sell the joints to his partners. In either case, the first experience of "turning on" his friends will really make him feel "boss" (superior). He must "have something going" for him; he must "really be into something," in the eyes of his partners.

A demand for marihuana and pills begins to increase with a concomitant growth of the rudimentary give-and-take bartering system among the cooler crowds. Having continuous access to marihuana may alter the way a young dude begins to experience himself. He may like the way grass gives him confidence when he tries to rap to his number one girl: "Hey, baby, what's goin' on. You wanna get high? You sure lookin' fine!" Here the little dude is starting to develop his conversation, and grass is helping him along. Over time, he may learn how to use grass to further advantage. Although everybody in his set seems to be getting high, not everybody can score their own grass. When he gets into high school, if he lives in certain Bay Area cities, he will have to have a "ride" (car) to really make it with his girls. He will also have to get his wardrobe together in mod fashion. This takes money, and money is scarce indeed. If he has made some pocket money by selling joints, and then picks up the enterprising spirit of the hustling world, he will begin to "game a little harder." The attraction of developing a "hustle" combines with the existence of petty dealing opportunities to orient dudes in the direction of hustling:

When you playin' gangster, you hittin' on dudes, just kick ass wherever you be. But then you start playin', you know, you try to jump sharp. Don't be wearing them bell-bottom jeans and actin' crazy. The thing is where you want to be mellow. So I was startin' to get my game together. You try to mack [pimp], or you shoot pool, or you start dealin' a little weed, or whatever. Everybody's got their little game and everybody's got their little front, and you're gonna get sharp.

Getting Your Game Together
Before a dude can make big money, "top dust," he must learn how to "get his game together." He must do "whatever is right." Whatever is right depends on the situation at any instant in time. You have to discover by yourself whatever is right for you. This may mean you have to "blow it" a few times

and get back in the "game." Drug dealing in the urban ghetto fits into the "whatever" dimension; it is right when the opportunity arises, and the individual is "ready."

It is the cool dude coming up on the set who is looking at the older cats, watching closely, listening, knowing that he better hear if he wants to survive as a physical being with a self worthy of respect. He soon learns that dealings in the hustling life are nothing like the amiable transactions among previous friends. To remain in the "fast life," the dude must have audacity, ingenuity, knowledge, skill and "luck."

I was still fighting, you know, but I started to dig weed, you know, and I wanted to have my own. I didn't want to be getting it off somebody all the time. So I began hustling. This cat gives me one connection, and I think I had been smoking dope about two months, you know, and my mind was getting a little advanced, you know. I was starting to game. I just wasn't running with my old partners as much because I got in this bag with this dealer. I mean I was steady talking to him, and I was starting to get deals from him, you know, matchboxes for two and three dollars. Well, one day I fell in, and I burned him. I did it on purpose, you know. I knew he was gonna find out about it, and I just took off two lids. So I come back the next day to see what the come down was gonna be, and he busts me. He says I burned him, and I told him, "Yeah, I burned you." And the dude dug me, you know. He says, "Well, that's all right." But I knew I had to watch him. . . .I was beginning to play now, you know, trying to be slick. I was trying to get myself together.

Getting Slick

The game starts to get cold; competition is keen; and everything a dude has learned "coming up" will be put to the test.

You can't be a so-called hustler now and then find out your game ain't so tight, or your money ain't right, or you don't know nothin' about dealing. Let me school ya' before they fool ya'. A lot of dudes have this here phoney act, tryin' to be dynamic and soulful when they don't have all the moves to back their hand. How you gonna tell the teller and sell the seller? You can't sell the seller shit 'cause he's sellin' you!

So after a while you read 'em, you know where they coming from. You know who to watch, what to say, when to say it, and how to play it. Let me tell ya', Jack. It's a cold game and you gotta be a cold dude. A poop-butt mother-fucker in there dealin' gets pushed aside, fucked over and stomped down.

It's a cold game, man. You got it down to where you don't care about anybody. You're trying to be slick, keeping your game tight, and that's all you care about. You're steady running, dealing some heavy shit, watching, doing a little bit of everything. You're that cold dude, and nobody's gonna mess with you. Whatever you say, they're gonna jump.

If he can remain in the game, a dealer will meet people coming from different directions in the social order. Through his work, he becomes increasingly aware of new opportunities for making money, meeting fine women, and gaining self-respect, respect that is always contingent on his rising prestige and the maintenance of his position in the "fast life." Yet, he discovers that to make money is not quite enough; he must also *show* that he is "qualified." This includes knowing how to "style." To be without sharp "threads" in the latest fashionable style, to be without classy jewelry or an expensive car means you are not ready yet. In addition, as most men know, in any game, "You got to have a *woman* or *women* in your corner." So you use the "dust" made from dealing dope, in order to "catch" yourself a girl, a bitch, a lady, or, if a dude is heavy enough, a full-blown woman. If your game is really together, you might even get a Queen or Star in your corner, and then you are *there*.

When dope is within easy reach and "you got your game up tight," you can deal in *weight*.[4] The heroin market, including the kilo connections, the ounce men, the dealers in cut ounces, the street dealers in $10 bags, the "hypes" who are "strung out," provides the opportunity for making "top dust," but the marketplace in cocaine is the place for the elite. Cocaine dealers move in the jet set of the underworld.

As a member of the elite, the cocaine dealer likes to "get down," likes to "blow," digs "jamming" with "girl" (cocaine), and knows what he can do behind it. His conversation is strong, and his mind is sharp; his game is tight, and he can move all night. He has reached the goal of all dealers in the "fast life," that point where "all you do, man, is lay back and dress n' rest, dress n' rest, man."

The illegal drug market, as it functions in the urban ghetto, may be viewed as a social and economic subsystem interpenetrating with the larger capitalist economy. The spirit of enterprise infuses the hierarchy of distributors and dealers, while consumers invest in and sustain the marketplace activity. The absence of regulations to ensure the manufacturing of quality drugs and the spy system fostered by repressive drug-control policies tend to generate chaos in the market. This makes for a "cold game," where the players and dealers must stand alone in order to survive. Dealing drugs, for many, is the only way to earn a living and still remain a man.

NOTES

1. The research techniques employed are described in more detail in Blumer, et al. (1967). Sutter (1969) presents a more comprehensive depiction of drug-use worlds, into which this analysis fits as one element. The more general ghetto context of social types and activities portrayed here is presented in Hannerz (1969) and Liebow (1967). See also Finestone (1957) and Milner and Milner (1973).

2. Elements of these themes have been presented with sensitivity by Carl Wertham (1967) and Harvey Feldman (1968).

3. See further John Irwin's (1970) treatment of the "disorganized criminal's" world and "state-raised youth."

4. For a fuller treatment of the heroin market in New York, see Prebble and Casey (1969). See also Woodley (1971) for a description of the workday, etiquette, and perspective of a New York cocaine dealer.

References

Blumer, H.; Sutter, A.; Ahmed, S.; and Smith, R. 1967. "The World of Youthful Drug Use." Add Center Project Final Report. Berkeley School of Criminology, University of California.

Feldman, H. 1957. "Ideological Supports to Becoming and Remaining a Heroin Addict." *Journal of Health and Social Behavior* 9 (June): 131-39.

Finestone, H. 1957. "Cats, kicks, and color." *Social Problems* 5 (July): 3,113.

Hannerz, U. 1969. *Soulside: Inquiries into Ghetto Culture and Community.* New York: Columbia University Press.

Irwin, J. 1970. *The Felon.* Englewood Cliffs, New Jersey: Prentice-Hall.

Liebow, E. 1967. *Tally's Corner: A Study of Negro Streetcorner Men.* Boston: Little, Brown.

Milner, C., and Milner, R. 1973. *Black Players.* Boston: Little, Brown.

Prebble, E., and Casey, J. 1969. "Taking Care of Business—The Heroin User's Life on the Street." *International Journal of Addictions* 4 (March): 1-24.

Sutter, A. 1969. "Worlds of Drug Use on the Street Scene." In *Delinquency, Crime, and Social Process.* Edited by D. Cressey and D. A. Ward. New York: Harper and Row.

Wertham, C. 1967. "The Functions of Social Definitions in the Development of Delinquent Careers." The President's Commission on Law Enforcement and Administration of Justice. *Task Force Report: Juvenile Delinquency and Youth Crime,* pp. 155-70. Washington, D.C.: Government Printing Office.

Woodley, R. 1971. "An Introduction to Flash." *Esquire* 75 (April): 79-83.

11

Street Status and Drug Use *

Harvey Feldman

On the evening of 24 March 1969, seven young men from the fictitiously named community of East Highland sat in my field office and listed the various substances with which they and their friends had experimented as a chemical means of getting high. The conversation had the animation of a reunion of baseball old-timers, each eager to contribute some mutually remembered segment of intoxicated glory or some sequence of drug-related error, now laughable in retrospect. The thirty-three substances they mentioned as triggers to autobiographical remembrances had become the core materials of many street activities among young men in the Italian working-class community of East Highland since drugs had been discovered as an alternative to alcohol some twelve years before.

*This work originally appeared in *Transaction/Society* 10, no. 4 (May-June 1973): 32-38.

With few exceptions, the drugs they talked about were the same as those used by the approximately 150 street youth of East Highland whom I had interviewed and observed for four years. Since 1957 when a small group of older adolescents had discovered that Tussar, a cough medicine with a strong component of codeine, produced a high more pleasurable in its intoxicating effects than alcohol and with fewer displeasing side effects, the street pharmacopoeia multiplied so that by 1969 any young man with even a casual interest in the street pastime of drug use had available to him the names, descriptions, and expected sensations of approximately three dozen assorted substances.

All reports indicated that marihuana was clearly the most frequently used substance in East Highland, but any street youth between the ages of fourteen and thirty could describe the distinctive features of the various highs that a panoply of other drugs and narcotics produced. Their knowledge, for the most part, was confined to descriptions of feeling states; and only a few street specialists had conscientiously acquired pharmaceutical sophistication and knew (or even cared) about the legitimate medical usage of each drug.

On the street, amphetamines like benzedrine and dexidrine were comonly known as mild "ups," but a diet pill locally called "black beauties" was stronger and created a nervousness that awakened conversational abilities and left an unwelcome residue of sleeplessness. Any corner boy knew that "beans," the street name for barbiturates—particularly seconals, tuonals, or carbitols—produced an alcohollike drunk without a telltale odor and with none of the hateful side effects of taste, nausea, or headache. Cough medicines, particularly Robitussin AC, induced a lazy comfort and an inexplicable nod that put a quiet gauze on an otherwise noisy and violent environment. For the experienced user of cough medicine, a four-ounce bottle of "Robbin" and a few beans could make sitting in a chair and listening to music a total evening's entertainment. LSD in its colorful variations—Orange Wedge, Blue Flats, Pink Swirl, Blue Owlsey—was a specialty drug reserved for weekends (usually Saturdays) because of the long-lasting effects of shifting colors and objects and the crash that created a nervous irritation that left the user exhausted but unable to sleep.

Opiates, it was commonly known, were injected with a hypodermic needle directly into the vein (no longer sniffed, snorted, or skin-popped) and produced on injection a rush whose description required a poet's facility with superlatives, all followed by a nod that users enthusiastically claimed was superior to the dreamy warmth cough medicine evoked. Even though only a small minority of drug experimenters had chanced the addicting powers of the opiates, most young men in the streets had a conversational familiarity with the methods of purchase and preparation of heroin. They had seen with regularity either friends or older acquaintances after an injection when their faces were slack, eyes half-closed, lazily scratching at invisible bites, and praising the wonders of a "dynamite bag." Fewer young men acquired the same intimate knowledge about other opiates but had heard that morphine, paregoric, dilaudid, and panapon were legitimately manufactured narcotics similar in their physical effects to heroin.

By 1969, drug use had become an integral activity in the street life of East Highland. One of the most frequently expressed opinions among young men in the streets was that the decision to avoid taking drugs was more difficult to make than a decision to use them. According to many respondents, drug use was such a common activity it could be found among members of every street-corner group in the community. One nineteen-year-old drug user claimed, for example, that of all the boys he knew and grew up with, he could name only two who had never used some kind of drug.

Yet when young men would discuss the ways they sifted and sorted through drug experimentation, it became clear that different youth preferred different drugs. On the surface, the process of selecting a preferred drug might seem simple enough. One had merely to experience an assortment of available drugs, carry out a kind of comparative analysis before selecting a high that was suited to the individual's taste—something like sampling multiple flavors of ice cream.

But the choice also took into account the risk factor—interlocking concerns over physical and social risks. Physical

risks were usually attributed to dangerous qualities inherent
in the drugs or narcotics themselves. Yet except for a few
especially well-read users, most young men were carriers of
misinformation. Their stories about the physical damage the
various substances caused the human body (and mind) were
garbled, exaggerated accounts of apparently well intentioned
but uninformed educational efforts from newspapers, television, or from concerned teachers whose aim, according to the
way respondents interpreted the material, was to frighten
young people away from all drug experimentation.

The social risks, perhaps more compelling as a determi-
nant of drug preference than the physical ones, arose from an
individual's realistic recognition that any given drug required
greater or lesser risks in the processes of purchase, distribution, and use. Even more important, he implicitly understood
the social context in which such activities took place. For
choice of drugs reflected the values, beliefs, and routes to
prestige (or loss of it) of young men who must decide where
they would like to fit within the local scheme of things.

Bylaws of Street Society
The East Highland street system offered its participants a
paradoxical sense of fear and protection. The young men (and
not-so-young men) who comprised and perpetuated the street
system became socialized to its unwritten bylaws early in life
through an informal arrangement of implicit directives. Unlike
the middle-class world where changes of college or bureaucratic position created a shifting pattern of relationships that
permitted failure in one period of life to be informationally
buried in a series of recurring fragmented friendships, the
street relationships of East Highland had a fixed, anchored
quality where adult relationships contained the memories of
younger years. The task, then, of every young man in the
streets was to project through actions and words the kind of
self he believed would be locally tolerated, welcomed, or
admired by persons who would know him throughout his life
and would, in the final analysis, be the measure of his worth.

For some, street life began early. Even in elementary-
school years, boys began seeking status positions among street

friends and participated in activities that had embryonic features of toughness, daring, and a willingness to show bravery in the face of pain. As boys grew into early adolescence, the excitement escalated to minor law-breaking activities such as joining friends in stealing cigarettes or vandalizing a school. The shared forbidden activities became the bonds that tied youth together in a sense of solidarity. Commitment to street life became a search for trust among one another both in carrying out exciting activities as well as in sharing intimate knowledge about them.

While the rewards of trust were comforting, within the close network of friends a dangerous undercurrent of competition made group ranking an uncertainty. This competition took the form of several kinds of status assertions, including verbal insult, fighting, and drinking. "Ball-breaking" was the local term for spontaneous verbal attacks that attempted to reduce someone's standing as a man through name-calling and other sarcastic humor. The way in which the intended victim dealt with the ball-breaking attempt—whether he retaliated with counterstatements of equal or superior verbal agility, became embarrassed, or lost his temper—determined the deference his friends showed him.

Fighting was another one of the principal instruments of ranking, since toughness was the most respected personal quality on the streets of East Highland. No youth could permit someone of lower or equal status to insult him, since failure to respond with appropriate action would lower his own status. There was, however, less fighting than the amount of talk about it would indicate. Since it often involved knives and other weapons, the anticipated gain in status had to be worth the risk of severe bodily injury.

Most respondents reported that their first experience with a drug-induced intoxication was not with marihuana but with alcohol. With other street boys as witnesses, a youth could demonstrate that he had flaunted prohibitions of law and family rule by daring an act denied him by reason of age. He did not need special qualities of physical strength; he did not have to pit skill or muscle against someone where defeat or victory might have lowered or raised his standing. He needed only to have an orientation and endurance to force down sufficient amounts of alcohol, and then wait for the intoxicating effects. Drinking was a street game anyone could play.

Hierarchy of Local Social Types

As he grew older, tests of manliness became part of the repertoire of activities that began to divide a youth's loyalties between insiders and outsiders. Those whose actions declared loyalty to the street became insiders, while police symbolized the opposition of outsiders. Loyalty to friends upheld in the face of personal disadvantages (such as arrests and police brutality) contributed to prestige. If the test for gaining entry had been successfully passed, even on a minimal basis, the youth was designated a "solid guy." He might have failings, but he could be trusted by other insiders even though he might hold low social ranking within the street-status scheme. In group actions, the solid guy would be depended on for support in illegal activities, defenses against outsiders, and pledged to an informal code of secrecy from parents and police. Aspirants to the solid-guy role could be charted on a continuum from low to high status:

"Faggots" constituted the lowest ranking in the status hierarchy. The designation did not refer to any homosexual aberration but merely to the individual's inability to manage manly actions. They were either physically weak or displayed inordinate fears and were unable to protect themselves from verbal or physical abuse from others. Most frequently, they hung out on the fringes of the street group.

The status of "asshole" or "jerk" was similarly low, but it was more a temporary designation, situationally induced. He might have put himself in a position where someone of equal status had outwitted him or reduced his manly claims. His failure to take action against an offender and his acceptance of humiliation without recourse to violence diminished the respect others might otherwise grant him. Under such circumstances, the individual became a figure of scorn.

The middle-ground position had no locally designed label, and I have called a youth in this status position simply "solid guy" (garden variety). He had sufficient qualitites of strength or daring to enable him to manage all other youth on the faggot/ asshole/jerk levels. He might lack physical qualitites of coordination or strength that would help him rise to a high position in the status hierarchy, but his willingness to chance daring behavior or to fight bigger and stronger opponents, even though losing was inevitable, demonstrated his courage. In the language of the street, he "had balls."

"Tough guys," for the most part, met and passed local tests of strength with a minimum of effort and seemed to have natural physical qualities of speed, stamina, and tenacity. They frequently fought opponents who were three or four years older or opponents whose high status had been generally recognized. In doing so, they developed a street reputation when they performed respectably or, in some outstanding cases, actually won. Some tough guys searched out situations that enhanced their street reputations, bringing with them an audience of friends who took the core truth and embroidered folktales of their strength. Others preferred a less hostile existence than their followers thrust on them. What held true, in either case, was the determination to avoid being con- sidered an asshole or a jerk in any situation that could be clarified with a fight.

"Crazy guy" was the highest rank. He was someone who conscientiously strived for a reputation that extorted fear and respect for his capacity to fight with such ferocity and brutality that inflicting physical pain or injury on his victims had little concern for him. His terms of battle were uncondi- tional surrender and total victory in which he used whatever means he had available: knives, broken bottles, bricks, lead pipes, pool cues, guns. Although his face-to-face relationships might be restricted to his own street-corner group, stories of his actions became widespread and legendary.

The crazy guy had a unique sociological function within the street system. To the individuals who surrounded him, apparent disregard of danger to himself gave him an air of heroism, a sense of being slightly larger than life. By the time his reputation as "crazy" had been secured he had chalked up a series of arrests; he might have survived one or two stabbings himself or have been on the receiving end of a shooting and converted injury into victory. As a hero, he was no distant gladiator performing in Madison Square Garden. He was local, and his victories had proximity. For young men growing up in a neighborhood where the code of the streets made toughness and risk-taking a necessity, these top-level solid guys were symbolic of the latent belief that with enough daring, enough masculine confidence, enough "balls," an individual—even one with humble physical qualifications—could master a threatening environment.

Street Hierarchy of Drugs and Narcotics

Just as individuals in the East Highland street system were ranked according to their willingness and ability to engage in risk-taking activities, there existed as well an unstated but identifiable hierarchical order of the drugs and narcotics in current use. By 1969, the collective experience with drugs had been distilled sufficiently for each person to recognize intuitively that the use of any given substance would thrust the user into higher and lower levels of risk. At the time of the study, street youth had developed a rational consensus on the relative dangers of the various substances available to them, not necessarily as the result of a planned, conscious effort but from the observable consequences of their own activities, their friends, and the local folktales of neighborhood drama.

The street ranking of drugs appeared to be based on five components of risk: 1) real or imagined physical dangers, 2) addiction potential, 3) chances of parental discovery, 4) potential for police harassment and/or arrest, and 5) competitive dangers from other drug users (see Table).

The principle governing an individual's drug preference was the relationship of his status in the street system to the drug's local ranking. Top-level solid guys, if they used drugs at all, preferred high risk ones that would be in keeping with their established reputations. The street reputations they had developed through other forms of risk-taking adventures were the credentials that permitted them to manage the difficulties associated with their drug selection. Similarly, for the young man aspiring to a top-level street position, his selection of a high-risk drug would provide an indicator of where in the

Table 11-1

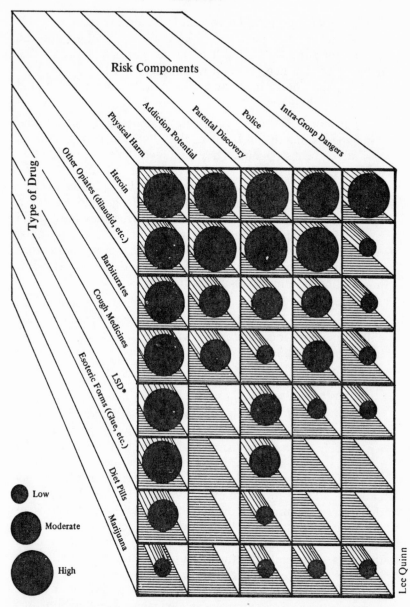

*Methedrine or "speed" was also used, but only rarely and by just a few LSD users. In 1968, its importance as a preferred drug was minimal. It was considered, however, to have great potential for physical harm but no risk in other areas.

hierarchy of solid guys he wished to locate himself.

Not everyone, however, had the qualifications for the successful pursuit of a top-level street position. Before using heroin, for instance, a youth would be required to assess his own capabilities to meet and overcome the risks associated with that substance.

For many solid guys, chancing the possibility of physical damage was one of the features that distinguished them from less adventurous friends. They managed the risk of addiction by believing that friends might develop heroin habits but they themselves had the inner resources of strength (as demonstrated in other street activities) to challenge and master a chemical competitor. They generally believed that they could successfully manage concealing use of heroin from parents. And if by chance parents uncovered their secret, users were in varying states of readiness to withstand the punishment, humiliation, or familiar disappointment.

Frequently, solid guys who moved into heroin use had had previous encounters with police and viewed agents of law enforcement as incompetent, corrupt, or cruel. In any case, heroin users believed they could outwit police, use influence (financial or political) to avoid arrest and conviction, or (other things failing) face the brutal tactics of the stationhouse and its aftermaths with a show of bravado and a legalistic coolness. The very fact of receiving special public attention from law-enforcement agents heightened both the adventure associated with heroin use and the user's claim to high street status. The more dangerous and most frequent risks, however, came from other seasoned heroin addicts whose recurring need for money had molded a multitude of exploitive skills so that even among themselves the phrase "never trust a junkie" was indicative of the desperate quality of their day-to-day activities.

If a street youth believed that he was unable to manage the risks, especially the intragroup dangers, he scaled down his selection of a preferred drug to a level that matched his abilities. One drug user, in explaining why he did not advance to heroin use after extensive involvement with barbiturates and cough medicines, analyzed his hesitancy not in terms of the dangers of the drug but within the context of the competition and style of the players, "The movement was too fast. It was a bigger league, like jumping from the Pony League into the majors. And I wasn't ready for that." Although the actual physical harm of barbiturates—brain damage, overdose, withdrawal seizures—was considerably higher than the opiates, most street users were unfamiliar with the scientific facts. They believed, nonetheless, that any illegal drug use—except perhaps marihuana—had its moral payoff in physiological deterioration. Without knowing the specifics, drug users sincerely subscribed to the belief that in the grand scheme of just rewards, evil behavior seldom went unpunished. The street expectation of physical decay was summed up in the view that drugs "gotta fuck you up somehow."

Except for a small minority of users dependent on barbiturates, most youth did not worry as much about addiction to "beans" as they did about heroin. Even with visible examples of barbiturate addicts, users attributed the cause of the addiction to the psychological makeup of the user rather than to the chemical property of the drug itself.

One of the major advantages of barbiturates was their easy concealment from parental discovery, since they lacked the telltale odor of alcohol. As one user who managed to keep all of his street behavior from his family explained: "Like they say, you can't smell nothing and everything. That's like a plus there in itself. If you want to go home, you know, they can't smell anything on your breath. You say you didn't have nothing to drink." Unless a user became careless and left pills around his house or if his parents had benefited from some of the educational material directed to identifying symptoms of drug use, he could conceal his barbiturate consumption almost indefinitely.

For the run-of-the-mill barbiturate user who was not involved in dealing, the risk of his arrest was also less than the heroin user's. With heroin, an addict might spend as many as eighteen hours a day in various illegitimate activities that put him in legal jeopardy. The barbiturate user, on the other hand, need not take more than a few minutes to purchase and use his drug. And if he carried additional pills with him for future use, the chances of impending arrest could be quickly eliminated simply by swallowing the evidence.

One of the unusual but socially functional consequences of barbiturate consumption was the manner in which it acted as an aid to violent behavior. Users discovered that in fighting off the drowsiness barbiturates induced, they could achieve a relaxed state free from anxiety, guilt, or remorse. An experienced user of barbiturates described his liberation from fear while high on seconals: "It's a sense of freedom from everything that inhibits you, you know. Like fear, you cease to fear. You cease to be anxious about anything. You cease to care, you now. The attitude is, 'Fuck everything.' You know, 'What do I care? So what if I die?' " For a neighborhood like East Highland where fighting proved toughness and provided a route to a high status and prestige, barbiturates could make traveling that route, if not physically less dangerous, at least emotionally less threatening.

Cough medicines were similar to barbiturates in their lower level of risk and acted as an aid to peaceful rather than violent behavior. Most drug users, once again, believed that physical damage from cough medicine resulted from heavy and prolonged use. Since law-enforcement surveillance of drug stores had by 1969 resulted in limited supplies, large amounts of cough medicines were not available so that, in most cases, users were unable to gather a supply sufficient to injure the body or develop dependency. And unless a user were caught at the point of purchase, he seldom ran the risk of arrest since the span of time involved in illegal activity was usually limited to a few moments to drink a four-ounce bottle of cherry-sweet syrup.

What the average street boy needed was a drug whose effects were mildly intoxicating, free of dependence and unpredictable behavioral reactions, and yet could still be viewed as a status assertion worthy of respect. Functionally, marihuana permitted street youth who were hesitant about using hard narcotics to join the illicit fun of drug use. It provided them with a behavioral link to activities that were viewed as exciting, daring, and adventurous. For the youth unqualified to participate in the turmoil of the major leagues of drug consumption, use of marihuana kept him at least on the fringes of the drug activity. In the eyes of his friends he had demonstrated (although minimally) that he was pledged to the new code of the streets.

Because controversy about the effects of marihuana had resulted in public positions in favor of its legalization, the East Highland youth were able to adopt a positive rationale for their choice of marihuana as opposed to other forms of drugtaking. Although it was listed in state and federal statutes as a narcotic, the usual opinion among street youth was that "grass" was relatively harmless, especially when compared to more dangerous drugs other local youth enjoyed. Of special importance, they were convinced that marihuana did not lead to addiction and discomforting withdrawal symptoms. Further, they were aware that the local police would frequently bypass marihuana smokers in favor of arresting heroin addicts. And once the users learned how to enjoy the effects of getting high, they were generally favorably impressed with the light, airy, and congenial sensations the drug induced. In addition, the effects were short-range and easily concealed from family. In fact, a user's increase in appetite frequently made parents believe that a boy had taken a positive step toward good health.

The minimal risk involved in selecting marihuana was illustrated by one respondent, an accepted but lower-ranked solid guy, who explained his rejection of other drugs: "I remember Nate Blane, like talking about seccies [seconals] being hate pills up at my house. And he said, 'How can anybody want to take seconals . . . when you can smoke and feel so good. You take those things and you want to kill everybody and everything.' You know, it [marihuana] seemed like such a nice experience. It makes you happy and everything."

In other aspects of his social interaction, the same boy admitted openly that he avoided fights, exchanged ball-breaking comments with only one heroin user his own age, and was generally respectful of those solid guys who were considered tough or crazy. When he was asked, for example, about the possibility of his exchanging verbal insults with a slightly older solid guy locally defined as crazy (and also a heroin addict), he answered emphatically, "I wouldn't even think of saying anything wrong to *him*." The possibility of dealing with solid guys with similar or superior credentials in the heroin system was even more remote.

On occasion, some drug users would consume substances that were apparently incompatible with their social ranking. How, one might ask, could marihuana use be explained among tough guys and crazy guys? Conversely, what were the chances of faggots, assholes, or jerks having a preference for heroin?

Marihuana use among top-level solid guys at some point in their drug-using careers was frequently reported even though use was intermittent. Unlike findings in other studies, marihuana in East Highland was not "a predisposing influence in the etiology of opiate addiction." Almost all the heroin users in East Highland reported use of both cough medicines and barbiturates prior to use of either heroin or marihuana. If anything, cough medicine would have been the precursory drug to heroin because of the similarity of effect in the nod. Rather, the more seasoned heroin users perceived marihuana as a qualitatively different experience from the opiates. The difference was both in the nature of the feeling state and in the level of risk. In either case, top-level solid guys looked on marihuana with the contempt or indifference of a heavyweight contender watching a boxing match at the neighborhood boy's club. One crazy guy, in reflecting on his earlier use of marihuana, claimed he resented the way it "made me silly." And a respected tough guy who was addicted to heroin viewed marihuana as nothing more than an amusing fill-in for empty time.

On the other hand, the most serious difficulty a lowly ranked solid guy faced when using heroin was to have others respond to him as meriting the street respect that heroin users from higher ranked solid guys normally commanded. One young man who had been placed in the faggot role, for example, genuinely attempted to join in heroin use. In all other aspects of his street life he was generally inept, uncertain, and frightened. A report from one of his street-corner associates illustrated total disrespect for him although the respondent's comments were flavored with mild but fleeting sympathy:

The other night he [the faggot] comes up. There's a kid selling rockets, right. So, something like $5 you could get a dozen of them. So [he] doesn't want to buy a whole dozen, you know. He didn't wanna waste the $5 'cause he knew everybody was gonn take 'em from him. So, he went home for a minute. When he come back out everybody threw fuckin' garbage at him. Boots, big, big bags of garbage, and shit. Right. Watermelon skins, papers, newspapers, cans. Like we just pelted him with everything, you know. Like that's pretty rotten like. How do you think the kid's gonna feel?

When he attempted to move into even minimal heroin experimentation, more confident street users aborted his efforts. Too frightened to make his own illegal purchases, he gave his money to others who in turn simply kept it, an act the street youth in East Highland called "getting beat." Possessing neither the physical attributes of strength nor the emotional will to injure, he suffered his loss with mild complaints. All of his friends agreed that his efforts to use heroin were laughable. By being identified as a failure in street life, he was unable to launch a career in heroin use.

Beneath all efforts to manage the drug problems in the United States—whether attempts to mobilize treatment services or to change public policy—there lies an articulated or implied theoretical explanation of the cause of youthful drug experimentation. Almost everyone, regardless of institutional or professional affiliation, has concentrated on the psychic flaws of individual users. But it is important to move away from an emphasis on the individual in isolation and more toward viewing young men as active agents who make choices regarding use of drugs within the social context of neighborhood life. In fact, the rise of drug use among blue-collar youth can best be understood as an extension of a street system rather than as an escape from it. Rather than viewing drug use as a retreat, it might more accurately be described as one of the important activities in sustaining and enhancing a street reputation that is admired and respected by persons who have a stake in the street system.

By employing a street perspective for the analysis of

differential drug preferences, the portrait of heroin users appears to differ sharply from the usual descriptions. Under the lens of psychoanalytic investigation, they appear to be nothing more than a composite of pathological traits— suspicious, hostile, lonely, frightened. In this respect, they may not differ markedly from nonheroin-using youth in their home community where the potential for violence and exploitation are everyday realities.

What apparently has escaped the scrutiny of psychiatrically oriented practitioners are the positive qualities of creativity, daring, and resourcefulness that provide the impetus for the top-level solid guys to rise to the top of the street hierarchy. Rather than retreating from the demands of their environment, they utilize the risks of heroin use to insure (or strive toward) a leadership position. Their use of heroin solidifies a view of them as bold, reckless, criminally defiant— all praiseworthy qualities from a street perspective. Rather than undermining their influence, efforts to limit their heroin use through legal sanctions merely serve to secure or enhance their status positions on the streets by providing them with opportunities for risk-taking adventures that previous generations of solid guys never knew or even imagined.

12

Drug Pushers: A Collective Portrait *

Richard H. Blum

"Get the dealer!" That is the cry today as the demands for change in the drug laws erupt on all sides. Soft on the user, hard on the dealer, that is the theme. And why not? Who is more malignant, more evil than the drug peddler? Can there be a criminal more loathed and feared than the pusher who is thought to seduce children into a life of slavery? He is the demon who spreads crime and corruption in the slums, who controls the minds and bodies of others by exploiting the cravings he has himself created. These are the images the drug peddler conjures up in the public mind. The question is, are the images correct? And is the criminal law derived from such conceptions likely to work?

*This work originally appeared in *Transaction/Society* 8, nos. 9-10 (July-August 1971): 18-21. This chapter was originally delivered to the Joint Bureau of Narcotics and Dangerous Drugs—Stanford Conference on Directions for Drug Research, 15-16 December 1970.

In order to answer these questions, we decided to find out
who drug dealers are by studying them. We could conduct only
a limited inquiry, and so we focused on the dealers in the San
Fancisco Bay Area. This report is a preliminary look at some of
our findings, findings based on interviews with just some of the
several thousand drug dealers that our interviewers have met
in the past several years. If that figure is surprising it should
be kept in mind that regular drug users and drug dealers are
the same people. Insofar as one is in contact with users, he is
also in contact with dealers. Out of these thousands, our
interviewers, many of whom were or had been drug dealers
themselves, selected various samples: all regular dealers in
one high school, for example, or all regular dealers in one
college, all in one block of the Haight-Ashbury, those passing
through a London legal-aid group, living in a commune,
and so on. We are also looking at dealing in institutions
and by professionals: in jails, juvenile halls, or psychiatric
wards; and among pharmacists, physicians, and detail men
and among narcotics officers themselves. We also constructed
an intensive sample of 454 Bay Area dealers who were
selected for their variability. That is, after we had interviewed
ten street amphetamine dealers in the Mission District of San
Francisco, we stopped and looked for a different type of dealer
defined by age, race, sex, neighborhood, dealing level, type of
drug, and so forth. We wanted a cross section. As is always
the case with the "dark number" problem in criminology, you
can never tell whether you have achieved a cross section or
not, but we do know we got a variety of dealers regularly
selling for profit, all of whom were interviewed for from two to
twelve hours. What we report here is a preliminary set of
observations.

What were the general characteristics of that intensive
sample of about 450? Most were between 19 and 35, most had
not finished college, about half earned their income only from
drug dealing, most were white, and most came from intact
families where the parents were not criminal, although a
fourth had one or more alcoholic parents. Most of our dealers
had begun drinking in their teens, most had become heavy
tobacco and marihuana smokers before their mid-twenties and

had used narcotics (opiates) by that same age. Nearly half had mainlined speed as well. Almost all had begun illicit use in their teens, receiving a drug from friends and acquaintances. Ten percent of our sample got their first drugs while imprisoned in juvenile halls or jails. The most common circumstances was that the first drug was a gift, not a purchase item. Most, by the way, said they were nervous prior to that initiation, which suggests that they were aware that the first use of a drug is a critical symbolic and social, if not health and legal, matter. By the time of their first actual sale, the majority of these young people said they were no longer nervous about arrest, although about ten percent told us they felt guilty about what they were doing.

We discussed with the dealers whether there was any circumstances that, if it had intervened in their lives, would have prevented them from making their first sale of illicit drugs. Just half replied that there was such a circumstance, and of these the most common reply (by only one-fifth) was that had they, in fact, been apprehended by the police prior to selling, they would have gone no further. We do not know if this is true; it is simply that, retrospectively, a small portion of the dealers felt that if formal and authoritative intervention had occurred early in their lives, it might have given them a different view of things. As it was, they learned and expanded their business, some taking great pride in it, and as of the time of our interviews, fifty-nine percent had yet to experience any sort of drug arrest, whereas fifteen percent had done more than six months' time. Aside from arrest, the most common interfering force of distress reported in connection with their early dealing was when their parents got wind of their drug-selling activities.

At the time of our conversations, thirty-five percent had stopped dealing, of whom about half were sure they would not go back to it. Among those still dealing regularly and for profit, three-fourths had considered quitting. Among those who had quit, as well as those still in business, the fact or fear of arrest looms largest as the reason for getting out. As for other pressures to quit dealing, those come mostly from one's intimates—parents, wives, girl friends, in that order. Some few dealers, less than ten percent, acknowledge moral qualms of their own that militate against peddling drugs. There is something to think about in the fact that even though after their first drug use nearly all recalled nothing but good or euphoric feelings uncontaminated by guilt or nervousness (15 percent to the contrary), after an average of four years of dealing, in addition to the predealing use period, 40 percent are now worried about their own drug use, that is, being dependent or addicted. Add here that two-thirds of the 450 people told of changes they had witnessed in other dealers, which, over time, had included addiction, death, criminalization, social alienation, drug obsession, and other pathological personality developments. Further, one-third of our sample commented that they were afraid of getting hurt, either by the occasional drug-using customer or acquaintance who flew out of control, or in the general rough and tumble of the criminal world.

And with respect to that criminal world, most of the dealers felt things were more violent now than when they had begun in the business. For one thing, more people were using guns. A quarter of our sample themselves carried a gun and half of these report having had occasion to use it. I can testify to the truth of at least some of these comments, having conducted one interview while a bodyguard covered me with a machine gun, and another while a dealer awaited an expected competitor's raid, a "ripoff" attempt, with a shotgun at hand.

The foregoing catalogue of worries indicates that the dealing life is not all roses. A large number of dealers are also concerned that their arrest or addiction or murder would make their families feel badly. With regard to that awareness of risk to others who care for them, we also find that whatever justification they have for their own activities—and it is important to realize that a sense of righteousness and superior morality, if not even religious dedication, characterize part of the drug-using and dealing world—fewer than ten percent would want their own children to be drug dealers. This stands in contrast to their feelings about the children's limited drug use, however: eighty percent would allow their children marihuana, two-thirds LSD, but only one-fifth would allow their children speed and thirteen percent heroin.

Let us turn now to dealers' views and reactions to the police, the laws, and to policy. Asked if an effective police could force them out of business, less than ten percent said they could. Dealers felt the drug business was too large and too well established ever to be eliminated by law enforcement. Some few claimed the police did not wish to stop traffic, others that they were too stupid to do so. The average narc (narcotics agent) was certainly not admired by dealers, and most demeaned his character and skills. Among narcs, the federals were considered most competent, locals least. Asked how to stop illicit traffic, half suggested legalizing drugs. Hitting the major suppliers was the most practical suggestion offered; almost none felt that increased penalties for sale would have any impact.

Only a few are sure that in five years they will still be dealing. Many hope—with varying degrees of realism or candor—to have legitimate jobs. Moreover, only a few are sure their dealing peers will be dealing in ten years; most seem unsure of their future. Although we may question their honesty in these predictions, one should keep in mind that when they describe the status of successful dealers, honesty ranks as the most prestigious characteristic, and being rich comes second. When they describe the personality traits linked to successful dealing, honesty ranks second—after friendliness. Given these very American virtues, the lack of self-identification as a criminal, and the relative youth of our group, why should not we expect many to be maturing cultural conformists going to legitimate endeavors?

At the same time, of course, we should also ask what factors may stand in the way of their moving into honest jobs. Their pleasure in drug use, and sometimes a drug dependency, is one factor; but this should be considered a general psycho-biological liability, for about one-third are also worried about being alcoholics. A second consideration is that they may feel unfit for straight work; about one-third are not sure they could make a living except in dealing. A third factor has to do with the pleasures of dealing; these are strong and include, first, relatively high, tax-free income under what many consider relaxed working conditions. The second-ranked gratification is access to drugs; the third is being with people they like.

Fourth ranked is the excitement of it. All in all, about half say it would be difficult to get out of dealing. As outsiders, we might also wonder, if as barriers to the straight life and attractions of the dealing one, personality disabilities may not play a role. We did not test this sample but did ask some basic questions and did some ratings. On the basis of these, I estimate that more than a quarter of this sample would be characterized, if seen psychiatrically, as having very serious personal problems.

One step in our data analysis was to create subgroups, comparing, for example, arrested with nonarrested, or younger with older dealers. Let me here refer only to findings when we compare those now dealing with those who have quit. A finding, by the way, is a statistically significant difference.

Those who have quit dealing were more often recruited for the study via the police or because they were in prison. Compared with those still dealing they are less well educated, are more often habitual criminals, come from lower socio-economic groups, having siblings with criminal histories, and themselves have more opiate and cocaine and less hallucin-ogen use. They began illicit drug use earlier and in the company of older lads.

The picture we get is of the more typical poor delinquent, the same fellow who emerges as a type when we compare those dealers arrested with those not arrested. It is for him that, realistically, the fear of arrest looms the greatest as a deterrent in limited dealing. One reasons that those who have quit dealing appear to do so primarily because they are arrest vulnerable and that vulnerability arises for many as soon as they begin dealing—although it is also a function of increasing exposure over time. It is among this group and among dealers who retire at public request that there is the greatest complaint about their suffering nervousness, being paranoid, disliking the rise in violence in the trade, and the fact that their customers tend to be heroin-using delinquents among whom police informants are readily recruited. Lest we be deluded into thinking that stopping drug dealing means going straight, consider that only slightly more than half are not earning some illicit income and those who are not include those in jail. Several in jail, by the way, are still active dealers.

That there is an attraction in resuming dealing can be understood when we learn that among those in the "having quit" group, one-fifth had been making over $1,000 per month as dealers. Note that this is not the group who consider themselves professional dealers or criminals; the professionals are among those who do not get caught. Since paradox is good for the mind, consider further that the people in this temporarily retired group are the most conventional in some ways; they are church members, want to settle down, want a straight job, are most strongly against any drugs for their children, seem least critical of the police, have the least interest in seeing drug laws abolished, and so on. This opiate-using, opiate-dependent, and opiate-selling group is, by the way, most in favor of keeping penalties for opiate sales.

Dealer Deterrence

What do these finding suggest about the control of illicit drug sales? First, enforcement does deter some dealing, especially for the arrest-vulnerable group; that is, the unsophisticated lower-class opiate user. The permanency of that deterrent is in doubt if we take our peddlers at their word; only some are sure they are permanently out of the business. On the other hand, even those converted by the sword—if not the scales—of justice, are generally agreed that law enforcement cannot eliminate drug dealing per se. We have heard their arguments as to why. There is other evidence as well, whether we look at fifty years of international treaty impotence, the rising rate of illicit use in spite of law-enforcement endeavors, or at the report of two-thirds of our sample that they have never had a sales slowdown due to insufficient drug supplies.

A second point is that among the less, as well as among the more conventional dealers—and the former are less vulnerable, higher class, less opiate-interested group—there are internal forces that do oppose drug dealing. These are moral forces elucidated more often by parents and wives than by dealers themselves—except when these young dealers contemplate their own children and begin to think as their own parents do when in that role. There are health factors, too, if we consider dependency fears to be a mix of mental and physical health concerns; and there are physical fears, especially in association with violence.

Pitted against these deterring factors are the attractions. Dealers use drugs and like them; most see only a minority of users suffering ill effects and the majority of users enjoying benefits. There are additional considerations that to be a dealer is to insure a supply of drugs, possibly to make lots of money, often to lead a happily undisciplined life with like-minded peers, and to accommodate to, if not to act out, whatever psychopathology is present.

Third, if deterrence is to be invoked, let it come early rather than late—whether by the police or by other authoritative intervention—and I include family here. It should come before regular drug use and subsequent dealing begins. Essentially, this is an argument for early case identification. Occasionally, deterrence, late in life by means of imprisonment, may be effective—and this comes from a few of our interviews plus extrapolation from other studies indicating that the sociopath can eventually tire of the hassle and long years in the bucket, being the burned-out case.

Fourth, to be effective, deterrence may require a preexisting receptivity in the dealer who does, in fact, accept the precept that the law is right; that is, drugs are primarily immoral and in addition, sometimes unsafe. That moral acceptance may be more common than the modern rhetoric hints, given the forces contravening drug use internal even to individuals among the "liberated" classes.

Fifth, one should entertain the possibility that among the middle and upper class, dealing may well be a self-terminating activity. That proposition rests not at all on our evidence of who terminates, but only on the uncertainty of dealer predictions about the future, the apparent drift toward the straight world—and the straight world's democratic drift to the psychedelic—and on the accumulation of jaundiced experience that seems to accompany staying in the dealing game.

Sixth, we should face up to the fact that much dealing will continue without bothering us because it is, as the Taoists would say, harmonious. That is, it is done discreetly by and among fairly sophisticated people who enjoy drugs without being sick, violent, or annoying. When so conducted, the police give it a rather low priority, if they know about it at all, and the community life moves along without disruption from either dealers or the law.

Seventh, much of our future rational effort regarding law-enforcement intervention in drug distribution will likely focus on a kind of case finding predicated on predictions as to what kind of users will make trouble, that is, pose a fiscal or moral emotional cost burden. Those who do—defined, I suspect, in terms of criminality, ill health, or indiscrete deviation—will be busted. Those who do not will not be. As for the suggestion by dealers and the sophisticated Bureau of Narcotics and Dangerous Drugs leadership that there be intervention at the top—hitting the biggest pushers—the tactics cannot be faulted. The strategic question here is a dynamic one linked to substitution. We must ask when one dealer is out, how many are in line to replace him; when one drug is out, how many are in line to replace it; and when one producing country is out, how many are poised to start planting?

Certainly, research should focus on substitution phenomena. It should examine the who, how, and how long of the replacement of dealer components in the marketing system as enforcement removes one and then another. It would study the replacement of one drug by another in the pharmaceutical bazaar, attending to cost and availability, as well as to individual acceptance of substituted products as controls become effective over a given substance. It would also examine the substitution of one region or country for another, as in response to international efforts, agricultural, and industrial production is subject to supervision. One wants to be able to predict which farmer Akbar Smith will move into the breach opened by the departure of farmer Guillermo Jones. Substitution studies are not unlike the cost effectiveness analysis of John Kaplan's recent book, *Marihuana, The New Prohibition*, which, when analyzing marihuana law enforcement, concludes that enforcement is just not worth it.

We might also ask to what extent our own policymaking rejection of the criminal law and its uses are, as applied to drugs in particular and vice in general, tied in hidden ways to our own unavowed punitiveness, fears of aggression, fantasies of pleasure, or joy in rebellion against authority. To ask is not to answer but I think we should keep the psychodynamic questions in mind.

There are other research enterprises to contemplate. We should learn at what age what kinds of people are aware of arrest risks and what effect that awareness has on their using and dealing behavior. We might go on to compare actual programs of maximal law enforcement with actual maximal educational and community organization endeavors in separate but matched communities so that through action research we could identify, within these natural laboratories, the effect of each in interaction with several constellations of family and personal dynamics, age, class, drug exposure, and the like.

Another effort would seek to develop a rational priority system for law enforcement. This, a systems-and-cost-effectiveness study, as well as one of local and regional dynamics, would presume different mixes of benign and malignant drug-user conduct and specific drug effects. It would specify varying levels of community morality and tolerance, of police capability and strategy, and of overall demands on public safety, health, and welfare resources. The product would at the very least be a list of alternatives for local or international agencies indicating the probabilities of achieving x effects at y cost with z side effects. When implementation is weak at best, as it is in the international efforts, there would be more unknowns in the predictions made. Whenever unknowns are great, they would remind everyone involved to be cautious with rhetoric as well as with spending.

Another need arises from our observations on narcs as dealers. We need to identify personnel selection and management procedures within police departments that would assist in making sure that the cops and robbers are not the same people.

I propose that there be an enhanced dedication on all our parts to governmental programs based on realistic estimates of the impact of new policies and programs. Naturally, political power, morals, and emotions will contribute to drug-policy development; yet I submit that we can treat these as factual components as well, coupling them with evaluation, the better to design programs that work with maximum benefit to the commonwealth.

13

The Culture of Civility *

Howard S. Becker and Irving Louis Horowitz

**Deviance and Democracy
in "The City"**

Deviants of many kinds live well in San Francisco—
natives and tourists alike make that observation. The city's
apparently casual and easygoing response to "sex, dope, and
cheap thrills" (to crib the suppressed full title of Janis Joplin's
famous album—itself a San Francisco product) astounds
visitors from other parts of the country who can scarcely
credit either what they see happening or the way natives stroll
by those same events unconcerned.

Walking in the Tenderloin on a summer evening, a block
from the Hilton, you hear a black whore cursing at a

*This work originally appeared in *Transaction/Society* 7, no. 6
(April 1970): 12-19.

policeman: "I wasn't either blocking the sidewalk! Why don't you mother-fucking fuzz mind your own goddamn business!" The visiting New Yorker expects to see her arrested, if not shot, but the cop smiles good-naturedly and moves on, having got her back into the doorway where she is supposed to be.

You enter one of the famous rock ballrooms and, as you stand getting used to the noise and lights, someone puts a lit joint of marihuana in your hand. The tourist looks for someplace to hide, not wishing to be caught in the mass arrest he expects to follow. No need to worry. The police will not come in, knowing that if they do they will have to arrest people and create disorder.

Candidates for the city's Board of Supervisors make their pitch for the homosexual vote, estimated by some at 90,000. They will not be run out of town; the candidates' remarks are dutifully reported in the daily paper, as are the evaluations of them by representatives of S.I.R., the Society for Individual Rights.

The media report (tongue in cheek) the annual Halloween Drag Ball, for which hundreds of homosexuals turn out at one of the city's major hotels in full regalia, unharassed by police.

One sees long-haired, bearded hippies all over the city, not just in a few preserves set aside for them. Straight citizens do not remark their presence, either by gawking, hostility, or flight.

Nudie movies, frank enough to satisfy anyone's curiosity, are exhibited in what must be the largest number of specialty movie houses per capita in the country. Periodic police attempts to close them down (one of the few occasions when repression has been attempted) fail.

The items can be multiplied indefinitely, and their multiplicity demands explanation. Most cities in the United States refuse to let deviants indulge themselves publicly, let alone tolerate candidates who seek their bloc votes. Quite the contrary. Other cities, New York and Chicago being good examples, would see events like these as signs of serious trouble, omens of a real breakdown in law enforcement and deviance control, the forerunner of saturnalia and barbarian takeover. Because its politicians and police allow and can live with activities that would freak out their oppositie numbers elsewhere, San Francisco is a natural experiment in the consequences of tolerating deviance. We can see from its example what results when we ignore the warnings of the custodians of conventional morality. We can see, too, what lessons can be learned about the conditions under which problems that perhaps lie deeper than matters of morals or life-style can be solved to the satisfaction of all the parties to them.

A Culture of Civility

We can summarize this low-key approach to deviance in the phrase "a culture of civility." What are its components, and how does it maintain itself?

San Francisco prides itself on its sophistication, on being the most European of American cities, on its picturesque cosmopolitanism. The picturesque quality, indeed the quaintness, rests in part on physical beauty. As the filling of the Bay and the destruction of the skyline by high-rise buildings proceeds to destroy that beauty, the city has come to depend even more on the presence of undigested ethnic minorities. It is as though San Francisco did not wish its Italians, Chinese, or Russians to assimilate and become standard Americans, preferring instead to maintain a panoply of ethnic differences: religious, cultural, and culinary (especially culinary). A sophisticated, livable city, on this view, contains people, colonies, and societies of all kinds. Their differences create a mosaic of life-styles, the very difference of whose sight and smell give pleasure.

Like ethnic minorities, deviant minorities create enclaves whose differences add to the pleasure of city life. Natives enjoy the presence of hippies and take tourists to see their areas, just as they take them to see the gay area of Polk Street. Deviance, like difference, is a civic resource, enjoyed by tourist and resident alike.

To enjoy deviance instead of fearing it requires a surrender of some common-sense notions about the world. Most people assume, when they see someone engaging in

proscribed activity, that there is worse to come. "Anyone who
would do that (take dope, dress in women's clothes, sell his
body, or whatever) would do anything" is the major premise of
the syllogism. "If you break one law or convention, who knows
where you'll stop." Common sense ignores the contrary cases
around us everywhere: professional criminals often flourish a
legionnaire's patriotism; housewives who are in every other
respect conventional sometimes shoplift; homosexuals may be
good family providers; some people, who habitually use the
rings from poptop cans to work the parking meter, would not
dream of taking dope, and vice versa. "Deviance," like
conforming behavior, is highly selective. San Francisco's
culture of civility, accepting that premise, assumes that if I
know that you steal or take dope or peddle your ass, that is all I
know. There may be more to know; then again, there may be
nothing. The deviant may be perfectly decent in every other
respect. We are often enjoined, in a generalization of
therapeutic doctrine, to treat other people as individuals; that
prescription comes nearer to being filled in San Francisco than
in most places in the United States.

Because of that tolerance, deviants find it possible to live
somewhat more openly in San Francisco than elsewhere.
People do not try so hard to catch them at their deviant
activities and are less likely to punish them when caught.
Because they live more openly, what they do is more visible to
straight members of the community. An established canon of
social psychology tells us that we find it more difficult to
maintain negative stereotypes when our personal experience
belies them. We see more clearly and believe more deeply that
hippies or homosexuals are not dangerous when we confront
them on the street day after day or live alongside them and
realize that beard plus long hair does not equal a drug-crazed
maniac, that limp wrist plus lisp does not equal child molester.

When such notions become embodied in a culture of
civility, the citizenry begins to sense that "everyone" feels that
way. We cannot say at what critical point a population senses
that sophistication about deviance is the norm, rather than a
liberal fad. But San Francisco clearly has that critical mass.
To come on as an antideviant, in a way that would probably

win friends and influence voters in more parochial areas, risks being greeted by laughter and ridicule in San Francisco. Conservatives who believe in law and order are thus inclined to keep their beliefs to themselves. The more people keep moralistic notions to themselves, the more everyone believes that tolerance is widespread. The culture maintains itself by convincing the populace that it is indeed the culture.

It gets help from public pronouncements of civic officials, who enunciate what will be taken as the collective sentiment of the city. San Francisco officials occasionally angle for the conservative vote that disapproves licentiousness. But they more frequently take the side of liberty, if not license. When the police, several years ago, felt compelled to close the first of the "topless joints," the judge threw the case out. He reasoned that Supreme Court decisions required him to take into account contemporary community standards. In his judgment San Francisco was not a prudish community; the case was dismissed. The city's major paper, the *Chronicle*, approved. Few protested.

Similarly, when California's leading Yahoo, Superintendent of Public Instruction Max Rafferty, threatened to revoke the teaching credentials of any San Francisco teacher who used the obscene materials listed in the standard high-school curriculum (Eldridge Cleaver's *Soul on Ice* and LeRoi Jones's *Dutchman*), the City did not remove the offending books from its curriculum. Instead, it successfully sued to have Rafferty enjoined from interfering in its operation.

In short, San Franciscans know that they are supposed to be sophisticated and let that knowledge guide their public actions, whatever their private feelings. According to another well-known law of social psychology, their private feelings often come to resemble their public actions, and they learn to delight in what frightens citizens of less civil cities.

We do not suggest that all kinds of deviation are tolerated endlessly. The police try, in San Francisco as elsewhere, to stamp out some vices and keep a ceiling on others. Some deviance frightens San Franciscans, too, because it seems to portend worse to come (most recently, users and purveyors of methedrine—"speed merchants" and "speed freaks"—whose

drug use is popularly thought to result in violence and crime).
But the line is drawn much farther over on the side of
"toleration" in San Francisco than elsewhere. A vastly wider
range of activities is publicly acceptable. Despite the wide
range of visible freakiness, the citizenry takes it all in stride,
without the fear and madness that permeates the conventional
sectors of cities like Detroit, Chicago, New York, Washington,
D.C., and similar centers of undaunted virtue.

Madames and Unionists

How does a culture of civility arise? Here we can only
speculate, and then fragmentarily, since so few cities in the
United States have one that we cannot make the comparisons
that might uncover the crucial conditions. San Francisco's
history suggests a number of possibilities.

It has, for one thing, a Latin heritage. Always a major
seaport, it has long tolerated that vice that caters to sailors
typical of such ports. It grew at the time of the gold rush in an
explosive way that burst through conventional social controls.
It ceded to its ethnic minorities, particularly the Chinese, the
right to engage in prostitution, gambling, and other activities.
Wickedness and high living form part of the prized past every
"tourist" city constructs for itself; some minor downtown
streets in San Francisco, for instance, are named for famous
madames of the gold-rush era.

Perhaps more important, a major potential source of
repressive action—the working class—is in San Francisco
more libertarian and politically sophisticated than one might
expect. Harry Bridges's longshoremen act as bellwethers. It
should be remembered that San Francisco is one of the few
major American cities ever to experience a general strike. The
event still reverberates, and working people who might
support repression of others know by personal experience that
the policeman may not be their friend. Trade unionism has
left-wing, honest base that gives the city a working-class
democracy and even eccentricity, rather than the customary
pattern of authoritarianism.

Finally, San Francisco is a town of single people.
Whatever actual proportion of the adult population is married,

the city's culture is oriented toward and organized for single people. As a consequence, citizens worry less about what public deviance will do for their children, for they do not have any and do not intend to, or they move from the city when they do. (Since there are, of course, plenty of families in the city, it may be more accurate to say that there are fewer white, middle-class families, that being the stratum that would, if family-based, provide the greatest number of complaints about deviance. Black, chicano, and Oriental populations ordinarily have enough to worry about without becoming guardians of public morality.)

The Place to Live

San Francisco is known across the country as a haven for deviants. Good homosexuals hope to go to San Francisco to stay when they die, if not before. Indeed, one of the problems of deviant communities in San Francisco is coping with the periodic influx of a new generation of bohemians who have heard that it is the place to be: the beatnik migration of the late fifties and the hippie hordes of 1967. But those problems should not obscure what is more important: that there are stable communities of some size there to be disrupted. It is the stable homosexual community that promises politicians 90,000 votes and the stable bohemian communities of several vintages that provide both personnel and customers for some important local industries (developing, recording, and distributing rock music is now a business of sizable proportions).

Stable communities are stable because their members have found enough of what they want to stay where they are for a while. If where they were proved totally unsatisfying, they presumably would move elsewhere, unless restrained. But no one forces deviants to live in San Francisco. They stay there because it offers them, via the culture of civility, a place to live where they are not shunned as fearsome or disgusting, where agents of control (police and others) do not regard them as unfortunate excrescences to be excised at the first opportunity. Because they have a place to stay that does not harass them, they sink roots like more conventional citizens: find jobs, buy houses, make friends, vote, and take part in political activities and all the other things that solid citizens do.

Sinking roots stabilizes deviants' lives, as it does the lives of conventional citizens. They find less need to act in the erratic ways deviants often behave elsewhere, less need to fulfill the prophecy that because they are deviant in one respect they will be deviant in other, more dangerous ways. San Francisco employers know that homosexuals make good employees. Why not? They are not likely to be blackmailed by enterprising hustlers. The police seldom haul them off to jail for little reason or beat them because they feel like pushing some "queers" around. Homosexuals fear none of this in San Francisco, or fear it much less than in most places, and so are less given to the overcompensatory "camping" that gets their fellows into trouble elsewhere.

Police and others do not harass deviants because they have found, though they may deny it for public relations purposes, that looking the other way is sometimes a good policy. It is easier, when a be-in is going on, to turn your back on the sight of open marihuana smoking than it is to charge into the crowd and try to arrest people who will destroy the evidence before you get there, give you a hard time, make a fool of you, and earn you a bad press—and have no conviction to show for it. At the same time, when you turn your back, nothing worse is likely to happen: no muggings, no thefts, no rapes, no riots. Police, more calculating than they seem, often choose to reach just this kind of accommodation with stable deviant communities.

The accommodation works in circular fashion. When deviants can live decent lives, they find it possible to behave decently. Furthermore, they acquire the kind of stake they are often denied elsewhere in the present and future structure of the community. That stake constrains them to behave in ways that will not outrage nondeviants, for they do not want to lose what they have. They thus curb their activities according to what they think the community will stand for.

The community in turn, and especially the police, will put up with more than they might otherwise, because they understand that nothing else is forthcoming, and because they find that what they are confronted with is not so bad after all. If homosexuals have a Halloween Drag Ball, the community discovers it can treat it as a good-natured joke; those who are offended discover that they need not go near the Hilton while it is happening.

No doubt neither party to such a bargain gets quite what he would like. Straight members of the community presumably would prefer not to have whores walking the downtown streets, would prefer not to have gay bars operating openly. Deviants of all kinds presumably would prefer not to have to make any concessions to straight sensibilities. Each gives up something and gets something, and to that degree the arrangement becomes stable, the stability itself something both prize.

Deviance and Democracy

What we have just described verges on the idyllic, Peace and Harmony in Camelot forever. Such a dream of perfection does not exist in San Francisco, though more deviants there have more of the advantages of such a bargain, perhaps, than in any other city in the United States. Nor is it clear that the system we described, even in its perfect form, would be such an idyll.

In San Francisco, as everywhere, the forces of decency and respectability draw the line somewhere and can be every bit as forceful and ruthless the other side of that line as the forces of decency and respectability anywhere else. When the Haight-Ashbury got "out of hand" with the overcrowded transiency of 1967, the city moved in the police Tactical Squad, the City Health Department, and all the other bureaucratic weapons usually used to roust deviants. They did it again with the growth of violence in that area associated with the use and sale of methedrine. In general, the city has responded with great toughness to those deviants it believes will not be satisfied with something "reasonable." In particular, political dissent has sometimes been met with force, though San Francisco police have never indulged themselves on any large scale such as that which made Chicago police internationally detested.

The system has beauty only for those deviants who do not mind giving up some portion of their liberty, and then only if the portion they are willing to give up is the same as what the community wants given up. This no doubt is the reason an accommodative system works well with those whose deviant desires are narrowly circumscribed, and may have less utility with those whose wants can be accommodated only at the expense of others who will not easily give up their privileges. In fact, current political difficulties clearly result from the breakdown of accommodation.

These considerations indicate the more general importance of San Francisco's experiment in tolerating and accommodating to the minor forms of deviance encompassed in sex, dope, and cheap thrills. How can a complex and differentiated society deal with variety and dissent and simultaneously with its own urges for centralized control? An accommodative relationship to difference, in which it is allowed to persist while it pays some minimal dues to the whole, is what San Francisco recommends to us, suggesting that the amount of the dues and the breadth of the license be set where both parties will, for the time being, stand still for it. The resulting working arrangement will be at least temporarily stable and provide for all concerned a tranquility that permits one to go about his business unharmed that many will find attractive.

But is this no more than a clever trick, a way of buying off deviant populations with minor freedoms while still keeping them enslaved? Beneath the rhetoric, the analysis is the same. The more radical statement adds only that the people who accept such a bargain ought not to, presumably because they have, if they only knew it, deeper and more important interests and desires that remain unsatisfied in the accommodative arrangement. So, of course, do those who hold them in check. Perhaps that is the ultimate lesson of San Francisco: the price of civilization, civility, and living together peacefully is not getting everything you want.

Limits of Accommodation

It is tempting to think that an accommodation based on civility and mutual interest provides a model for settling the conflicts now wracking our urban areas. Our analysis suggests that this is a possibility, but no more than that. Peace can occur through accommodation, the example of the potheads and pimps tells us, only under certain not so easily attained conditions. Those conditions may not be present in the ethnic and political problems our major cities, San Francisco among them, are now experiencing.

Accommodation requires, as a first condition, that the parties involved prize peace and stability enough to give up some of what they want so that others may have their desires satisfied as well. But people take that point of view only when the accommodation leaves them enough of a share to want no more. Some urban groups no longer believe that they are getting that necessary minimum, either because they have learned to interpret their situation in a new light or because they have lost some advantages they once had.

Members of black communities may be no worse off than ever, but they are considerably worse off than whites and know it. For a variety of historical reasons, and as a matter of simple justice, some of them no longer regard the little they have as sufficient reason to keep the peace. All the discussion about how many blacks feel this way (is it ten percent or fifty percent?) and how strongly they feel it (are they willing to fight?) is irrelevant to the main point: enough feel strongly to make a lot of trouble for the white community, thus changing the balance of costs to the whites and insisting on a new division of rights as the price of stability.

Some members of white communities probably are objectively worse off and may resent it sufficiently to give up peace and stability in an effort to raise the costs to others and thus minimize their losses. Many whites in civil-service positions, in the skilled trades, and in similar protected occupational positions have lost or are in danger of losing competitive job advantages as governments act to do something about the injustice that afflicts black communities. Without a general expansion of the economy, which is *not* what blacks demand, injustices inflicted on blacks can be remedied only by taking something away from more favorably situated whites. It may be possible to improve the education of poor black children, for instance, only by taking away some of the privileges of white teachers. It may be possible to give black youths a chance at apprenticeships in skilled trades only by removing the privileged access to those positions of the sons of present white union members. When whites lose those privileges, they may feel strongly enough to fracture the consensus of civility.

The deviant communities of San Francisco show us cases in which the parties involved agree in a way that leaves each enough. But that may only be possible when the interests to be accommodated involve morals and life-styles. When those interests include substantial economic prizes, major forms of privilege, and real political power, it may be that nothing less than a real-life assessment of relative intensities of desire and ability to inflict costs on others will suffice. That assessment takes place in the marketplace of conflict.

This suggests a second, more procedural condition for the achievement of urban peace through accommodation and civility. Mechanisms and procedures must exist by which the conflicting desires and resources for bargaining can be brought together to produce a temporarily stable working arrangement. The accommodations of enforcement officials and deviants typically occur in a host of minor bargaining situations. Hassles are settled by the people immediately involved, and settled "on their own merits"—which is to say, in a way that respects the strength of everyone's feelings and the amount of trouble each is prepared to make to have his way. The culture of civility works well because the myriad of separate local bargains respect and reflect what most of the involved parties want or are willing to settle for.

We do not allow ourselves this extreme degree of decentralized decision making with respect to many important problems (though many critics have suggested we should). Instead, we allow federal, state, or city bureaucracies to make general policies that inhibit local accommodation. While government might well intervene when circumstances make bargaining positions unequal, we know now that it is not ordinarily well equipped to reach accommodative agreements that will work at the grassroots. Unable to know what the people who inhabit local areas will want and settle for, officials turn to technocrats for solutions.

Thus, when we confront the problem of slums and urban renewal, we send for the planner and the bulldozer. But the lives of urban residents are not determined by the number or newness of buildings. The character of their relationships with one another and with the outside world does that. Planners and technocrats typically ignore those relationships, and their influence in shaping what people want, in constructing solutions. They define "slums" impersonally, using such impersonal criteria as density or deterioration, and fail to see how awakened group consciousness can turn a "slum" into a "ghetto," and a rise in moral repute turn a "ghetto" into a "neighborhood."

Too often, the search for "model cities" implies not so much a model as an ideology—a rationalistic vision of human interaction that implies a people whose consistency of behavior can nowhere be found. We already have "model cities": Brasilia at the bureaucratic end and Levittown at the residential end. And in both instances, the force of human impulses had to break through the web of formal models to make these places inhabitable. In Brasilia the rise of shantytown dwellings outside the federal buildings made the place "a city," whereas the Levittowners had to break the middle-class mode and pass through a generation of conformity before they could produce a decent living arrangement. To design a city in conformity to "community standards"—which turn out to be little more than the prejudices of building inspectors, housing designers, and absentee landlords—only reinforces patterns of frustration, violence, and antagonism that now characterize so many of America's large cities. To think that the dismal failure of large housing projects will be resolved by their dismal replacement of small housing projects is nonsense. Minibuildings are no more of a solution than maxibuildings are the problem.

In any event, centralized planning operating in this way does not produce a mechanism through which the mutual desires, claims, and threats of interested groups can sort

themselves out and allow a modus vivendi, if one exists, to
uncover itself. The centralized body makes bargains for
everyone under its influence, without knowing their circumstances or wants, and so makes it possible for the people
involved to reach a stable accommodation. But centralized
planning still remains a major solution proffered for urban
problems of every kind.

Accommodations reached through the mechanism of
old-fashioned city political machines work little better, for
contemporary machines typically fail to encompass all the
people whose interests are at stake. Richard Daley demonstrated that when the Chicago ghetto, supposedly solidly under
his control, exploded and revealed some people his famed
consensus had not included. Lyndon Johnson made the same
discovery with respect to opponents of the Vietnam War.
Insofar as centralized decision making does not work, and
interested parties are not allowed to make bargains at the
local level, accommodative stability cannot occur.

So the example of San Francisco's handling of moral
deviance may not provide the blueprint one would like for
settling urban problems generally. Its requirements include a
day-to-day working agreement among parties on the value of
compromise and a procedure by which their immediate
interests can be openly communicated and effectively adjust-
ed. Those requirements are difficult to meet. Yet it may be that
they are capable of being met in more places than we think,
that even some of the knottier racial and political problems
contain possibilities of accommodation, no more visible to us
than the casual tolerance of deviance in San Francisco was
thinkable to some of our prudish forebears.

14

Scapegoating "Military Addicts": The Helping Hand Strikes Again*

Thomas S. Szasz

One of the most clear-cut regularities of social behavior is the scapegoat principle: When things do not go well, people blame the difficulty on individuals or groups who are innocent but defenseless. Through this moral exchange, the scapegoat becomes guilty, and the scapegoater innocent. The persecution of the scapegoat and the ideology and rhetoric that justify it authenticate this moral inversion so irresistibly that the "problem" and its "solution" become obvious or self-evident. To the German people in the 1930s, it was obvious that the Jews were a problem. To Americans today, it is obvious that drug addicts are a problem. These problems and the solutions built into them can thus be challenged only by challenging the ideologies that support them—a task most people, perhaps wisely, prefer to avoid.

*This work originally appeared in *Transaction/Society* 9, no. 3 (January 1972): 4, 6.

In the 1960s, Americans were promised a Great Society. What they got was a Great Mess. Racial troubles. Economic troubles. And then, the inevitable fiasco in Vietnam. Such frustrations create the social climate that typically generates a search for scapegoats. Countless Americans feel frustrated by crime in the streets, unemployment with inflation, a disintegrating educational system, and an interminable land war in Asia. The more helpless they feel vis-à-vis these real but apparently invincible adversaries, the more tempted they might become to turn their rage against an illusory but seemingly more easily conquerable enemy. I believe we are now witnessing the birth of new wave of scapegoating. Unless we halt this process now—and the prospects of this seem dim—it will, I predict, grow rapidly, with results disastrous for scapegoats and scapegoaters alike.

The selection of the scapegoat is largely a matter of cultural circumstances. In Christian countries, the Jews have, for obvious reasons, long served as scapegoats. In the United States after Pearl Harbor, Japanese-Americans were cast in this role. Who will be the scapegoats for the consequences of our accumulated failures and especially for our blunders in Vietnam? They will have to be persons who fulfill our present-day requirements for scapegoats; in short, they must be individuals:

who are politically unorganized and hence unable to defend themselves;
who exhibit characteristics generally regarded as defects or diseases or to whom such defects or diseases must be easily attributable; and
who lend themselves to being persecuted and injured in the name of helping or treating them.

In recent months we have been authoritatively informed, with hardly a serious voice dissenting:

that most Ameican servicemen in Vietnam smoke marihuana;
that vast numbers of them are now using heroin and have become addicted to it;

that the abuse of prohibited drugs is a disease called addiction; and

that this disease has reached epidemic proportions and hence its control justifies and requires the involuntary diagnosis and treatment of those who suffer from it.

Like the Germans after World War I who claimed that their troops were stabbed in the back by pacifists and other "unpatriotic elements" at home, we claim that our troops are being stabbed in the back by heroin and the pushers responsible for supplying it to them.

I shall make no attempt to discuss the pharmacology of so-called habit-forming drugs, or the history, ethics, and politics of drugtaking. There is ample information about all this. Those seriously interested in these facts can and should obtain them. Here I want to do no more than warn of a grave impending danger: of making scapegoats of innocent Americans—mainly servicemen and other young persons; and of letting guilty Americans—mainly politicians and physicians— become inquisitors in a holy war on drug addiction.

I shall frame my warning in the form of four brief questions, and two brief statements.

Question 1: Is the reportedly high incidence (twenty percent and more) of heroin use among American servicemen in Vietnam accurate? Or are these figures deliberately inflated to justify the proposed countermeasures? Are we dealing here with a pharmacological Gulf of Tonkin?

Question 2: President Nixon has announced that "drug abuse" has assumed "the dimensions of a national emergency," and has appointed Jerome H. Jaffe to head a new Special Action Office of Drug Abuse Prevention. Jaffe is a physician and a psychiatrist. Are we to assume, then, that drug abuse is a medical and in particular a psychiatric problem, and that drug addiction is a disease?

Question 3: Dr. Jaffe is considered an expert on drug addiction because, "When he arrived in Illinois in 1966 from the Bronx [reported the New York Times, 18 June 1971, p. 22], there was not a single state-supported bed for the treatment of drug addicts in Illinois. This first year he got 300 beds. Now there are 1,800." Are we to infer from this that drug addicts are sick? Indeed, that they are so sick that they need beds to lie in all day? What is the proper duty of the physician: To create beds for people who do not want to lie in them? Or to offer treatment—in or out of bed—to those who want it, and to those *only*?

Question 4: American troops in Vietnam appear to have a big problem with drugs. We never hear of the Vietcong having a similar problem. Why? Are the Vietcong immune to the "disease" of heroin addiction?

Fact 1: The usual newspaper accounts of the drug problem in Vietnam (and at home) imply that an individual who habitually uses marihuana and/or heroin cannot "function." This is false. Field Marshall Hermann Goering was, while a morphine addict, a competent pilot, host of admiring foreign dignitaries, and second in command of one of the most powerful nations in the world. On a less dramatic scale, we might recall that thousands of Americans were using opium habitually before 1914, and Englishmen before 1920 (these drugs being obtainable then as easily as cigarettes or aspirin are now), and were functioning perfectly well in their customary social roles.

Fact 2: It is repeatedly and authoritatively stated that heroin causes crime. This is also false. Heroin does not cause crime. The prohibition of free trade in heroin does.

In short, as we deescalate against the Vietcong, we escalate against heroin. No doubt, we shall find it easier to control Americans who shoot heroin then Vietnamese who shoot Americans. This is the perennial advantage of fighting scapegoats: they cannot fight back.

15

The Politics of Drugs *

Matthew P. Dumont

The American response to drug abuse demonstrates how a nation both creates and controls anxiety for political purposes. It also demonstrates that repression is possible in a pluralistic system. Both lessons should have been learned long ago. But the knowledgeable left in this country has tormented itself about whether a government can at the same time be incompetent and manipulative, and power both fragmented and persecutive.

Drug-abuse programs partake of the same forces as racism and anticommunism, but being more focused and explicit they offer the observer of American society a perfect laboratory for the study of its social-control capacities.

I have a simple model to offer. Victimization and persecution will take place in a pluralistic society when a confluence

*This work originally appeared in *Social Policy*, July-August 1972. Reprinted by permission.

of vested interests is threatened by a confluence of powerless groups.

Specifically, in the area of drug abuse, we are witnessing a confluence of the usually distinct forces of national politics, social science, medicine, and law enforcement as they perceive a confluence of youth, blackness, and social deviance in the form of drug addiction.

Persecution in this light is not the victimization of an exploited under class by a conspiratorial power elite. Confluent vested interests are not generally aware of their confluence and do not perceive themselves as having malicious or self-serving intentions. The effect of their joint behavior is nonetheless to identify, monitor, isolate, and neutralize individuals whose collective identities are threatening. It amounts to the control of enemies of an established order.

Not long ago President Nixon described drug abuse as "the most serious threat this nation has ever faced." This is a remarkable statement. It is colossally false. It demands attention not so much for itself as for what it portends for the future. It is designed either to divert a nation's anxiety from more palpable and vulnerable concerns or to serve as a distant early warning of some monstrous program.

When illicit drug use was largely confined to urban ghettos, it was not a matter of great national concern. It was a criminal matter without many victims outside the black and poor themselves. As long as that was true, a comfortable symbiotic relationship existed between the drug "problem" and the perfunctory law-enforcement officials assigned to it. Police corruption became rampant. To this day it is a matter of popular wisdom in the ghetto that a black or Puerto Rican drug dealer will be arrested only if he sells to a white purchaser. Racism therefore attempted to protect white America from the "drug menace." But racism was no more functional for this purpose than for any other. Illicit drugs escaped the ghetto and found more affluent and whiter souls responsive to their seductions. Like everything else that emerges from the ranks of an under class, this was perceived with rage and terror by middle America.

The anxiety became focused on heroin, despite the

relatively small role heroin played and still plays in drug abuse. Heroin was called a "killer" and a "hard" drug, while other chemicals were accorded less deference.

In reality, what needs constant emphasis is that heroin, along with the other opiates, is among the most innocent drugs that nature or the mind of man has produced. It is the unpredictability of concentration and quality and contaminated needles that cause the poisonings, overdosages, and infections, but the heroin itself is benign. In any case approximately 1,200 deaths per year are attributed to heroin in New York City. While that makes it a killer of no small determination, there are also 1,200 reported suicides per year. The true number is almost certainly higher by several magnitudes, but suicide has not captured the anxiety of the American public nor provoked the outrage of its leaders. More significantly, in New York City, the "drug capital of America," there are 6,000 deaths each year caused by alcohol. Heroin is not the outrageous killer we are told to believe it is. Indeed, what risks to life it does entail are generally the result of the criminal and clandestine circumstances of its use rather than of the properties of the drug itself.

Even its association with crime is exaggerated. Heavy heroin addicts do indeed need to resort to crime to support their habit. But less than fifty percent of heroin users use it daily; that is, not all users are addicts. And the great majority of addicts rely on shoplifting, drug dealing, prostitution, and breaking and entry for their sustenance. While these are distressing unsocial acts, they are not as serious as murder, rape, and armed robbery, which are less associated with heroin than with alcohol. Even those crimes against property that are the consequence of heroin use would disappear if the laws against heroin use would disappear first.

It has become functional for political leaders to focus the public's concern about crime in the streets onto the drug issue.

By every physical, psychological, and social parameter, barbiturate and amphetamine abuse should warrant at least as much public concern as heroin addiction. But the fact that these chemicals are produced by the most profitable and respectable industry in the nation and are, in large part, distributed by the most prestigious group of people seems to have helped blunt the edge of political indignation.

Identifying Political Victims

Let us look for a moment at the macropolitical environment of this issue. The Nixon administration in particular has generated an ambience about social deviancy that can be epitomized as the "fed-up-to-here" syndrome. It is manifested, for example, in the trial balloon report of Dr. Huntschecker's recommendation to the President that at an early age "delinquency-prone" individuals be identified, segregated, treated, if possible, and, if not, isolated indefinitely.

The statements of Vice-President Agnew are also utilized to plumb the depths of American "fed-upness." In 1970, during a trip abroad, he was quoted as saying:

> There are people in our society who should be separated and discarded. I think it's one of the tendencies of the liberal community to feel that every person in a nation of 200 million people can be made into a productive citizen.

> I'm realist enough to believe this can't be. We're always going to have our prisons; we're always going to have our places of preventive detention for psychopaths; and we're always going to have a certain number of people in our community who have no desire to even fit in an amicable way with the rest of society.

> And these people should be separated from the community, not in a callous way, but they should be separated as far as any idea that their opinions shall have any effect on the course we follow [italics added].

This is a revealing statement not only because of its lucid substance but also because it coincided with a particular course followed by the administration, the "incursion" into Cambodia, which precipitated a new wave of antiwar activity.

It is as ancient as politics itself. Unpopular, deviant, minority populations have been clustered, labeled, and segregated by political leaders for political purposes. They have been blamed for social ailments whose real sources are more deeply embedded in the normative behavior of society. They have been disenfranchised, incarcerated, and at times killed; Sophists, Jews, Christians, Bolsheviks, atheists, the "Yellow Peril," the "foreign, pauper insane," and on and on. The tradition is almost sacred, and at a time of popular unrest when political destinies are at stake those of us left who are concerned with social justice ought routinely to ask, "Who is about to be victimized?"

We need to depart from drug abuse for a moment to emphasize the importance of identifying "prone" individuals. With sophisticated computer programs and large enough samples, the most thoughtless and uncreative social scientists can both win their tenures and destroy what is left of democracy. It is now possible to predict socially dysfunctional behavior in individuals or groups before it takes place. A notable example was a study undertaken in the late 1960s by liberals at the American Council of Education supported by liberals at the National Institute of Mental Health to illuminate what was then a burning social issue, student-protest behavior. The investigation had already determined that very high predictors of "protest proneness" in incoming freshman were having Jewish sounding names and having no religious preferences. The study was supported to flesh out in more specific detail those qualities that were statistically related to proneness to demonstrate in 30,000 freshmen entering thirty-three participating colleges.

The people involved were asked how they could justify the development of information that could be used to discriminate against certain individuals based on group identities. They were also asked how they could justify human research that violated the "informed consent" principle. The response was an expression of indignation at an assault on the sanctity of pure science. The ultimate utility of knowledge can never be gauged. The role of the scientist is to illuminate the frontiers of the universe, not to burden himself with petty and transient issues of partisan politics. If the knowledge generated by science is misused, that is the responsibility of government, not of science itself. So cloaked with the righteousness of Galileo, some social scientists provided the means for a quota system that only the rarest deans of admission could resist.

What has happened since President Nixon declared drug abuse to be the "the worst threat the nation has ever faced"? He has created a new office for "special action" in the White House with unprecedented authority to coordinate the drug-related activities of every branch of government. From DOD to OEO, from NIMH to LEAA, the whole federal alphabet will be sifted through a White House filter commanding a billion bureaucratic dollars with as yet unsounded legislative and executive authority.

The director of this office, Dr. Jerome Jaffe, is a psychiatrist with a heavy bent to pharmacology. Although he was responsible for a "multimodality" program in Illinois, his publications and pronouncements indicate a heavy preference for methadone maintenance in the treatment of heroin addicts. Right now he and his colleagues in the Bureau of Narcotics and Dangerous Drugs of the Justice Department are concerned about the potential for "misuse" and "diversion" of methadone from government-controlled programs. He is exploring a variety of methods for dealing with this. The administrative ones, though not yet formalized in FDA regulations, are expected to prevent private physicians from prescribing and private pharmacies from filling prescriptions for methadone. The only methadone available for addicts will then be through those programs approved and supervised by the government. At the same time Jaffe is exploring some technical mechanisms for monitoring the patients themselves—footprint or voiceprint systems, called the "unique identifier." Even a nationwide registry for addicts is under consideration. Urinalysis surveillance is already a familiar component of methadone programs.

The *New York Times* carried an interview with Dr. Jaffe datelined April 11 under a headline that read "Vietnam Methods of Heroin-Control Urged for U.S." It began: "Dr. Jerome T. Jaffe said today that American medical techniques, including 'quarantine,' now provide the means to 'break the back' of what he called the heroin 'epidemic' in this country, much, he said, as the use of heroin by the military in Vietnam was curbed. . . . (He) feels that heroin addiction in the United States has reached a point of 'crisis.'. . . 'Because we know that one drug user communicates the drug experience to another, as in a flu expidemic,' he said, 'the armed services isolate individuals identified as hard-drug users, keeping them away from nonusers. . . .If one could just identify and take out of circulation the early users, we could break the whole chain,' he said."

Getting civilians to take tests and getting the ones identified as users to submit to the same sort of detention and treatment imposed on military users raises civil rights problems, but Dr. Jaffe believes that with sufficient support from the media the public could be persuaded to support tests in schools and other institutions [italics added].

While Jaffe's references to early case finding, quarantine, and epidemics might seem to bespeak a public health sophistication, what he is in fact doing is making a sloppy metaphor of questionable validity and acting as if it were literal truth. While peer pressure is a major influence on the incidence of drug abuse, it is unjustified to assume that addiction is "communicated like a flu epidemic," rather than being a complex arrangement of predispositions, learned behavior, and social options. It would take a desperate literary talent to do so, but one is no less entitled than Dr. Jaffe to refer to "epidemics" of sales of air-conditioned cars, births of triplets, or charter flights to Europe. It would be something less than Aristotelian logic to suggest quarantine for the early cases as a method of control. Drug addiction is not an infection with incubation periods, vectors, and carriers. Each decision to use the drug, even after physiological addiction, is a conscious decision chosen from alternatives.

The model of success in the Vietnam experience of heroin control is also subject to question. By Jaffe's own reports, the original estimates of heroin use in Vietnam were grossly exaggerated. The great majority of heroin use was not intravenous. A good deal of the heroin was dusted onto cigarettes and smoked as a way of getting high less conspicuously than marihuana smoking.

Treating the Fifth Column Addict

The thirty-day detoxification and treatment imposed upon those "addicts" discovered by mass urine surveillance has not been particularly successful. The VA programs, which are heir to these patients, are no more capable of treating them with anything beyond methadone maintenance than the Army was. Representative John Murphy has introduced a bill that would place veterans certified as addicts by the armed services under the jurisdiction of the Narcotic Addict Rehabilitation Act of 1966 (N.A.R.A) making *compulsory treatment possible.* He stated what has been obvious to many, that the current system has not worked.

The belief that compulsory treatment would work is shared by many despite experience and data to the contrary. Neither the national experiment with NARA nor the examples of New York and California can muster evidence that forcing unmotivated addicts into "treatment" significantly interrupts a pattern of drug use. Despite the lack of a specific and effective treatment, a demand for enforced treatment persists. Involuntary civil commitment is the purest culture of this foolishness and most clearly articulates what the real agenda is, social control masquerading as public health.

The New York and California state institutions to which "patients" are civilly committed are concerned more with security and custody than with treatment. They function as prisons but are called *rehabilitation centers* to soothe the roughened conscience of a public that does not like to perceive itself in illiberal terms.

We are now confronted with a major initiative to create a federal involuntary civil commitment program. Congressman Louis Frey, Jr., of Florida has introduced such legislation, which carries an appropriation to build or modify existing structures for the purpose of "treating" the civilly committed addict. I suppose the camps lying fallow since the McCarran Act days would serve admirably.

Congressman Frey has provided us with another illustration of an unwholesome confluence of politics, medicine, and social science in a statement in the *Congressional Record* of 9 February 1972:

Mr. Speaker, recently a new system has been developed and brought to my attention dealing with the important problem of identification of the drug abuser. The study was completed by David B. Vinson, Ph.D., with the cooperation of Drs. George Constant and John Quackenbush of the Devereus Foundation and J. O. Molly, M.D. The procedure has been named "DUP" for drug-user profile.

Basically, it is a procedure to identify by behavior profile the actual drug user or the *drug-prone individual*. One attractive facet of this system is that it is applicable to large groups [italics added].

The current national drug-abuse control effort is a serious threat to freedom in America. The usual law-enforcement paraphernalia are being extravagantly focused on people who are neither sick nor criminal, but who are being called *sick*, as they are treated as criminals. Preventive detention, no-knock entry, undercover agents, the "dropsy rule," the heroin hot line for anonymous charges against pushers, and the geometric increase in local, state, and federal narcotic officers suggest a major preoccupation by the police in drug-abuse control. American medicine, dominated by a short-sighted perspective on the walking wounded and obsessed with technology, has found itself using cingulectomies, massive doses of shock therapy, carbon-dioxide treatments, and operant conditioning on individuals who choose to use drugs for complex reasons existing as much or more outside their skins as within them. Social scientists, grasping for identity and security, having never developed a professional sense of responsibility, accountability, or discretion, are in command of powerful instruments of prediction and surveillance of social behavior.

Political pulses are running high this year. The public is frustrated and angry about the war, unemployment, inflation, and public safety. The addict is perceived as a dangerous and unwanted representative of unpopular social groups. When a scientific perspective dominated by a short-sighted medical model in conjunction with powerful technologies of prediction, monitoring, and control occupies a commanding position in public policies on drug abuse, then we need to be more than anxious.

C. P. Snow delivered the Godkin Lectures at Harvard in 1960 on the subject of the role played by scientists in the British government during World War II. Snow was intimate with the events surrounding the reciprocal roles played by Henry Thomas Tizard and Lindemann, the most influential British scientists of their time. After his detailed account and analysis of those critical years, Snow wrote:

> We ought not to give any single scientist the powers of choice that Lindemann had. It is even clearer, in my mind at least, that there is a kind of scientist to whom we ought not to give any power of choice at all. . . .Various kinds of fear distort scientific judgments; just as they do other judgments: but, most of all, the self-deceiving factor seems to be a set of euphorias. The euphoria of gadgets; the euphoria of secrecy. . . .Any scientist who is prone to these euphorias ought to be kept out of government decisions or choice making, at almost any cost. It does not matter how good he is at his stuff. It does not matter if the gadgets are efficacious like the atomic bomb, or silly like Lindemann's parachute mines for dropping on airscrews. It does not matter how confident he is; in fact, if he is confident because of the euphoria of gadgets, he is doubly dangerous. . . .The point is, anyone who is drunk with gadgets is a menace.[1]

Our political leaders are, as always, preoccupied with power. They continue to be responsive to vested interests. They seem to be ever ready to unleash massive energies and manipulate public attitudes to provoke and focus rage on people who are already the victims of abuse and neglect. Now medicine, law enforcement, and social science are walking a common path with politics in the persecution of the addict. It is an agonizing persecution for the few hundred thousand addicts directly threatened by it; it is a persecution fraught with risk for the concern for freedom we like to believe America stands for.

NOTES

1. C. P. Snow, *Science and Government* (New York: Mentor, 1962).

16

Cannabis, Alcohol, and the Management of Intoxication*

John Auld

It might be argued that there are more pressing matters of public concern in Britain today than the issue of whether cannabis (in the form of either marihuana or hashish) should be decriminalized or should at least be officially subject to more lenient sentencing policies. Considerations of newsworthiness aside, it nevertheless seems at first sight rather surprising that a subject so fervently and lengthily debated in the late 1960s and early 1970s should recently have aroused so comparatively little attention. The most recent concerted attempt to resuscitate and remobilize the so-called propot lobby (promarihuana), in the form of the setting up in July 1973 of the Cannabis Action Reform Organization (C.A.R.O.), was greeted by an almost total lack of response. One can only conclude that the four million potsmokers alleged to exist by a national survey carried out for the B.B.C. television program

*Printed with the permission of the author.

261

"Midweek" at around the same time were not prepared to
compaign publicly for the right to engage in an activity that, in
its private form, offers few problems.

However, there are growing indications that factors other
than the pursuit of self-interest on the part of the politically
influential, and anxiety over the possibility of police harassment among the politically weak, may underlie the attitude of
relative indifference with which the issue of the ban upon
cannabis seems to be widely regarded at present. To accept
the finding that four million people have at one time or another
smoked pot in no way obliges one to refrain from questioning
any implication that all these people are, have been, or indeed
ever will be regular and continuing users of the drug. Nor need
one suppose that all these people would be outspoken critics of
the existing law if only they dared or could be bothered to raise
their voices. Although precise epidemiological data are as
lacking here as they so often are elsewhere, what little
evidence we do have at the moment seems to suggest the need
for a rather different interpretation of the current state of
affairs—and, correspondingly, a rather different prognosis.
Putting matters quite bluntly, it suggests that the activity of
potsmoking tends to lack consistent appeal.

Such an interpretation is prompted by the nature of
disparate information that has been steadily accumulating
recently on both sides of the Atlantic. The survey carried out
in 1972 by the United States National Commission revealed, for
example, that "41 percent of the adults and 45 percent of the
youth who have ever tried marihuana reported that they no
longer use the drug." When asked why, "the overwhelming
majority of adults (61 percent) specified, among other reasons,
that they had simply lost interest in the drug" (Schafer, et al.
1972, p. 34).

This in itself requires explanation. Perhaps more significant in the British context, however, is the following statement
that appeared in the news pages of the April 1973 edition of
the London underground magazine Oz, the penultimate one to
appear before it ceased publication: "Let's be frank, booze is
back. The bottle's in vogue again and the fab fashionable
everywhere are saying Out of the window with that dowdy old

LSD, that dreary pot, or even those merely ephemerally amusing white powders. Instead it's a return to liquor, drink, hooch, grog, whatever you want to call your own personal tipple."

Such an endorsement of alcohol is particularly curious when published in a magazine that—as one of the foremost exponents of the possibility of accomplishing social revolution through the diffusion of "dope, rock music, and fucking in the streets"—at one time regarded the drug with something like contempt. However, lest this apparent rejection of illegal drugs should be interpreted as a response merely to the growing realization that their use was failing to promote this revolution after all, it is worth referring again to the American situation. The detailed 1972 report of the United States Consumers Association reported a similar reversal of the erstwhile tendency for young people to reject alcohol in favor of other drugs. Moreover, "marihuana users were said to be drinking the alcoholic beverages *along with* smoking the marihuana joints. One survey even suggested that the heaviest marihuana smokers were also the heaviest alcohol drinkers" (Brecher, et al. 1972, p. 433).

By 1974 this trend appeared to have become consolidated still further. Alcohol had not only returned to favor among the young, but had also done so to a degree that was viewed by many adults with alarm. Figures released by the Home Office in October revealed that proved offenses of drunkenness among boys aged fourteen to seventeen had increased by thirty-two percent compared with the previous year, and throughout the year the media devoted much coverage to the new social problem presented by "teenyboozers" or "teeny-drunks," as they chose to label them. If potsmoking, correspondingly, was becoming increasingly unfashionable, there were indications that such a trend was merely paralleling what appeared, once again, to be the American experience. A report in the *London Daily Telegraph* of 9 October 1974 headed "Why U.S. Parents Are Happy To See Youngsters Taking To Drink" contained an illustrative testimonial: " 'A lot of us used to smoke pot.' a 17-year-old student in Washington [D.C.] explained, 'but we gave that up a year or two ago. Now we drink a lot. In my book, a high is a high'."

For the time being, then, it seems as if those who with every seriousness once posed the question of whether cannabis could replace alcohol have received a fairly decisive answer. But how can we explain such apparent anomalies? How, for example, can we explain the seeming paradox of people simultaneously using two drugs whose reputed effects —the one heightening awareness, the other diminishing it— appear at first sight to be diametrically opposed? To say that changes in drug preference or patterns of drug use occur either at random or as the result of supposed loss of interest is unsatisfactory. After all, we would probably think it a little strange if somebody told us that he had decided to become teetotal because alcohol no longer "interested" him—although we might be willing to credit any number of other reasons. I shall argue that a more fruitful approach to the problem is one that focuses attention upon the ways in which the constellations of meanings assigned to different drugs affect the character of social interaction in the settings of their use. Such an approach seems particularly appropriate in the case of cannabis, which has often been described as the "new social drug." Presumably this designation has largely to do with the fact that most potsmoking has traditionally occurred within a group context. However, this in itself tells us very little: acknowledgment of behavior being social need not imply that it is also sociable, in the sense of positively facilitating or strengthening relationships among those who engage in it. Nor does it follow from observation that if such behavior is sociable at one point in time, that it will continue to be so at another. We need both to distinguish between the structure and the content of such relationships and to examine the ways in which both of these are likely to change over time.

In view of the apparent trends I have just outlined, an appropriate place to start is with a closer consideration of the social attributes of alcohol. Although criticism of the prevalence and frequently disruptive consequences of its use continues unabated, there can be no question that alcohol remains the dominant social drug in our society. Its enormous popularity may be attributed to the subtle interweaving of

several related factors. First, and partly of course because of
its legality, its potential effects are known by almost everybody. Second, these are almost universally thought to involve a
certain variably defined dulling of awareness, impairment of
judgment, or—at the extreme—loss of self-control. Since
knowledge of such effects is assumed to be shared, any display
of them is relatively unproblematic. And certainly, there is no
recent tradition in Western culture that explicitly links alcohol
with the pursuit of self-knowledge and insight. Third, the
consumption of alcohol seldom constitutes what Goffman
(1963) has termed a *dominant involvement* in any given
situation; just as people are not usually preoccupied with the
changes in their subjective experience when they drink (Orcutt
1972), so they by no means always drink explicitly in order to
get drunk. Indeed, the multiplicity of motives surrounding the
use of a drug whose consumption, despite the objections of its
critics, is usually a pleasurable activity in itself makes it
possible for people to deny any implication that their primary
motive for indulgence is intoxication for its own sake. This,
along with the fact that the pharmacological action of the drug
itself tends to be cumulative rather than immediate (in the
sense of involving a sudden qualitative shift in the character
of conscious mood), succeed in making the activity and
experience of drinking relatively unlikely to impede the flow of
interaction with others.

Taken together, all of these factors help to tilt what
Goffman has described as the delicate balance between
individual privacy and social accessibility more or less
markedly in the direction of the latter. The lowering of
inhibitions thus implied is what informs the popular belief that
a drink or two will help to "break the ice" at social gatherings
—a belief seemingly assumed to be shared by all. Billboard
posters depicting scenes of social merriment and carrying the
exhortation to "drop in at your local"; advice in the women's
glossies that a fundamental requirement for a successful
dinner party is plenty of wine; the recent series of advertise-
ments showing two apparently ill-matched individuals sharing
a joke accompanied by the caption "Beefeater Gin mixes
people perfectly"—all these combine to provide the clear

suggestion that people *expect* one another to become talkative
and gregarious under the influence of alcohol. In an increasingly mobile and pluralistic society in which the conditions for
friendship are seldom prestructured and where people of
diverse backgrounds, values, and interests must nevertheless
be provided with the means to form relationships and get along
with one another, alcohol may thus perform very signficant
integrative functions.

Cannabis, in contrast, seems in many ways to be quite
different. For a start, as is now well known, the process of
becoming a user of the drug involves an elaborate process of
learning. Not only must the subject learn the appropriate
technique of smoking the drug, itself a somewhat problematic
(and not infrequently unpleasant) enterprise, but he must also
acquire the ability to both identify and enjoy its effects. These
are neither self-evident nor intrinsically pleasurable (Becker
1963). Moreover, acknowledgment should be made of a
growing body of opinion that regards the drug—especially in
the potencies in which it is commonly used (Jones 1971;
Fairbairn, et al. 1974)—as being pharmacologically not dis-
similar to a placebo, whose principal function is to increase
the user's suggestibility. David Matza (1969), for example, has
persuasively argued that it merely predisposes him to an
alteration of conscious mood by making him drowsy or half-
asleep; whatever he experiences subsequently, Matza suggests,
is largely a product of the interaction between this physiological condition and the kind of reflective thinking induced by a
situation whose prime (if implicit) directive is that he "wait for
something to happen." More recently, Andrew Weil, himself
an expert in pharmacology with much research on the drug to
his credit, has described the drug as an *active placebo*, in
which "the influence of set and setting dwarfs the influence of
the drug itself" (1973, p. 76).

Now the multiplicity of factors that may affect the
character of these elements of set and setting naturally makes
an attempt at analyzing their impact upon the nature and
pleasurability of the drug experience somewhat hazardous.
This alone may account for the paucity of research in this
area. Unfortunately the widespread rejection of the traditional

positivist belief in the existence of a direct and unvarying link between the drug ingested and the mental effects derived from it seems recently to have given rise, in some quarters, to an equally unfortunate tendency to suggest that the variables influencing such effects are too numerous for one to be able to talk about their possible impact at all. Pushed to the limit, such a view is totally incapacitating. Nevertheless, I believe that it *is* possible to extract certain themes that make sense of the available findings. In discussing these, however, I should point out that I shall be referring primarily to those cannabis users whose commitment to the utilitarian values dominant in our society is sufficiently stable and highly developed as to insulate them from any desire to pursue the existential implications of experiencing an altered reality to the point of abandoning the life-style around which their *normal* reality is structured. Thus I shall have little to say that is of direct relevance to the case of the drugtaker who is also a committed hippie. Here an additional set of factors must be taken into consideration, and there currently appears to be no shortage of those willing to suggest what these might be.

One of the implications of what has already been said on the subject of set and setting is that the character, meaning, and behavior expression of the drug experience will tend to vary in accordance with the prior expectations that the people in question have of it. Where the neophyte cannabis user is concerned, these expectations will typically be based at least to some extent upon the kind of drug-related imagery available in the wider culture. In the past, such imagery has for the most part contained little mention of any mind-expanding or psychedelic properties of cannabis. Rather, it has tended to associate use of the drug with episodes of unusual or unpredictable behavior and a more or less marked loss of self-control. As I have suggested elsewhere (Auld 1973), this view owes much to the publicly reported statements of those who have a pesonal interest in sustaining the idea that the drug "causes" deviant behavior. Foremost among these, perhaps not surprisingly, are deviants themselves. Any survey of the press publicity given to court cases over the last few years will reveal many instances in which people arrested on

criminal charges have attempted to plead diminished responsibility for their actions by citing the supposedly disinhibiting
effects of cannabis. One fairly recent example of this tendency
was a report in a leading Fleet Street newspaper, The Sun (5
July 1973), which described how two barmen were jailed after
they had "savagely attacked and nearly choked a chamber-
maid." One of the defendants apparently told police that they
had both been smoking cannabis: " 'It makes you high, and you
want to have sex,' he explained."

Second, and simultaneously both drawing upon and
enhancing the plausibility of such accounts, there are the
romanticized statements issued by groups such as policemen,
magistrates, and politicians—presumably with the primary
aim of deterring people from experimenting with drugs. One of
the more colorful examples is the statement made by a police
superintendent before an audience of Liverpool schoolchildren
in April 1971: "In plain language this cannabis sends you
absolutely round the bend, and make no bones about that."
More recently, the 27 April 1974 edition of The Guardian,
another Fleet Street newspaper, reported an Old Bailey judge,
Mervyn Griffith-Jones, as saying the following: "Day after day
these courts are dealing with persons who have committed
atrocious crimes of violence, and indeed other crimes as well,
which they would never have committed had they not been
acting under the effects of cannabis."

These are both extreme views, of course, and ones that
few potential users of the drug would accept at face value. But
a more moderate version of them nevertheless lingers on in the
form of an association of the drug with a general loss of
inhibitions. In this form, such a view resists repudiation even
by established members of the potsmoking subculture itself.
For though they may lay stress more upon changes in
experience than in behavior, they are unlikely to disabuse any
potential recruit of the notion that the drug will do something
to him.

It is perhaps in the light of this enduring association
between cannabis and disinhibition that the documented
behavior of so-called naive users of the drug can best be
understood. For there are frequent suggestions in those

studies that have looked at this area that either they appear to
expect a dramatic change of some kind, and, when this fails to
occur, claim that the drug has no effect upon them; or else,
complying (perhaps unconsciously) with the presumed expectations of others, they display what they have been led to
believe is a prevalent response to the drug and become
noticeably more uninhibited and expressive. In the latter case
the drug experience then comes to acquire the status of a
dominant involvement in which they become totally engrossed.

Regular cannabis users, by contrast, have frequently
been noted as typically quieter and more subdued, even to the
point of appearing withdrawn (Grinspoon 1971, p. 136;
Hochman 1972, p. 18; Tart 1971, p. 127). Hitherto, there has
been a tendency to explain these differences either in terms of
the supposedly deleterious long-term effects of the drug upon
mental functioning, or in terms of some notion of there being a
basic maladjustment on the part of the kinds of people who end
up becoming regular cannabis users. At first glance, for
instance, the following extract from the report of the United
States National Commission might seem to lend support to
either of these theories: "The social adjustment of the daily
users, when judged from a traditional psychiatric viewpoint,
was impaired. Individuals tended to be more withdrawn and to
interact less with each other than the intermittent users,
regardless of the type of activity or state of intoxication"
(Schafer, et al. 1972, p. 39).

Such statements provide useful ammunition for those
anxious to find ways of discrediting cannabis and its most
committed users. Equally tenable and possibly more helpful,
however, is an explanation in terms of the notion of *learning*.
There are several different types of learning that may occur,
some fairly general, others more specific to the values of the
drugtaking subculture in which the user finds himself. The
first type falls into the former category. To begin with, and
perhaps as long as the drug experience remains a novelty
capable of sustaining a shared sense of excitement and
discovery, the cannabis user may well be quite open and
uninhibited in expressing the extent of his newfound insight
into realms of meaning normally obscured by the taken-for-

granted attitude of everyday life. At the same time, he may experience intense rapport with those at a similar stage in their drugtaking career; while more experienced users, conscious of their own early experiences and anxious to ensure that the neophyte defines the activity as enjoyable, are likely to take an indulgent attitude toward such expressions of naive enthusiasm and wonderment. Over time and with more intensive use, however, the subject learns to become less demonstrative in his behavior. For, if he is to appear an experienced user, to become somebody who controls the drug rather than being controlled by it, he must appear to take its effects for granted. Only thus can he effectively resolve the contradiction between society's claim that it causes loss of self-control and his peers' belief that it heightens self-aware-ness. Gradually, therefore, he is constrained to become someone who is manifestly adept at maintaining expressive control (Lyman and Scott 1970). In a word, he must become *cool*.

However, the respect accorded those whose behavior visibly contradicts the stereotypes erected in its defense is not the only way in which the ban upon cannabis serves to constrain the expressivity of the regular user. Besides the more familiar argument that uncool behavior may be consid-ered likely to attract the unwelcome attentions of third parties —probably only of relevance in this context if the user chooses to enter straight company when high—one must also consider the consequences of the ban upon the supply of the drug and the notorious lack of standarization in its quality. Awareness of pharmacological variability, it may be argued, is equally likely to render the behavioral display of intoxication problematic to the extent that it has the effect of making it difficult for the user to know whether such a display is warrantable in terms of the quantity and quality of the drug he has ingested. On the one hand, the somewhat disdainful or patronizing attitude known to be reserved for the person (other than the neophyte) who starts expostulating after a mere few puffs on the proffered joint may encourage him to think that it would probably not be. At the same time, however, he may be concerned that a *failure* to offer such a display may be construed, particularly by the person who has offered him the joint, as an indication that he has remained unaffected by it and considers its contents to be inadequate or of mediocre quality. Individualistic responses are therefore hazardous: the pressure to seek orienting cues in the actions of others considerable. The attempt that is thus likely to be made to negotiate the reality of the drug's effects through an exchange of exploratory gestures (Cohen 1955, p. 60) may itself partially account for the sensations of heightened interpersonal sensitivity commonly reported by cannabis users (Tart 1971; Berke and Hernton 1974).

It is worth noting, however, that the interpretative difficulties I have mentioned are not entirely—or perhaps even largely—attributable to the operation of social control. They also owe something to the technological aspects of potsmoking and the widespread persistence of the tacit rule that the joint be shared by all those present. For it is frequently the case that knowledge of the probable potency of the joint is possessed only by its manufacturer. Unless they are unusually sophisticated users of the drug and are capable of accurately judging the quality and quantity of the substance merely be tasting it, others are required to infer such potency from the character of any changes in their subjective experience that the act of smoking appears to generate.

As with most other commodities of indeterminate value, then, there is a sense in which it may be rather better to give cannabis than to receive it. Yet the paradox remains, here as elsewhere, that for all his inside knowledge, the giver is typically the person most reluctant to state what the value of his gift should be to its recipients. What perhaps distinguishes cannabis smoking from most other types of ritual gift sharing is that in this case there is the strong possibility that nobody will feel much inclined to express an opinion on the subject.

But if the rule of passing and not "bogarting" (holding on to) the joint is to a large extent a legacy of the once close association between potsmoking and the ethic of property sharing, this is not the only contribution that the ideological inheritance of the activity has made to the growth of an emphasis upon being cool. One must also give consideration to the consequences, largely unforeseen, of the rhetoric advanced in the late 1960s by those people concerned with both defending the use of cannabis and attacking the values of a society that condemned it. Even if they were primarily an outgrowth of the settings in which it was used (Matza 1969), the psychedelic—or consciousness raising—properties attributed to the drug during this period were given an additional symbolic potency by virtue of its comparison with alcohol, the recreational drug clearly favored by the hostile members of straight society. Such a context provided fertile ground for the development of somewhat romanticized ideas about the effects of the drug and its potential as an agent of social change. Like LSD, it was commonly credited with the power to produce enlightment and insight. Moreover, partly by virtue of the ascendancy in this country of what Young (1973) has termed the *middle underground*, many of whose (largely middle-class) members were "tuned in" to the semimystical ideas of Timothy Leary and his followers, this state of enlightenment was considered most likely to be achieved through the medium of peaceful contemplation. As a mode of interpersonal communication, speech was largely devalued (Adelman 1973). In a culture heavily imbued with ideas appropriated from Eastern philosophy, the aphorism, "he who knows does not speak: he who speaks does not know," acquired for many the status of a guide to conduct. The mystique surrounding the use of cannabis in such a context may thus be regarded as having derived not simply from its illegality, but also from its subcultural reputation as a means whereby this state of knowing could be made more easily accessible. As such, however, it became an essentially *privatized* activity. The person who continued to verbalize his experiences was increasingly likely to feel that not only was he engaging in an essentially pointless endeavor whose consequences would merely be to inhibit the likelihood of his acquiring true insight: by forcing his attentions upon others he was making the achievement of such a goal difficult for them, too. Either he was undersocialized in the values prevalent within the culture, or else—paradoxically—he was being antisocial.

For those people who were exposed, even if only

peripherally, to the values of the middle underground, the political and cultural meanings of expressive behavior thus further increased the disincentive toward manifesting it. And yet, in the last analysis, the existence and dissemination of such values was not a necessary condition for such a devaluation of expressivity to occur. In a relatively stable and unchanging environment, the ability to continually extract new insights from the drug experience is as finite as the tolerance of others for their expression. What were once revelations eventually become merely commonplaces; a way of looking at the world that was once new and exciting increasingly becomes *the* way of looking at the world. In such circumstances as these, *any* individual who persists in drawing attention to the profusion and profundity of his so-called insights, who is continually collapsing in laughter at the quite ordinary remarks made by others (Margolis and Clorfene 1970, p. 31; Goode 1970, p. 167), who continually exclaims—like Matza's subject (1969, p. 138)—"Golly gee, look at that chair!" (or whatever), is likely to become considered at best as experientially naive—at worst, as a rather dim-witted "drag." After all, why comment upon something that others, in their cool wisdom, already take wholly for granted? Why, indeed, continue to take the drug at all if one does not precisely anticipate undergoing experiential changes of one kind or another?

The irony was, however, that similar questions could also be directed at those who withdrew into a privatized world of silent contemplation. Here again, it seems that the passing of time accomplished a subtle redefinition of the meanings attached to such behavior. For when it almost inevitably involved the the creation of communication barriers between people, its moral justifications became increasingly ambiguous. The basic problem was succinctly stated by Ann-Marie Bax, assistant director of the celebrated Paradiso Club in Amsterdam, who was reported in the B.B.C. journal *Radio Times* (26 April 1973) as saying: "We are trying to change our whole image. It has been like this too long. We need people to get involved, to understand each other again instead of getting lost in a wall of music." Apparently wishing to make a similar point, the London underground newspaper *I.T.* had a few months earlier carried a cartoon showing a group of freaks staring vacantly at the wall, accompanied by the somewhat acid caption "The Silent Minority."

The emergence of such misgivings, coupled with the fact that the structure of the "Alternative Society" was in an advanced state of decay by this time anyway (see Young 1973), served in turn to encourage a gradual restoration of the kinds of meanings that are *conventionally* assigned to silence in social settings and that tend to identify it as a major source of social embarrassment. Eventually, therefore, any appearance of engrossment in the drug's effects to the point of actually discouraging social accessibility came to acquire negative connotations, too, signifying as it seemed to either naivete, calculated insensitivity, or social maladroitness. Here again, though for different reasons from those suggested above, a high premium came to be placed upon the demonstrated ability to treat the activity of smoking as essentially routine: a mere gloss upon an interactional process that would have taken place anyway and that would remain to all intents and purposes unaffected by it. Once again, in short, actions that might be construed as evidence of intoxication were rendered problematic.

As might be supposed, the business of steering a safe path between the two extremes of being too cool and being over-expressive, and all the while being alive to the other interpretative dilemmas mentioned, demanded a very high level of interactional competence. Contrary to the assumptions and allegations of pathology contained in much public rhetoric on the subject, I would argue that those drug users whose successful pursuits of this path led to their remaining regular cannabis users were likely to have been highly endowed with such competence. Unfortunately, however, not only were interactional skills of this order in limited supply, but also the necessity of deploying them at all constituted something of an anomaly in the context of an activity that had also been assigned a preeminently *recreational* status by its adherents (Matza 1969; Goode 1970; Young 1971). A further important paradox should also be noted: for unlike the use of alcohol, it appears that much of the "enjoyment" associated with the use of cannabis relies upon not just the desire but, more important, the *ability* to explore and experience one's environment in unconventional ways. Whether the chosen avenue for such exploration be "hot hedonism" or "cool hedonism," uninhibited immersion *in* the world or privatized contemplation *of* it, each involves a certain degree of emancipation from the kinds of moral rules that conventionally constrain people to observe minimally acceptable levels of involvement with, accessibility to, and even comprehensibility by others (Goffman 1963). Now the implicit (or indeed explicit) directives typically offered the cannabis user in the early stages of his career serve to sanction and thus facilitate such "rule evasion." Historically, too, it received legitimation from the ideological emphasis upon the uncontestable right of the individual seeking personal liberation and self-realization to "do his own thing." However, once an emphasis upon coolness prevails, social constraints gradually become reestablished. Once felt inhibitions upon the display of intoxication emerge, the possibility develops of there occuring an uncomfortable or dysphoric disjunction between the individual's subjective experience and the socially available opportunities for giving it expression: a "sensed discrepancy between the world that spontaneously becomes real to the individual, or the one he is able to accept as the current reality, and the one in which he is obliged to dwell" (Goffman 1972, p. 40).

It might be thought that for the person who increasingly finds himself in social situations where his enjoyment is inhibited by such problems as these, one solution might be for him to seek out alternative smoking partners with whom a new set of meanings and understandings might be negotiated. However, the process of meeting and interacting with other smokers is hardly free of difficulties either. In contrast once again with the case of alcohol, and partly because of the lack of a public body of knowledge other than of a highly negative kind, there appears to be a certain amount of disagreement as to what the typical effects of cannabis are. Insofar as any common set of beliefs about these effects exists at all, it seems to center upon the rather vague notion that it heightens awareness. Yet for the purposes of socializing and breaking the ice, such a notion—even if only implicit—is not at all helpful. For either people are likely to believe that they can tell where one anothers' heads are at almost at a glance, and that verbal "games" are meaningless; or else they merely become *more* aware of one anothers' differences. In either case the likely result is the direct opposite of that which might be expected to occur with alcohol. Here, as seen in the earlier setting, the balance between individual privacy and social accessibility is shifted in the direction of the former.

In such circumstances as those I have tried to outline, the introduction of alcohol and the social meanings associated with its use may do much both to smooth the flow of interaction and broaden its potential scope. To the extent that this does in fact occur, people who use the two drugs conjointly may come to believe that not only are they entirely compatible, but also in certain situations actually serve to potentiate one another. Then again, as an alternative to smoking the drug on their own, people may restrict their use of cannabis to those settings where they know and trust their smoking companions sufficiently well as to have confidence in their ability to negotiate a satisfactory definition of the drug's effects without falling victim to the difficulties mentioned above. In this case, of course, the activity is likely to become intensely cliquish. However, if on the other hand the drug is difficult and costly to obtain, as increasingly seems to have become the case in England since the setting up of the Central Drugs Intelligence Unit in March 1973, this may not be experienced as any very great loss. Such a view receives added support from the statements made by some of the more sophisticated members of the drug subculture itself, who have claimed that there are few effects of the drug that cannot be replicated without it.

All such possibilities prompt the conclusion that no adequate understanding of the effects of cannabis is likely to be achieved until researchers pay at least as much attention to the meanings that its users assign to it as to its pharmacological properties. On the face of it, there seem to be good reasons for disputing its designation as the "new social drug." So long, at least, as it is predominantly regarded as a drug that heightens rather than dulls awareness, it seems unlikely to present a serious threat to the position held for so long and with such success by alcohol. While these remarks are admittedly speculative, a more immediate implication is that research in the field of drugtaking might do well to focus rather less upon such issues as why and how many people start using drugs in the first place, and rather more upon those of why and how they cease or alter their patterns of drugtaking. In view of the kind of scaremongering so prevalent in the 1960s (and indeed up till just a short while ago), it is somewhat ironic that the average cannabis user should now appear to stand a very much greater chance of deescalating to alcohol than he does of escalating to heroin.

REFERENCES

Adelman, Clifford. 1973. *Generations: A Collage on Youthcult.* Harmondsworth, England: Penguin.
Auld, John. 1973. "Drug Use: The Mystification of Accounts." In *Contemporary Social Problems in Britain.* Edited by R.V. Bailey and J. Young. London: Heath
Becker, Howard S. 1963. *Outsiders: Studies in the Sociology of Deviance.* New York: Free Press.
Berke, Joseph, and Hernton, Calvin. 1974. *The Cannabis Experience.* London: Peter Owen.
Brecher, Edward, and the Editors of Consumer Reports. 1972. *Licit and Illicit Drugs.* Boston: Little, Brown.
Cohen, Albert K. 1955. *Delinquent Boys: The Culture of the Gang.* Glencoe, Illinois: Free Press.
Fairbairn, J. W.; Hindmarch, I.; Simic, S.; and Tylden, E. 1974. "Cannabinoid Content of Some English Reefers." *Nature* 249: 276-78.
Goffman, Erving. 1963. *Behavior in Public Places.* New York: Free Press.
_____. 1972. *Encounters.* Harmondsworth, England: Penguin.
Goode, Erich. 1970. *The Marihuana Smokers.* New York: Basic Books.
Grinspoon, Lester. 1971. *Marihuana Reconsidered.* New York: Bantam Books.

Hochman, Joel S. 1972. *Marihuana and Social Evolution*. Englewood Cliffs, New Jersey: Prentice-Hall.

Jones, Reese T. 1971. "Tetrahydrocannabinol and the Mari-
huana-Induced Social 'High': Or the Effects of the Mind on
Marihuana." Paper presented at the New York Academy
of Sciences Conference on Marihuana Chemistry,
Pharmacology, and Patterns of Social Usage, New York.

Lyman, Stanford M., and Scott, Marvin B. 1970. "Coolness in
Everyday Life." In *A Sociology of the Absurd*. Edited by
S. M. Lyman and M. B. Scott. New York: Appleton-
Century-Crofts.

Margolis, Jack, and Clorfene, Richard. 1970. *A Child's Garden
of Grass*. New York: Pocket Books.

Matza, David. 1969. *Becoming Deviant*. Englewood Cliffs, New
Jersey: Prentice-Hall.

Orcutt, James D. 1972. "Toward a Sociological Theory of Drug
Effects: A Comparison to Marihuana and Alcohol."
Sociology and Social Research 56: 242-53.

Schafer, Raymond, and the National Commission on Mari-
huana and Drug Abuse. 1972. *Marihuana: A Signal of
Misunderstanding*. Washington, D.C.: U.S. Government
Printing Office.

Tart, Charles T. 1971. *On Being Stoned: A Psychological Study
of Marihuana Intoxication*. Palo Alto, California: Science
and Behavior Books.

Weil, Andrew. 1973. *The Natural Mind*. London: Jonathan Cape.

Young, Jock. 1971. *The Drugtakers: The Social Meaning of Drug
Use*. London: Paladin.

_____. 1973. "The Hippie Solution: An Essay in the Politics of
Leisure." In *Politics and Deviance*. Edited by L. Taylor and
I. Taylor. Harmondsworth, England: Penguin.

17

Invitational Edges of Corruption: Some Consequences of Narcotic Law Enforcement*

Peter K. Manning and Lawrence John Redlinger

Prior to the early years of this century, the nonmedical use of narcotics was largely unregulated and distribution and sales were routinely handled by physicians and pharmacists. However, sparked by international obligations and fervent moral crusaders, a series of legislative acts and court decisions were enacted and enforced. The enforcement of the laws resulted in marked changes in the population of users and drove the trafficking of narcotics underground.[1]   Since the early twenties, then, federal, state, and local agents have been engaged in enforcing the law and attempting to eradicate the illicit trafficker and his activities. Even though it can be demonstrated by official statistics that large numbers of users and dealers are arrested and prosecuted each year, narcotic law-enforcement problems continue to generate considerable governmental and public concern. Our purposes in this chapter

*Printed by permission of the authors.

are to examine the dominant or operative mode of enforcement, to point out the particular problems associated with it, and to indicate how these problems are not unique to narcotics enforcement.

The enforcers of the narcotics laws stand on the invitational edge of corruption, and the problems they encounter while regulating and attempting to eradicate illicit trafficking of drugs reveal similarities to regulation of other markets. Study of their problems and of the corruption that can, and does occur, will lead to insight into the structural problems of regulation, and to an understanding of the stress or tension points in regulatory apparatuses of the government.

As Robert Merton has noted, there are many similarities between legitimate and illegitimate businesses: *"Both are in some degree concerned with the provision of goods and services for which there is an economic demand"* (Merton 1958, p. 79). Thomas Schelling (1967) has noted that there must be many similarities between illicit and licit markets, and Redlinger (1959) analyzing heroin markets demonstrated remarkable similarities to licit markets. Likewise, Moore's analysis (1970) indicates that the economics of heroin distribution are similar to those of other consumer products. So the question is, then, what are the similarities and differences, and how do these effect variations in the regulation of the market?

Licit and illicit markets share several structural properties in common.[2] Both involve willing buyers and sellers. The buyers make demands for goods and services, and the sellers provide these for some reimbursement. In both licit and illicit markets, the sellers have in mind the making of a profit, and ideally maximizing that profit. Both types of markets are regulated by agencies whose mission is to do so, and both types of markets have sellers within them who seek effective control over the manner and type of regulations that will be applied to them. However, there are some differences and these stem from the moral intention of the regulatory statutes, the loyalties of those applying the regulations, and the nature in which they are applied.

The moral intention of regulatory statutes either legitimizes particular behaviors, goods, and services, or it jades them. Some goods and services (for example, the production, distribution, and possession of alcoholic beverages) become morally transformed; first they are defined one way, and then another. The nature of the definition structures the manner in which regulation is to be accomplished. Where products are determined to have "legitimacy" those who buy and sell them often are *licensed*. The license is part of the regulatory process and identifies dealers. These dealers in turn are regulated by a set of standards that are set by the various jurisdictions: for example, federal, state, and local. Consumers are assured, insofar as sellers adhere to the standards, that products are of sufficient quality. The moral intention of the regulation, then, is to insure the adequate *delivery* of goods and services and to insure the delivery of *adequate* goods and services. This is not the case for markets that have been morally transformed into "deviant" markets. Demand for products that are defined as illicit places a stigma on the consumer; selling such products places the dealer in a criminal and highly sanctionable position; the regulation seeks to collapse distribution channels, reduce supplies, and effectively reduce demand. Markets that are defined as immoral become "legally suppressed" and the regulatory functions become "enforcement" functions rather than compliance functions. Strictly speaking, there is no difference between compliance functions of regulations and enforcement functions because both seek to persuade and coerce sellers to "comply" with the regulations. The difference between the two arises out of the intent of the statute. In legal markets, the actions of distribution, production, and consumption are not illegal in themselves, and the persons doing this activity are not subject to criminalization. The regulation seeks to insure the channels of distribution and seeks to insure the quality of the product. Licensing of dealers performs this function, and in addition secures revenue for the licensing agent who in this case is the state.[3] The revenue provides resources for the licensing and for compliance agents to continue their performances. This is not the case with illicit markets. Regulations do not insure product adequacy, cannot provide revenue intake, and thus cannot generate their own resources. Finally, the regulations seek "compliance" only in the sense that they wish *no one* to engage in the activity.

In a similar manner, the loyalties of licit market regulators are focused in a different manner than those agents regulating illicit markets. Very often, the regulators of licit markets are products of those markets. The staffing of regulatory agencies is accomplished by using industry executives who are "experts" in the field. Thus, the loyalties of the people as agents is not wholly to the regulation process. They have an "insider's" view of the marketing structure and are able to consider both the regulations and their effects on the sellers. Obviously, this type of interpenetration between regulators and sellers is not extant for illicit markets. The regulators are never drawn from the ranks of sellers, and one can imagine why.[4] The sellers of illicit products are typically viewed as unwholesome characters, and the aim of the regulations is to put them permanently out of business.

The ways in which the regulations of licit markets are applied vary considerably from the manner in which illicit markets are regulated. Compliance sections of regulatory agencies frequently warn the seller to correct his practices, or at best take him to court where the process of advocacy litigation is applied. The seller when convicted is often fined or reprimanded. Since the regulators are often drawn from the industries they regulate and since the regulations legitimate, albeit regulate, the market, the same moral stigma is not applied to violators. Indeed, the violators may not view themselves as having committed a violation (see Sutherland 1949, on this point). Suppressive enforcement has some similarities, but is ultimately geared toward bringing about virtual *cessation* of activity. Agents may warn a seller of narcotics whom they cannot arrest, but in general, they seek to catch him in the act (although these patterns vary by size of city and patterns of seller's activities). Once caught, they seek to remove him from the market or immobilize him, since removal and immobilization are the only manners in which he can be forced to comply with regulatory standards. Some of the differences we have been discussing between legally regulated and legally suppressed markets and their relationships to regulatory agencies can be summarized in Figure 1.

FIGURE 1

A Comparison of Selected Aspects of Legally Regulated versus Legally Suppressed Markets

Legally Regulated Markets	*Legally Suppressed Markets*
1. Willing buyers and willing sellers	1. Willing buyers and willing sellers
2. Sellers seek to maximize profits	2. Sellers seek to maximize profits
3. Intent of law to set and maintain standards of goods and services	3. Intent of law to suppress all activity
4. Law licenses and legitimates dealers	4. Law stigmatizes and illegitimates dealers
5. Law legitimates use	5. Law stigmatizes use
6. Agents of regulation often drawn from sellers' ranks	6. Regulators never drawn from sellers' ranks
7. Agents seek compliance and seek maintenance of market at established levels	7. Agents seek eradication of market
8. Buyer quality protected	8. Buyer quality unprotected

Variation in moral intention, reflected in legal definition, creates differences in the kinds and types of influence sellers have on regulators and regulations. As we noted earlier, sellers of a product will seek to maximize their profits and will seek to have effective control over market conditions. Legally regulated markets offer the seller more opportunities for influence than do illicit ones. One reason we have already noted; in licit markets very often the regulators are drawn from the ranks of sellers, and often return to those ranks when they leave the regulatory agency. Second, in legally regulated markets, sellers have other means available for political influence. Because their activities are defined as creditable, they can utilize legislative means to attempt effective control. That is, they can attempt to have regulations set, sustained, or altered in line with their wishes rather than the wishes of other partisans in the market (for example, agents and consumers). They can lobby and thus attempt to influence the legislative process, and they can appear before congressional committees as "expert witnesses." When they appear, they can produce market data to support their position, and their legal staffs can actively seek changes in the law through aggressive court action. They can engage in negotiation with regulatory agents and attempt to mitigate the regulatory effects, or have them apply only after a certain period that will allow for industry "adjustment." They can engage in reactive challenging of regulations; that is, when they are charged formally and brought into court, they can initiate challenges to the law. They can band together into associations on the basis of common interests and utilize these associations to voice their collective position. Finally, they can resort to bribery, blackmail, extortion, pay offs, and a variety of other corrupting measures in pursuit of their goal of effective control. These corrupting attempts can be made both at higher official levels (since they have access to the personnel at this level of the regulatory process), and at agent-enforcement levels. Thus, legally regulated sellers have *both* licit and illicit means of influence available to them.

Sellers operating in illicit markets do not possess the same credibility of licit sellers and, consequently, they do not have the same types of access to influence over their market.[5] Regulators usually view the sellers as morally reprehensible, and take a hostile position vis-à-vis their activities. As a result of the moral intention of the regulations, then, illicit sellers have limited capacity for legitimate political influence. They do not engage in lobbying in a traditional sense, and they do not actively and voluntarily come forth as "expert witnesses" during drug-law hearings. They do not engage legal staffs to construct alternatives to present regulations and to initiate active resistance to present statutes through litigation. To challenge regulations, they usually must wait until the regulation is applied to them, and thus their posture is defensive. They cannot band together and have an association represent them and their collective views. Presumably, in the United States, their access to officials higher up in the regulatory apparatus and other government agencies is severely limited, and thus they have minimal opportunities to corrupt upper echelons of regulatory agencies. *Thus, for sellers in illicit markets, their focal points for effective control of their market must be enforcement agents.* Retail sellers in licit markets, to be sure, concentrate at this level since their span of control and resources warrants attempted intervention only at this level. However, wholesalers and producers are able to intervene successfully at higher levels. In legally suppressed markets, even wholesalers must focus on enforcement levels since influence at higher levels is denied them.[6]

The *structural constraints* of legally suppressed markets expose the agent to an accumulation of attempted influence. Because sellers want effective control over their markets, they must find ways to neutralize enforcement agencies. If they cannot avoid at least arrest and charge, and it is probable that eventually they cannot, then they must attempt to gain favorable influence with agents. The differences between legally regulated and legally suppressed markets is summarized in Figure 2.

We want to point out that we are not attempting to explain why individual enforcement officials become corruptible and corrupted, nor are we making comparisons between corrupted agents and those who are creditable. Furthermore, we are not arguing that all enforcement is corrupt or that a sizable number of agents are corrupt. We are specifying the structural conditions that focus pressure and tension on agents, antecedent to the actual day-to-day occasions of enforcement. Each department of agents makes varying adjustments to these conditions: the department may be cognizant of the pressures, demand high agent accountability, and thus be relatively immune to seller influence; or, individual agents within a department may be either "clean" or "on the take" and the problem is isolatable to individuals; or, the entire department can be involved in aiding seller control of the market; or,

finally, the department itself can, or agents within the
department can be selling in the market resulting in interpenetration of seller and regulator.[7]

FIGURE 2

Indicators of Degree of Access To and Influence Upon Sources of
Legitimate Authority for Sellers in Legally
Regulated versus Legally Suppressed Markets

Legally Regulated Markets	*Legally Suppressed Markets*
1. Sellers have potential political influence	1. Sellers have limited potential for political influence
2. Sellers can engage in lobbying to change and to maintain laws	2. Sellers cannot, do not lobby
3. Sellers can testify as expert witnesses	3. Sellers do not testify
4. Sellers can engage legal services to actively challenge existing laws and to create alternatives	4. Sellers do not actively challenge laws
5. Sellers can engage in negotiation on regulations with officials	5. Sellers cannot engage in negotiation
6. Sellers can engage in reactive challenges to charges under regulations	6. Sellers can engage in reactive challenges to charges under regulations
7. Sellers can form visible voluntary associations that can take collective positions	7. Sellers cannot form visible voluntary associations
8. Sellers can engage in the corruption of officials	8. Sellers cannot engage in corruption of officials
9. Sellers can engage in the corruption of compliance agents	9. Sellers can engage in the corruption of enforcement agents

There are additional structural constraints on agents that promote infractions of other laws in the performance of their assigned duties. Because the narcotics market involves willing buyers and sellers, agents must find ways of obtaining information that are not "victim" centered. That is, agents do not have a victim willing to give information. Thus, they must buy information or attempt to gain information from others within or near to the sellers. Moreover, having once obtained access to information about seller activity, agents must find ways of keeping their channels of information open. The manner in which they do so may involve them in infractions of other laws. As we shall detail later, there are structural pressures on enforcement agents that promote both infractions in enforcement of regulations and obstruction of legal proceedings. All of these considerations gradually lead to a corruption of regulations and negotiated law-enforcement practices.[8]

The focus of strain upon the agent points up a structural problem of regulation in general, and specifically the regulation of lucrative illicit markets. By looking at some of the enduring patterns of corruption, we may be able to locate and sensitize ourselves to more general problems of the structuring of regulation. There is little irony in the generalization made by the Knapp Commission in their report on police corruption when it states that "a corrupt police officer does not necessarily have to be an ineffective one" (1972, p. 55). Agent corruption is a product of the requirements of narcotic law enforcement and a theme found in the history of the enforcement enterprise.[9] The structural nature of narcotic law enforcement has historically created the problem of agent corruption, and is reflected by the social organization of enforcement agencies.[10]

Organizational Aspects of Drug-Enforcement Agencies

Narcotics squads, whether specialized sections within police departments or subsegments of vice divisions, are characterized by internally and externally generated pressures to produce visible evidence of their activity and achievements. Because the "products" of such organizations are essentially ineffable and difficult to measure, agencies *reify* specific measures of performance. These measures then become powerful inducements to organizational conformity, for in order to show adequate performance, agents must produce data in conformity with the established measures (Manning 1976). The pressures to produce, and the implied sanctions for failing to produce are the structural mechanisms by which policies of agencies become agent conduct.[11]

Internal pressures can be analytically separated from those external to the agency. In addition, we can separate pressures in terms of their impact. Some pressures induce agents to violate laws to enforce the narcotics laws, while others induce agents to obstruct justice. The translation of pressure is very indirect; "varying efforts to enforce these [vice laws] undermines the possibilities for strict supervision because the work obliges the men to engage in illegal and often degrading practices that must be concealed from the public" (Rubinstein 1973, p. 375). Furthermore, the application of successful techniques on the street (discussed below) produces a continuing ambivalence to law-abiding conduct. As Rubinstein (1973) notes, no department "had found ways of fulfilling its obligation to regulate public morality without resorting to methods that constantly provide policemen with temptation and encourage ambiguous attitudes toward official standards of conduct." That is, narcotic law enforcement is virtually always secretive, duplicitous and quasi-legal, and is extremely difficult to effectively regulate.[12] Greater pressures lead to, at least, greater encounters with problematic situations containing opportunities for corruption. The more pressure there is to enforce the law, the less opportunity for close supervision, and the greater the opportunities for corruption. Ironically, increasing the effectiveness in vice enforcement brings with it the increasing likelihood of corruption.

Internal pressures for excessive enforcement are created by: (1) aspirations for promotion, salary, and "easy numbers" within the unit; (2) quotas for arrests or stops insofar as these are tied to notions of success and enforced on agents[13]; (3) directives from administrators either in conjunction with "dope drives" (departmental efforts to round up users and pushers) or individual officers' attempts; (4) self-esteem maintenance produced by attempts to achieve success in terms of the conventional markers of arrests and buys; (5) moral-ideological commitments by officers to "protecting the kids" by "locking up the junkies and pushers" and thus, "winning the war against dope" and achieving a final E.N.D. ("Eradicate Narcotics Dealers"—a recent Detroit campaign against dealers).

Pressures to obstruct justice flow from similar sources to those mentioned above insofar as to be successful one must: (1) protect informants who constitute the agent's vital link to the underworld; (2) create informants through threats of prosecution on pending cases if cooperation is not forthcoming, and when they do cooperate persuade officials to drop charges against them; and (3) suppress information on cases pursued by other officers (for example, where one's informant is also responsible for a burglary). The last category of obstruction also occurs when there is interagency competition and federal agents, for example, will suppress their information about the case so that other agents (for instance, state agents) will be unable to "break" the case before them, or even with them and get "credit."

Internal pressures are complemented by external pressures to enforce the law and to obstruct justice. Law enforcement, shading into excess, is facilitated by: (1) political pressures from formally elected or appointed political officials translated through the chain of command to agents; (2) media pressures in the form of editorials, feature stories, comments on the rising crime rate (cf. F. Davis 1952; Cohen 1973); (3) grand jury, prosecutor's office, and judicial pressure (which can work in a "negative direction" as it has in Washington, D.C., where District Prosecutor Silvert urged officers not to bring him cases of personal possession of marihuana to prosecute); (4) ad hoc community groups and community associations; (5) external funding agencies such as O.D.A.L.E., D.O.J., and L.E.A.A., which provide money and additional manpower (in the form of strike forces or tactical units).

The obstruction of justice occurs as a result of pressures generated by: (1) bribes to agents from users or dealers either to protect their operations or to avoid a charge once arrested; (2) competition and cooperation between and among agents and agencies (this is especially crucial when informants are needed in cases where both state and federal agents are involved, cf. Daley 1975); (3) grand juries that encourage the development of "big busts" or big cases to show the public that "something is being done" also encourage the protection of snitches in order to have them work bigger cases and to protect them in the interim from prosecution on other pending charges.

Each of these pressures, it should be emphasized, is not directly translated into the conduct of agents. The point we wish to underscore is that the organizational ambience of narcotics law enforcement is such that rather than providing inducement to conformity to the law, it is more likely to underscore the virtues of avoidance of the more obvious requirements of law enforcement. It encourages rather more excess in pursuit of the job and modification of procedural rules to maximize arrests and buys. In the course of doing so, one learns to view with only minimal concern somewhat less obvious consequences of systematic obstruction of justice.

Patterns of Agent Corruption in Narcotics Law Enforcement

Corruption, in the sense that we are using the term, refers to departures from correct procedure in exchange for some goods, services, or money. That is, the agent modifies what is expected of him by the nature of his employment and thus affects the outcome of enforcement. The corruption of enforcement can occur in seven principle ways:

1. Taking Bribes

If we eliminate for the moment everyday/anyday favors and gratuities, considerations and presents that are exchanged between police officers and the public, bribe-taking is the most common form of corruption (on this point, see Stoddard in Sherman 1974). In the area of narcotics enforcement, bribe-taking manifests itself in two ways. First, there is a pay off to officers from dealers for advance-warning information concerning raids, or other such warning information. This type of pay off is made on a regular basis. Second, there are pay offs made at the time of a raid or arrest. In the first instance, the bribes are made by a single organization or person, whereas in the second, officers accept bribes from a variety of persons; that is, officers accept the bribe from whomever they are arresting. At the time of the arrest, the individual being arrested will make explicit or implicit remarks concerning money or drugs that he may have available. The officers may take the dealer's stash money and then let him go (see Knapp Commission 1972, p. 94). If the dealer has no money, the officers may confiscate his drugs but this case does not occur as often as the taking of stash money. However, the opportunities for bribery do not end with the making of the arrest, for the agent or agents still has the option of "making the case" badly. That is, the agent can write the case up in such a manner that it will be thrown out of court. And there are other ways:

> [A] police officer who is skillful or experienced enough can write an affidavit that appears to be very strong, but is still open-ended enough to work in favor of a defendant when coupled with appropriate testimony from the arresting officer. For example, an officer could state in his complaint that the suspect threw the evidence to the ground at the approach of the police. Should that officer later testify that he lost sight of the evidence as it fell, the evidence and the case could well be dismissed. The Commission learned that it was not uncommon for defense attorneys in narcotics cases to pay policemen for such favors as lying under oath and procuring confidential police and judicial records concernin their clients' cases. (Knapp Commission 1972, p. 97)

The Knapp Commission data are substantiated by evidence gathered by other researchers (cf. Sherman 1974). For example, Sanders (1972), studying the court experiences of middle-class drug users, was able to show that police officers, working through defense attorneys, were willing to later drop narcotics charges for a fee. The attorney acted as a middle-man in the situation. He would take money from his client, take a percentage for his "service," and pass on the remainder to the

292 DRUGS AND POLITICS

officer. The money may buy a change in the charge (for example, a reduction from a felony to a misdemeanor), but more likely the money was in exchange for "sabotaging" the trial. The officer would make errors such as incompetent testimony or not being able to find evidence (see Sanders 1972, pp. 242-43).[14]

The Knapp Commission also uncovered evidence of bribes in several diverse forms:

[I]t was quite common for an apprehended suspect to offer to pay his captors for his release and for the right to keep part of his narcotics and cash. This was especially true at higher levels of distribution where the profits to be made and the penalties risked by a dealer were very high. One such case was that of a suspended Narcotics Division detective who was recently indicted in Queens County and charged with taking bribes to overlook narcotics offenses. The indictment alleged that this officer accepted $1,500 on one occasion for not arresting a suspected drug pusher who was apprehended while in possession of $15,000 worth of heroin. There is evidence that on another occasion this detective was paid $4,000 by a different narcotics pusher for agreeing not to confiscate $150,000 worth of heroin. The detective has pleaded guilty to attempting to receive a bribe, and his sentence is pending. (1972, p. 96)

2. Using Drugs

Agents have been known to use illicit drugs. For example, Harris (1974), interviewing three ex-narcotic agents, reports the smoking of marihuana by agents as they sat "surveillance." In another case witnessed by one of us, an agent about to participate in a late-night raid discussed the fact that he was tired, and promptly produced a nonprescription vial of amphetamines from which he took and swallowed three capsules. Undercover agents, to show their loyalties to the people on whom they are doing surveillance, often must "turn-on" (use drugs) with them. In several observed cases, officers went to parties and carried their own stash as evidence that they were users.

3.   Buying/Selling Narcotics

Evidence gathered by journalists suggests that many observers believe that dealing in narcotics exists among agents, especially local agents in Los Angeles and New York. *New York Times* reporter David Burnham wrote:

> [S]ome policemen wonder whether the transfer of two hundred plainclothesmen, a highly cynical group of men, to the narcotics beat might not result in a net increase in the flow of narcotics into the city. . . . "The moral jump from making illegal drug deals to getting evidence and dealing in drugs to make money is not as big as it might look to an outsider," one experienced narcotics detective said. (Burnham in Sherman 1974, pp. 309-310)

In Gary, Indiana, near Chicago, seven policemen were convicted in February 1975, of conspiracy to deal in drugs and of drug trafficking (*Washington Post*, 9 February 1975). In 1974, the same group was convicted on trafficking charges. The Knapp Commission discovered in the testimony of two "ex-addicts" that eleven Harlem policemen would supply them with narcotics in exchange for cigarettes, whiskey, power tools, a minibike, and stereo equipment. The addicts had collected the goods through burglaries (Daley 1975, p. 339). Several other variations on this pattern occur: the selling of narcotics to informants for resale to other addicts, and the use of narcotics to pay off informants for information useful in making a buy or a buy and bust. Narcotics officers also financed heroin buys for others when the aim was not eventual arrest (Knapp Commission 1972, pp. 91-92); they also accept narcotics as bribes, which in turn they sell. In New York, no informant fees were paid officially: narcotics seized in one arrest can be used to pay off informants (Whittemore 1973, p. 323) (a case of both arrogation of seized property and dealing illegally in narcotics). A more elusive type of corruption is simple conspiracy to deal, such as introducing potential customers to dealers. Since the latter is a requirement of undercover work for informants, it is hardly surprising that agents might introduce, directly or indirectly, clients to a pusher. Without such introductions, the enforcement of most narcotics dealing laws would be impossible.

4.　Arrogation of Seized Property

Since the law in most states requires that any property relevant to the crime must be seized until the trial has been held, large amounts of property—typically automobiles, guns, money, and drugs—are confiscated as evidence. The control of evidence of this type is extremely difficult as well as expensive for large police departments.[15] A series of scandals in the New York Police Department in 1973 involved missing or stolen property, including well over one hundred kilos of high-quality heroin taken from the Property section of the Department (Pileggi 1973b). Further, the arrest situation often entails large amounts of money involved in the exchange that led to the arrest, as well as other monies that may be a part of the dealer's crib or bank. During the Knapp Commission testimony, Patrolman Phillips (one of the corrupt policemen "turned" by the Commission) testified he saw a plainclothesman leaving the scene of a multimillion dollar drug raid with $80,000 confiscated earlier in the raid. In March 1975, the officer identified by Phillips was indicted, and charged with stealing more than $1,500 in cash and heroin (the minimum amount for a grand larceny charge) (New York Times, 21 March 1975). Although the money used in the actual exchange (used by the informant or the agent to buy the drugs) is marked and the serial numbers registered prior to the buy, other confiscated money becomes the responsibility of the agents to collect, record, and to insure its safe deposit with I.R.S.

5.　Illegal Searches and Seizures

There are several ways in which illegal searches and seizures can be initiated, and each is used at one time or another (see Harris 1974; Sanders 1972; Wambaugh 1973; see also Johnson and Bogomolny 1973, for a study of reported arrest data). One way illegal searches are conducted is for the narcotics officer to claim there was a "quantity of alleged drugs" in "plain sight" (see Wambaugh 1973; Sanders 1972), and then search the house, apartment, or vehicle of the person. In the case of a vehicle search, often the outward appearances of the person or the vehicle provide clues to officers that a drug violation *may* be occurring, and, in addition, that a "stop" on the vehicle is warranted (Johnson and Bogomolny 1973, euphemistically refer to these as "ancillary" or "consumption-related" offenses). The officers then stop the vehicle, "see" contraband in plain sight, and initiate a search of the vehicle. Another variant on the vehicular search is to claim, as with marihuana, that "smoke could be smelled" and that the search had "probable cause." "Flaking" is a term referring to the act whereby the officer plants illicit drugs on the person (see Knapp Commission 1972). When an officer has made an illegal search, he may "find" drugs that have been "flaked." Narcotics officers may possess a "sure bust kit" that contains several types of drugs and allows them to select the appropriate contraband that will justify their illegal search. Reiss (personal communication) indicates that a narcotics officer working the Washington, D.C., area told him that he had never made an arrest *without* flaking the person. Still other officers have reported to us that, "If you're gonna' search 'em, it's wise to come up with sumthin'."

A variation on "flaking" is "dropsey." An officer will report that he came upon the subject just as he was throwing contraband away. The "overt act" of throwing the contraband away allows for the search; however, in the case of "dropsey" the officer actually supplies the contraband. Pileggi (1971) quotes one New York City judge as saying: "Surely, though, not in *every* case was the defendant unlucky enough to drop his narcotics at the feet of a policeman. It follows that in at least some of the cases the police are lying."

"Padding" occurs when the officer adds drugs to the already confiscated evidence either to increase the quality of the substance seized and make the evidence more acceptable in court, or to raise the charge from a misdemeanor to a felony after the arrest has been made (Knapp Commission 1972, p. 91). In one case, agents seized several ounces of lactose and a dealer, but no narcotics. A Marquis field test was done on the seized lactose and produced negative results. At that point the officers "sweetened" the seizure so that a field test would render it positive. In cases where drugs are added to raise the charge, often the motive is to use the more serious charge as a threat and thereby gain greater leverage over the arrestee. This presure can be used to "turn" the arrestee into a "confidential informant," or extort money from the arrestee, or to persuade the arrestee to offer bribes or service to the officer (for example, sexual favors).[16]

6.   The Protection of Informants

Informants are the heart of the enforcement of narcotics laws. Detectives either pay their "snitches" out of their own pockets, or the department provides a "confidential informant" fund.[17] All major federal enforcement agencies allocate money for payment of information (F.B.I., D.E.A., and so on), as do most major police departments. At least four consequences issue from the use of informants in narcotics law enforcement. First, agencies may have to compete for information, and informants have the option of accepting the best deal. In one instance, a confidential informant who was "working off cases" found that federal agents were willing to pay more and consequently began working for them. In another instance, local agents were unable to get the prosecuting attorney to drop charges against a potential snitch, so the "confidential informant" went to the federal agency and the charges were dropped a short time thereafter. Daley (1975) provides another example: federal agents, in protecting their confidential informant incognito and incommunicado, inhibited local agents from obtaining necessary information to move on local cases. As noted by Skolnick (1966) and Van Maanen (personal communication), and as we have observed, confidential informants often are protected from prosecution on other charges while they are working. That is, the confidential informant in one case was caught breaking and entering a home, but the agents "fixed" the charge with the prosecuting attorney's office on the basis that the informant was "one of the best." The officer then added five cases to the informant's caseload. Second, informants may be working for several agents or agencies. This occurs more frequently in areas where interagency cooperation is virtually nonexistent. The informant is thus able to receive payment from more than one agency and, in addition, perhaps keep more charges off his back. Even in the instance where the informant is working for only one agency, a third consequence results. Most informants are drug users themselves, and the agents provide money or drugs in payment. Thus, the agents become a link in the marketing of narcotics. The fourth consequence we have already briefly noted: informants are oftentimes protected from prosecution. As Skolnick (1966) suggests, informants in effect reverse the hierarchy of criminal penalties in that they are allowed to work off charges, receive no penalty, and may even be paid for their services. In cases where officers hope to reach "Mr. Big," the costs of protection from prosecution spiral. Each level of the dealing chain must be granted some measure of immunity from prosecution, or some consideration for turning state's evidence. For some of those in the dealing chain, charges will never be filed and thus justice will be obstructed in order that someone deemed higher up can be caught.[18]

7. Violence

Sometimes the information desired from an informant is not forthcoming and some "physical therapy" is necessary (Redlinger 1969). The potential for violence in narcotics enforcement is high; often addicts are roughed up in attempts to gain information from them. Moreover, violence can be used to force informants to engage in illegal behavior such as stealing *for narcotics officers* (see Knapp Commission 1972, p. 92). Agents also have the option of turning the name of the informant over to interested dealers, and can effectively use this threat to gain information. Sometimes, of course, especially on informants who may turn out to be quite unreliable, they do turn the names over. The use of unwarranted violence can also occur during raids. Officers can claim that the dealer "went for his gun" and proceed to blow him away; such a procedure has merits in that the dealer is no longer able to testify otherwise, and in addition the officers make a good case

and obtain the rewards. Other features of narcotics enforcement make very likely the unfortunate possibility that agents
will shoot other agents in the same agency (for example, in a
shoot-out involving an undercover agent who is indistinguishable from the targets of police bullets), or uniformed officers in
another agency may shoot narcotics officers (or vice versa) as
occured in Cali, Colombia, in February 1975, and in West
Germany in March 1975. In both of the last cases, United
States agents killed foreign police officers in shoot-outs
touched off by raids.

Violence can be used to restore face after the agent errs,
as happened in Boise, Idaho:

> The narcs hired operatives, at $3 an hour, to make
> connections with dealers. Near Sun Valley, agents gave one
> such operative $1,000 and waited outside a bar while he
> went in, strolled through, and left by the back door. Burned
> on another buy when a dealer passed off powdered aspirin
> as heroin, agents returned posing as Mafia hoods and
> retrieved their money at gun point. To support this cover,
> agents offered to buy guns in the underworld: this sparked a
> wave of sporting goods-store burglaries around Pocatello.
> When police figured out what was going on and complained,
> the narcs accused them of being involved in the drug trade.
> (Newsweek, 27 January 1975).

Comment

Licit and illicit markets have many features in common,
but they differ substantially as a result of the moral intention
of regulatory statutes, the loyalties of those applying the
statutes, and the manner of application. We have noted that
sellers in licit markets have both legitimate and illegitimate
means to influence regulatory policies and action. Sellers of
illicit goods and services (such as narcotics) have recourse only
to illicit means, and, moreover, because of the nature of their
incredulity, they ordinarily must focus their efforts on enforcement agents. Hypothetically, then, if illicit sellers could effect
control over their markets through higher, more powerful
channels, they would attempt to do so. It is critical to understand that the structural features of society, and in particular

regulatory agencies and the activities they regulate, dispose specific elements to be exposed to corruption. Agents, thus, are more often placed upon an invitational edge of corruption, and are a major point of tension in the regulation of legally suppressed markets.[19]

Our discussion should not be taken as limited to the dramatic instances of corruption in the narcotics field, but rather should be viewed as pointing out areas of corruption that one might find in other regulatory agenices. Since the structural features of both markets and their regulatory-enforcement agencies are similar, evidences of corruption in one should instruct us to look for such features in other agencies and their personnel. The nature of licit markets allows for that corruption to occur at more varying levels than in legally suppressed markets. That is, the same *forms* of corruption occur and exist, but the structural positions where they can occur appear to be more numerous. In addition, because markets and their goods and services are defined as licit, some areas deemed "corruption" in illicit markets are not seen as such in licit ones, and this bifurcation of vision only serves to point out the structuring features of moral intent.[20]

Although some of the similarities are quite obvious, we would like to compare types of corruption found in licit and illicit markets. In both markets, *bribery* is to be found. The history of American politics is punctuated with pay offs, bribes, gifts, and the like forwarded by legitimate businessmen to regulatory agents. The *use of the product* is in many instances obvious, and most often is not seen as a case of corruption. That is, members of regulatory agencies such as the F.A.A. often ride in planes; members of the F.C.C. often watch television; members of the F.D.A. often use drugs. We have already noted that in regulated markets, it is quite common for sellers to be asked to accept positions in agencies that regulate the very markets they come from. The interpretations of regulators, sellers, and producers is hardly considered remarkable in this country. There is circulation of elites through, for example, the Defense Department, military, large armaments, shipbuilding, and aircraft manufacturing companies. Furthermore, as Lieberson (1971) indicates, the Senate committees that are supposed to regulate spending and investment in markets are committees composed of senators from the very states that have vested intersted in those areas.[21] *Buying and selling of products* one is supposed to regulate occurs in both regulatory and enforcement agencies, as does the *arrogation of seized property.* For example, automobiles seized in raids by drug agencies supply vehicles for many enforcement agents at both lower and higher echelons of the agencies, while such arrogation is a common process in bankruptcy proceedings. The use of wiretaps and bugging, *modes of illegal entry and/or surveillance* is common in virtually all federal agencies; recent headlines have revealed the use of spying and taps by the Internal Revenue Service, Department of Defense, and other agencies. Moreover, private industrial concerns have utilized taps to illegally spy on their regulators. *Informants* were an inimicable part of all prosecutorial activity and immunity granted to witnesses is common throughout not only courts but congressional hearings as well. Watergate is only a most recent example, but policies regarding immunity are also found in the Internal Revenue Service, the F.A.A., the Armed Services, and in the Department of Justice in civil as well as criminal cases.

Finally, *violence* is found more often in the regulation of illicit markets primarily because sellers do not have recourse to contracts and corporate law, but must deal with agents directly in the same way that agents must deal with sellers. The independence of the market from conventional conflict-modifying mechanisms produces conditions where violence must be used to settle differences; that is, there is no legitimate or "civilized" locus for the negotiation of disputes and no "dispassionate" third party to resolve them. Moreover, violence may be more common in illicit markets because most sellers operate at low levels of dealing (small clientele and capitalization) and with clientele that are from social classes normally associated with high rates of violence. Put in another manner, most of the narcotics dealer robberies occur at lower levels of the markets *as do robberies of legitimate sellers.* It is possible that clandestine raids, undercover work, and the competition between and among agents and agencies produces greater opportunities for interpersonal violence than does the regulation of, for example, legitimate pharmaceuticals.

We advance these similarities to indicate that there are specific structural reasons why narcotics agents are more often thrown onto the invitational edge of corruption. However, any serious student of social control and regulation should not stop with analysis of enforcement agents and agencies, but should look farther and ask the very same questions about regulatory agents and agencies. After all, objective analysis of social control should begin by being minimally encumbered by society's morality and its blinders.

NOTES

1. Extensive research on the early years has been done by several scholars, and the reader interested in how the drug problem was socially constructed, how legislation was passed, and how initial attempts at regulation gave way to the enforcement mode, should look at such works as Brecher, et al. 1972 (part one); Lindesmith 1965; Musto 1972; and King 1972. One result, however, deserves mentioning primarily because it set up the now-accepted linkage between urban crime, poverty, and narcotics addiction. Whereas, prior to criminalization, narcotics users were mostly women who self-administered the drug for a variety of medicinal reasons, after criminalization males became the primary users. In addition, the social class of the user steadily declined so that in contrast to the late 1800s when use was spread throughout the class structure and even concentrated more in the middle and upper classes, the majority of users are today from the lower classes (this does not, of course, include physician addicts who obtain their drugs in other manners). In addition, prior to criminalization, the average age of a user was between forty and fifty years of age, whereas today, the user is more likely to be under thirty. Thus, resulting from criminalization and the enforcement of the laws, the patterns of addiction and use changed remarkably. Today addiction is most often associated with poor, young, urban males, usually from one of the minorities.

2. The literature on "legitimate" versus "illegitimate" markets and their associated regulatory activity is growing. Sociologists have long recognized that police control crime rather than eliminate it. For example, Hughes (1971) has written on "bastard institutions" that provide desired products not otherwise available, and Schur (1966) analyzed some of the consequences of making illegal certain con-

sumatory patterns. N. Davis (1973) has provided an intensive and detailed analysis of the changing patterns of regulation associated with abortion, and sociologist Gusfield (1963) and political scientists such as Lowi (1969) and Edelman (1962) have examined the symbolic fictions of regulation. In a sense, all regulation is an additional price or value-added cost, and while the cost of regulation is passed onto both seller and buyer, more often than not the seller is able to transfer his costs to the buyer. Thus, the buyer becomes the taxpayer. Corruption is a variant on the cost, coming as it does, directly as one resultant of the enterprise of morality regulation.

3. Associations, such as the American Sociological Association and the American Medical Association, also license practitioners, and collect revenues for their agents. The agents through their certification attest to the credibility of the licensed persons' claims to be what they are and to be selling what they claim to be selling.

4. This can be seen through our later analysis to not always be the case. Numerous examples from nations other than the United States will indicate complicity between those who seek to suppress the illicit marketing of products and the sellers of those products. Given the extremely lucrative nature of illicit narcotics, unscrupulous entrepreneurs and power-driven people, whether in legitimate occuptions or illegitimate ones, will be tempted. In a society where money is equated with social respectability and power, lucrative ways to make money become extremely attractive, and constraining themes in morality can be neutralized.

5. The foregoing analysis operates with the assumption that illicit sellers of narcotics do not sell licit goods and services. This assumption is, of course, not totally warranted. Licit sellers may be engaged in selling illicit goods, and in fact, at higher dealing echelons, this may be a rule rather than an exception. Thus, licit sellers of one set of goods, may be able to indirectly use their political influence through these channels to effect the regulations surrounding their "other business." What the nature and extent of effects seller interpenetration may have is difficult to measure due to the relative paucity of data. However, there are several suggestive remarks one can make. In instances where the interpenetration is political in nature, illicit sellers may have direct and enduring influence in the enforcement of regulations and the nature of these regulations. Where mayors or governors, for example, are also sellers of illicit goods and services through illicit organizations or act as middlemen between illicit producers and regulators, the types and kinds of police-enforcement capacity are often affected. In some countries other than the United States, the interpenetration between licit and illicit markets and control may be

greater. Percentages of the take may be typically allotted to the political structure so that influence will be exerted and the seller can maintain effective market control. Recent cases in this country of government corruption accent the possibility of greater seller interpenetration than heretofore might have been thought.

6. Evidence suggests that in America, there are no producers of heroin per se (it is smuggled in in a refined form). However, even in cases of producers of other illicit substances, the producers rarely have recourse to influence a higher echelon official unless, as noted in an earlier footnote, this official has "interpenetration" with the illicit market.

7. It is not our argument that these are the sole features conducive to the patterns of corruption we describe below. There may be others. However, these are the most important. Insofar as the market features distinguishing the legitimate from the illegitimate markets for illicit substances obtain, and the differences in patterns of regulation obtain, we would expect to find analogous patterns of corruption, that is, agent-focused. Many Anglo-American societies follow the regulatory model we have described, and would be expected to possess similar corruption patterns. For example, Gabor (1973) reports that in Melbourne, Australia, narcotics squads utilized blank search warrants. The warrants are signed en masse by a judge and agents could then search the premises of anyone they chose. During or after the search, a name is placed on the warrant. The practice came to light when "following a raid carried out in the usual manner, drug-squad officers left behind a folder of papers. On examination the folder was found to contain, among other things, four blank search warrants—but with the signature of a Melbourne JP alrady attached" (Gabor 1973, p. 20). Other features of a society, for example, high levels of violence such as occur in Latin American countries, obviously contribute to the likelihood of discovering violence in drug-enforcement operations.

8. Sykes, in *Society of Captives* (1958), makes a similar argument concerning prison guards. Caught in the bind of being accountable for maintaining order, yet having to rely on the inmates to maintain order, the guard must make trade-offs with the inmates. Redlinger (1970) offers a similar explanation for the negotiation of order in homes for emotionally disturbed children.

9. It may be, too, that certain individuals are channeled into being agents and that these individuals are more corruptible than some hypothetical average; this we doubt. For one thing, many police departments work their men on a rotation basis and thus narcotics agents are policemen transferred into and out of sections. Second, given the nature of regulation, other officers have the opportunity for

bribe-taking, extortion, and so on, as is amply documented in the literature on police corruption (Sherman 1974). Assessment on this proposition would require data most difficult to gather. Among other things, one would need detailed life histories of agents that would indicate any and all prior involvement in corruption, and these would necessarily have to be matched against a comparable sample of nonagents. Another way of approaching the problem would be to follow a cohort of "clean" agents through their tenure as police officers noting along the way the temptations to corruption. In either case, the officers, especially those who have something to hide, are not likely to voluntarily subject themselves to close scrutiny.

10. King (1972) reports that in 1917, two years after the passage of the Harrison Act criminalizing nonmedical use, "the first narcotic agent was caught and convicted for taking a large bribe." In that same year, Treasury agents, who were held responsible for enforcing the regulations, began seizing activities (previous to this time, agents did not seize large amounts of drugs). As King notes, agents even in 1917 needed a way to show they were doing their job, and one way they did and do is to account for their activity in terms of the dollar value that can be attached to what they have acquired:

By 1917 increasing numbers of civic leaders and responsible citizens were calling for federal intervention and strict federal controls to stop the drug traffic. In that year the first caches of illegal drugs were seized by Treasury agents; and Treasury then started the deceptive practice, continued ever since by drug-law enforcers, of announcing each seizure in terms of how many millions of dollars the contraband substances might have been worth if they had been sold at maximum prices in the illegal market. (1972, p. 25)

11. Regulatory agencies of all kinds reside and act in a competitive, symbolic domain that includes other agencies sharing similar goals and clientele. Drug agencies seek not only to control their clientele (dealers and users) but also to maintain an *image* of control vis-à-vis their public. The public includes not only the taxpayers external to the government but other agencies and members within the government as well. Within all organizations, there are pressures to survive as an organization and to satisfy the needs (economic, social, and the like) of the members (Clark and Wilson 1961). At least one formal defining characteristic of organizations is their public obeisance to a set of formal goals (as associative pressures to achieve at least a semblance of these goals) and mechanisms to systematically evaluate organizational achievements.

12. Modes of supervision and control of narcotics agents tend to replicate the dissembling, duplicity, lying, and threat used by officers *against* drug offenders. The Knapp Commission, for example, "turned" four patrolmen to spy on fellow officers, often leading to massive misunderstandings (because the other Knapp agents were not known to them). Of the four, three had been essentially blackmailed into working for the Commission (arrests for corruption-type offenses led to their being invited to work undercover) and were given consideration for this work in their own charges. Further, the borders of entrapment were always skirted, if not violated (Wainwright 1972; reprinted in Sherman 1974; Whittemore 1973, pp. 364-83). This mode of under-cover and secretive enforcement of disciplinary rules is typical in large police departments, and it creates an ambiance of doubt and suspicion of colleagues. It is always possible that a fellow officer is working for internal affairs, or will inform to them. This condition furthers the already suspicious frame of mind of the officer, and sets him against the administrative strata in a very profound fashion. Consequently, when the agent wishes to resist the control of superiors, resistance takes the form of either complicity with the targets of control (in this case, users and dealers in narcotics), or work slowdowns (see Manning 1977, ch. 6, for a further discussion of the question of internal rule enforcement and its organizational consequences).

13. In one department the informal quota rules were summarized by a detective in the rhyme: "Two a day keeps the Sarge away." The Knapp Commission (1972) studied the New York City quota system and for many reasons we cite here recommended that it be abandoned, and as a result the system was phased out formally shortly thereafter.

14. A vice officer presented these rationales to Sanders concerning the deals that go on behind the scenes:

> I'm sure that there are lawyers who are paying off policemen in some cases. You'll always have this. But this is controlled by the police department because you have the I.I.D. (Internal Investigation Division) and the policeman now is making $12,000 a year—he's making good money. I've heard a lot of stories about a lot of policemen and I've learned one thing—if you don't have something good to say about someone, don't say anything at all. So I don't carry tales. Some cases are dealt with between the lawyer and the police officer or through other channels, but I think this is really good. I think it is beneficial to the individual that gets busted. If he can pay $300 or $400 to get out of it, good, you're out of it. That's the type of society this is. This is what was built by other people. We are going to have to realize that it is a good point. Sure, there are a lot of

policemen making money on it through lawyers. The reason is that it is an easy dollar and the chances of getting caught are slim. I really believe it is good for the citizen. It may sound fascist but it is good to have a way out of something. When you get busted you need a way out. This is the game. (Sanders 1972, p. 235)

15. Its legal status is under present review, see Johnson and Bogomolny, Technical Papers of the National Drug Abuse Commission, Appendix, Volume 3.

16. One Vermont narc allegedly propositioned a young girl after giving her some cocaine (Time, 10 March 1975). When she refused, he busted her two weeks later for selling him drugs. This case of alleged corruption, uncovered in Vermont, was one of some six hundred convictions that resulted in a letter from a county prosecutor to the governor asking that all six hundred convictions based on the officer's testimony be pardoned. The officer, in addition to attempted extortion, is suspected of confiscating the drugs he planted on an apparently large number of arrestees, and of converting money assigned for buys to his personal use.

17. Robert Daley, former deputy commissioner of the New York Police Department, describes the present New York system that replaced the previous informal arrangement whereby detectives paid $5 fees to their informants:

> [Informants] are listed with the Police Intelligence Division under a code number and usually a code that they have been obliged to sign onto the equivalent of a bank deposit card. Their verifiable signatures are important, because they must sign receipts for money paid them. Each informant is further classified by specialty, and by the area he knows. (Daley 1973, p. 31)

Of course, as the Knapp Commission pointed out, it is possible to create fictitious informants and for an officer to collect the fees himself.

18. The informant system facilitates extortion, lying, blackmail, and violence. Information sold to an officer, or given during questioning, can be used for the officer's own interests. Likewise, the informant can turn the information to his. By informing a dealer that officers are coming, for example, the informant may be able to avenge some affront. Informants often do turn in people they have quarrels or grudges with, and the informant system allows for the turning of the process around. The informant may be able to "set up" an officer much the way he sets up dealers. Too, informant information may be

used by an officer who is also dealing to effectively eliminate his competition.

19. While agents regulating licit markets are located in a similar position, there is not as much focus for effective control upon their position. Licit sellers have other potentially more powerful means for effecting control over their markets. Thus, while the potential for corruption of these agents exist, its return in terms of effective market control is not as great. Agents regulating licit markets have relatively little power to change policy, and licit market sellers have access through both legitimate and not so legitimate channels to persons of greater power.

20. Space does not permit the outlining of what might be called a *phenomenology of corruption*. Suffice it to say that elements in such an outline would be the nature of the *relationship* among the *recipient*, the *donor*, and the *object* transmitted. The *definitions* given to such transactions, as well as the *structure* of the exchange (tertiary, seconary, or primary exchange; short- or long-lag systems, cf. Blau 1964 and Levi-Strauss 1969) would also have to be taken into account. By holding constant *some* of the structural features of regulatory agencies, and examining what is *defined* as corruption, we are suggesting an analytic strategy that we hope to puruse in subsequent analyses.

21. For example, the House Agriculture Subcommittee on Tobacco is a seven member committee that has six members from the tobacco-producing states; the Minerals and Fuels Committee is "loaded with senators from states with relatively large segments of the labor force engaged in these extractive industries" (Lieberson 1971, pp. 579-80). Likewise, the Senate Armed Services Committee has a disproportionately high membership from states that would stand to lose when arms are cut back, and in contrast, "the small Subcommittee on International Organization and Disarmament Affairs is disproportionately composed of senators from states that stand to gain through a military cutback" (Lieberson 1971, pp. 580-81).

References

Blau, P. 1964. *Exchange and Power in Social Life.* New York: Wiley.

Brecher, H. W., et al. 1972. *Licit and Illicit Drugs.* Boston: Little, Brown.

Clark, P., and Wilson, J. Q. 1961. "Incentive Systems: A Theory of Organizations." *Administrative Science Quarterly* 6 (September): 129-66.

Cohen, S. 1973. *Folk Devils and Moral Panics.* London: Palladin.

Daley, R. 1973. *Target Blue.* New York: Dell.

_____. 1975. "Inside the Criminal Informant Business." *New York* 8 (March 24): 31-35.

Davis, F. J. 1952. "Crime News in Colorado Newspapers." *American Journal of Sociology* 57 (January): 325-30.

Davis, N. J. 1973. "The Abortion Market: Transactions in a Risk Commodity." Ph.D. dissertation, Michigan State University.

Edelman, M. 1962. *The Symbolic Use of Politics.* Urbana, Illinois: University of Illinois Press.

Gabor, I. 1973. "Drug Squad Inquiry." *Drugs and Society* 3 (November): 1.

Gusfield, J. 1963. *Symbolic Crusade.* Urbana, Illinois: University of Illinois Press.

Harris, D. 1974. "An Inside Look at Federal Narcotics Enforcement: Three Ex-Agents Tell their Tales." *Rolling Stone,* December 5, pp. 65-71, 84-89.

Hughes, E. C. 1971. *The Sociological Eye.* Chicago: Aldine.

Johnson, W., and Bogomolny, R. 1973. "Selective Justice: Drug Law Enforcement in Six American Cities." In *Drug Use in America: Problem in Perspective. Technical Papers of the Second Report of the National Commission on Marihuana and Drug Abuse.* Volume 3, Appendix, pp. 498-650. Washington, D.C.: U.S. Government Printing Office.

King, R. 1972. *The Drug Hang-up.* New York: Norton.

Knapp Commission. 1971. *Report* [on Police Corruption]. New York: George Brazillier.

Levi-Strauss, C. 1969. *The Elementary Structures of Kinship.* Boston: Beacon Press.

Lieberson, S. 1971. "An Empirical Study of Military-Industrial Linkages." *American Journal of Sociology* 74 (January): 562-84.

Lindesmith, A. 1965. *The Addict and the Law.* Bloomington, Indiana: Indiana University Press.

Lowi, T. 1969. *The End of Liberalism.* New York: Norton.

Manning, P. K. 1977. *Police Work: Essays on the Social Organization of Policing.* Cambridge, Massachusetts: M.I.T. Press.

Merton, R. K. 1958. *Social Theory and Social Structure.* New York: Free Press.

Moore, M. 1970. "Economics of Heroin Distribution in New York City." Hudson Institute Mimeo Report.

Musto, D. F. 1972. *The American Disease.* New Haven, Connecticut: Yale University Press.

Pileggi, N. 1971. "From D.A. to Dope Lawyer." *New York Times Magazine,* May 16, pp. 34, 35, 38, 40, 42, 45, 47-48, 50.

––––––. 1973a. "How Crooks Buy Their Way Out of Trouble." *New York,* November 19, pp. 45-52.

––––––. 1973b. "Further Developments in the 'French Connection' Case." *New York,* September 24, pp. 42-48.

Redlinger, L. J. 1969. "Dealing in Dope." Ph.D. dissertation, Northwestern University.

––––––. 1970. "Making Them Normal: Notes on Rehabilitating Emotionally Disturbed Children." *American Behavioral Scientist* 14 (December): 237-53.

Rubinstein, J. 1973. *City Police.* New York: Farrar, Straus and Giroux.

Sanders, C. 1972. "The High and the Mighty: Middle-Class Drug Users and the Legal System." Ph.D. dissertation, Northwestern University.

Schelling, T. 1967. "Economics Analysis and Organized Crime." In *Task Force Report: Organized Crime.* President's Crime Commission. Washington, D.C.: U.S. Government Printing Office.

Sherman, L. W., ed. 1974. *Police Corruption.* New York: Doubleday-Anchor Books.

Schur, E. 1966. *Crimes Without Victims.* Englewood Cliffs, New Jersey: Prentice-Hall.

Skolnick, J. 1966. *Justice Without Trial.* New York: Wiley.
_____. 1975. *Justice Without Trial.* Second ed. New York: Wiley

Sutherland, E. C. 1949. *White-Collar Crimes.* New York: Dryden Press.

Sykes, G. 1958. *Society of Captives.* Princeton, New Jersey: Princeton University Press.

Wambaugh, J. 1973. *The Blue Knight.* New York: Dell.

Whittemore, L. W. 1973. *Super-Cops.* New York: Bantam Books.

Contributors

John Auld graduated from the University of Leicester and subsequently carried out research at the London School of Economics. At present he is a lecturer in sociology at Middlesex Polytechnic, England, where he is completing a study of the changing social meanings of cannabis use.

Howard S. Becker is professor of sociology and urban affairs at Northwestern University, where he also teaches photography. He is the author of The Outsiders and co-author of Boys in White and Making the Grade.

Richard H. Blum is the director of the Program in Drugs, Crime, and Community Studies at the School of Law, Stanford University. He has been a consultant to numerous government agencies and is the U.S. delegate to the United Nations Narcotics Commission. He also chairs an international drug group headquartered in Geneva, as well as the Democratic National Committee Advisory Council of Elected Officials, Drug Abuse and Alcoholism Subcommittee.

John A. Clausen is a professor in and chairman of the department of sociology at the University of California at Berkeley. He has also served as chief of the Laboratory of Socioenvironmental Studies at the National Institutes of Mental Health and as director of the Institute of Human Development at Berkeley.

William P. Delaney received his doctorate from the University of Illinois at Urbana-Champaign in anthropology. His interests include Buddhology, aging and thanatos, and the study of political change.

Donald T. Dickson received his J.D. from the University of Chicago and his Ph.D. in sociology from the University of Michigan. He is currently an associate professor at the Graduate School of Social Work, Rutgers University. In addition to his narcotics research, he has co-authored studies in juvenile corrections and has written articles on the impact of law on social welfare organizations.

David Downes is a senior lecturer in the department of social science and administration in the London School of Economics and Political Science, University of London. He has worked with the British National Council of Civil Liberties on drugs and is the author of *The Delinquent Solution* and *Gambling, Work, and Leisure.*

Matthew P. Dumont is a psychiatrist and the director of a mental health center in Chelsea, Massachusetts. He was formerly the director of the Division of Drug Rehabilitation in the same state, and is the author of *The Absurd Healer.*

Harvey W. Feldman worked six years as a street-gang worker with a settlement house in New York's Lower Eastside. He has been a fellow with the Drug Abuse Council in Washington, D.C., and received his Ph.D. from the Heller Graduate School of Advanced Studies of Social Welfare, Brandeis University. He is currently an associate professor at the School of Social Service at St. Louis University.

Irving Louis Horowitz is professor of sociology and political science at Rutgers University, director of *Studies in Comparative International Development,* and editor-in-chief of *Trans-*

action/Society. He is the author or editor of a number of works in political sociology and social development, including: *Genocide: State Power and Mass Murder; Cuban Communism, Third Edition; Sociological Realities: A Guide to the Study of Society;* and *Social Science and Public Policy in the United States.*

Peter K. Manning is professor of sociology and psychiatry at Michigan State University. He has published several books and numerous articles; his latest book on narcotics enforcement is entitled *The Narcs' Game.*

Andrew Moss, currently a Ph.D. candidate at the University of California at Berkeley, has served as a journalist for the *Mid-Peninsular Observer* and was an editor for Ramparts Press. He is also a consultant to the Berkeley Education Authority.

Lawrence J. Redlinger is an associate professor of sociology at the University of Texas-Dallas. He has published a number of articles and is co-author with Peter K. Manning of a forthcoming book on social control.

Paul E. Rock is senior lecturer in sociology at the London School of Economics and Political Science, University of London. He is the author of *Making People Pay, Deviant Behavior,* and a number of articles.

Alan G. Sutter, before his untimely death in 1974, received his Ph.D. in sociology from the University of California at Berkeley and was affiliated with that department when his article appeared.

Thomas S. Szasz is professor of psychiatry at the State University of New York in Syracuse. He is the author of eleven books, including *Ceremonial Chemistry: The Ritual Persecution of Drugs, Addicts, and Pushers.*

Jock Young is principal lecturer of sociology at Middlesex Polytechnic, England. He is a member of the committee of the National Deviancy Symposium in England and is the author or co-author of numerous books, including *The Drugtakers, Media as Myth,* and *The Genesis and Solution to Social Problems.*

Index

*Italic numbers refer to
illustrations*